W9-CEE-799

OF ALL THE GIN JOINTS

ALSO WRITTEN BY **MARK BAILEY**

AND ILLUSTRATED BY **EDWARD HEMINGWAY**

Hemingway & Bailey's Bartending Guide to Great American Writers

Books for Children:
Tiny Pie

Of All the Gin Joints

Stumbling through Hollywood History

WRITTEN BY **MARK BAILEY**

ILLUSTRATED BY **EDWARD HEMINGWAY**

ALGONQUIN BOOKS OF CHAPEL HILL 2014

Published by
ALGONQUIN BOOKS OF CHAPEL HILL
Post Office Box 2225
Chapel Hill, North Carolina 27515-2225

a division of
WORKMAN PUBLISHING
225 Varick Street
New York, New York 10014

Text © 2014 by Mark Bailey.
Illustrations © 2014 by Edward Hemingway.
All rights reserved.
Printed in the United States of America.
Published simultaneously in Canada by Thomas Allen & Son Limited.

DESIGN BY JEAN-MARC TROADEC

CONSULTING BARTENDERS
Drew Jacobson and Paul Keo of Luminosity Entertainment

CONSULTING WRITER
Keven McAlester

SENIOR RESEARCHERS
Timothy Mackin, Emily Schlesinger

RESEARCHERS
Jordan Cohen, Joel Dando, Michelle Hovanetz, Aily Nash, Georgia Stockwell

Library of Congress Cataloging-in-Publication Data
Bailey, Mark, [date]
Of all the gin joints : stumbling through Hollywood history / written by Mark Bailey ;
illustrated by Edward Hemingway.
pages cm
ISBN 978-1-56512-593-3
1. Hollywood (Los Angeles, Calif.)—History.   2. Los Angeles (Calif.)—History.   3. Scandals—California—
Los Angeles—History.   4. Crime—California—Los Angeles—History.   5. Hollywood (Los Angeles, Calif.)—Biography.
6. Los Angeles (Calif.)—Biography.   7. Hollywood (Los Angeles, Calif.)—Social life and customs.   8. Los Angeles
(Calif.)—Social life and customs.   9. Cocktails.   I. Hemingway, Edward, illustrator. II. Title.
F869.H74B36 2014
979.4'94—dc23   2014014693

10 9 8 7 6 5 4 3 2 1
First Edition

For Ed Bailey, who liked a good laugh
and a good drink, too.

—M.B.

For Sophie, Sergio, Brian, and Johnny—bonne santé!

—E.H.

*"We are sitting at the crossroads
between Art and Nature, trying to figure out
where Delirium Tremens leave off
and Hollywood begins."*

—W.C. FIELDS

CONTENTS

FOR THE COCKTAILS that call for simple syrup, please refer to this recipe.

RECIPE FOR SIMPLE SYRUP

. . . .

1 CUP GRANULATED SUGAR

1 CUP WATER

ONE-TO-ONE RATIO, AS MUCH
AS DESIRED FOR USE OR
STORAGE

Stir sugar and water in a saucepan over medium heat. Bring to a light boil and then let simmer until sugar is completely dissolved. Remove pan from heat and let cool.

If storing, pour cooled syrup into a glass bottle or jar, cap tightly, and refrigerate. Should keep for up to a week.

OF ALL THE GIN JOINTS

Part One

THE SILENT ERA

1895–1929

"To place in the limelight a great number of
people who ordinarily would be chambermaids
and chauffeurs, give them unlimited power and
instant wealth, is bound to produce a lively
and diverting result."
—ANITA LOOS, screenwriter

ROSCOE "FATTY" ARBUCKLE

1887–1933

ACTOR AND COMEDIAN

"The only place in America to get a drink is the police station."

At five foot ten and 275 pounds, Fatty Arbuckle earned his nickname. Of his over 150 films, the best known are *The Rounders* (with Charlie Chaplin, 1914) and the unconventional Western *The Round-Up* (character name: Slim Hoover, 1920). Arbuckle also wrote and directed most of his own films. In 1918 he became the first $1-million-per-year movie actor. In 1921 he was implicated in the sexual assault and accidental death of actress Virginia Rappe. Arbuckle was acquitted after three trials, but he did not receive a film contract for the next eleven years. With no means of employment, in 1928 he opened the popular, though short-lived, nightclub Plantation Café, in Culver City. His acting comeback finally began in 1932. A year later, the night before he was to sign his first talkie, Arbuckle had a party to celebrate. He left early, went straight to bed, and died in his sleep from a heart attack.

★

EARLY ONE MORNING IN 1920, housekeepers at the Sunset Boulevard mansion of actress Pauline Frederick heard a commotion outside. They emerged to discover a car blithely parked in the middle of the front lawn and three utility workers digging toward a leaky gas pipe. The housekeepers screamed for the workers to stop; Frederick had just paid an enormous sum to have the 150-foot lawn perfectly manicured, and now her flawless grass was being destroyed. The workers were unmoved. *There could be an explosion, for God's sake.* Finally, Frederick herself dashed out of the house in a bathrobe, shouting and weeping. But as she neared the truck, her screams abated and something entirely unexpected occurred: Frederick broke into laughter.

Two of the "gasmen," it turned out, were none other than superstar Fatty Arbuckle and his newest partner in crime, Buster Keaton—both well in their cups.

Arbuckle's unquenchable thirst for good scotch was already legendary inside Hollywood. He threw lavish parties on any occasion, however slight. One such party was for the wedding of two dogs. The basement of his Tudor mansion on West Adams was stacked floor to ceiling with expensive wine and scotch. He owned a custom $25,000 Pierce-Arrow phaeton car with a bar and toilet inside. Perhaps that is worth repeating: He had a toilet inside his car.

> **Arbuckle's unquenchable thirst for good scotch was already legend inside Hollywood. He threw lavish parties on any occasion, however slight. One party was for the wedding of two dogs.**

A typical Arbuckle night involved lobster, scotch, a party (his or someone else's), and the occasional orgy. It was thus that he ended up on Polly Frederick's front lawn. The idea for the prank had been born several weeks earlier, when Arbuckle drove past Frederick's home and deemed the front lawn insultingly well kept. Resolved to do something about it, he hatched the gasman plan, enlisting best friend, Keaton.

For her part, Frederick was gracious about the entire affair. After explaining to her housekeepers what was happening, she scolded the pranksters with a smile and invited them inside for breakfast. ★

the HOLLYWOOD HOTEL

NORTHWEST CORNER OF
HOLLYWOOD AND HIGHLAND

BUILT ON A THREE-ACRE strawberry patch fronting the dusty, unpaved road that would become Hollywood Boulevard, the Hollywood Hotel was the town's first proper nightspot. Stucco, Moorish style, it was a mecca for arriving talent, as well as the early giants of the industry: actors, directors, producers.

Originally named the Hotel of Hollywood, but always called the Hollywood Hotel, the establishment had two watershed moments within its first decade. The first came in 1906, when sixty-three-year-old heiress Almira Hershey (of the chocolate dynasty) rode up from her Bunker Hill mansion to eat lunch at the hotel and ended up buying the place. Apparently things like this actually did happen, once upon a time.

The second was in 1910, when New York's Biograph Studios sent director D. W. Griffith to shoot three films in Los Angeles, and he discovered the charms of its suburb (Hollywood)—and its freedom from the expensive patent licenses required to film in New York. Within five years, most of the film industry had relocated to Hollywood, and virtually everyone's first home was the Hollywood Hotel. Its registry is now in the Smithsonian.

During those early years, it was the only acceptable hotel in Hollywood in which to reside, with a Thursday night dance that became quite the scene—the city's very first "place to be seen." Hershey didn't allow drinking or cohabitation, but she was the only person who enforced those rules—and she was in her seventies and nearly blind. The result, to read contemporary accounts, was some combination of a frat house and an insane asylum, with ill-behaved actors drinking openly in the very dining room she policed. A besotted Fatty Arbuckle was known to use his napkin to catapult butter packets onto the ceiling, which then melted and dropped down at the next seating.

The most famous room, 264, was the honeymoon suite out of which Jean Acker locked Rudolph Valentino on their wedding night, afraid to tell him she was a lesbian. Legend has it that Miss Hershey paid a visit to one bed-hopping actress every night to assure that no untoward activity was taking place. The actress always timed her trysts accordingly, until one night Hershey caught her. She was evicted at dawn. Two hours later, the actress returned with a new hairstyle, fake accent, and a pseudonym. Miss Hershey checked her right in.

Inevitably, stars bought mansions, and new hotels and nightclubs emerged; by the time Hershey died in 1930, at age eighty-seven, the Hollywood Hotel had become a quaint relic. It was torn down in 1956, and today the location houses an abominable megamall, the only graceful note of which is the Dolby Theatre, which hosts the Academy Awards on the same plot of land that sprouted the film industry a century before. ★

JOHN BARRYMORE

1882–1942
STAGE AND SCREEN ACTOR

"You can't drown yourself in drink. I've tried; you float."

John Barrymore was universally considered by peers and critics to be greatest actor of the early twentieth century. A theater legend, his 1922 turn as Hamlet (on Broadway and in London) is still considered the definitive performance of the role. Barrymore was perhaps the most prominent member of the multigenerational Drew-Barrymore acting dynasty. His father Maurice, grandmother Louisa Lane Drew, and uncles John Drew, Jr., and Sidney Drew were all thespians. His brother Lionel, sister Ethel, daughter Diana, and granddaughter Drew were all film actors. Working exclusively on the screen after 1925, Barrymore hated film but loved the money. Of his fifty-seven movies, he is best known for his leads in *Dr. Jekyll and Mr. Hyde* (1920), *Don Juan* (1926; the first film to use sync sound), *A Bill of Divorcement* (1932), and a comic turn in *Grand Hotel* (1932). From 1933 through to his death in 1942, Barrymore's acting ability and looks crumbled due to excessive drinking; his final roles were painful self-parodies. But even his worst work would not tarnish Barrymore's eulogy: greatest actor of his time.

★

THE NURSE COULD NOT BE TAMED. Three months prior to his death, the great John Barrymore was bedridden in his Tower Road home, and his few remaining friends wanted desperately to see him. But Barrymore's nurse, an unyielding and apparently quite large woman, simply would not allow it. Painter John Decker tried a ladder; she pushed it over. Actor Errol Flynn tried to wrestle her and lost. The nurse had been sternly advised that any friendly visit would involve the smuggling of alcohol, and that, she couldn't have. Alcohol, after all, was the very thing that had brought him to death's door.

Now we all know that each Hollywood generation has its most handsome leading man, its most admired acting talent, and its most raucous party animal. John Barrymore had the distinction of holding all three titles at once—for twenty years. His striking good looks earned him the nickname "The Great Profile," and his Broadway version of *Hamlet* alone would have assured his place in the acting pantheon: Freud had recently published his theory of Hamlet's Oedipal desire, and Barrymore embraced the idea, giving the doomed prince an unusual touch of sex appeal.

Barrymore's success with the gambit was no accident: As a teenager, he had lost his virginity to his own stepmother, Mamie Floyd, a tryst that saddled Barrymore with a mistrust of women and a guilt that accelerated his growing fondness for booze. Both the mistrust and the fondness would last the rest of his life.

Although Barrymore would arguably never fully translate his stage magic to the silver screen, Warner Brothers and their $76,250 per picture kept him in Tinseltown. And once he got over the feeling of slumming it, he was just simply bored. "On a movie lot," Barrymore once said, "you're nothing but a bloody stooge, a victim of some inept director who doesn't know his ass from a Klieg." By the time sound arrived, he was known as much for his off-screen antics as for his acting. His nicknames reflected the shift; The Great Profile had become, among his acquaintances, "The Monster."

Barrymore ran with a group of fellow revelers and derelicts—W. C. Fields, Errol Flynn, John Decker, John Carradine, and screenwriter Gene Fowler—christened the Bundy Drive Boys. According to Fowler, they showed up at the draft office in 1941 sloshed and anxious to serve; the registrar looked them over and asked, "Who sent you? The Enemy?"

The other Bundy Drive Boys worshipped Barrymore, whose most affectionate nickname for someone was "shithead." They all drank like devils, but even Fields was no match for him. The volume of fluid he could consume was untouchable, as was, accordingly, his need to relieve it. The Great Profile was famously indiscriminate in his choice of urinals. First it was sinks. Then it was windows. Soon it became anywhere—elevators, cars, the sandbox at the Ambassador Hotel (which banned him), nightclub draperies. (Decades later, Robert Mitchum would demonstrate a similar proclivity.)

One story goes that, while out on a binge, Barrymore accidentally walked into a women's restroom. Finding no urinal, he proceeded to relieve his bladder in a potted plant. A woman standing nearby reminded him that the room was "for ladies exclusively." Turning around, his penis still exposed, Barrymore responded, "So, Madam, is this. But every now and again, I'm compelled to run a little water through it." Roughly fifty years later, the incident made its way, verbatim, into the film *My Favorite Year*.

It was not surprising that, over time, such debauchery started catching up to Barrymore. And thus, by 1942, did he find himself confined to bed in his Tower Road home, forbidden all drink, with a quite large nurse barring all visitors. The only exceptions were his brother Lionel, his daughter Diana, and doctors. Then there was the insurance adjuster who showed up one day dressed in the black flannel suit of a pallbearer and introducing himself as Harleigh P. Wigmore. The nurse led the man into Barrymore's room. No sooner had she left, than poor, haggard Barrymore brightened, "What is this, a dress rehearsal for my obsequies?" The adjuster smiled back and pulled something out of his briefcase: an ancient bottle of Napoleon cognac. The man was, in fact, Barrymore's close friend, director Raoul Walsh, who'd concocted the ruse to get past the nurse.

The nurse had been sternly advised that any friendly visit would involve the smuggling of alcohol, and that she couldn't have. Alcohol, after all, was the very thing that had brought him to death's door.

"Ingenious," Barrymore told him, as they sat sharing a bottle for what would be the very last time. Barrymore was now more animated than ever. He told Walsh that he'd be donating his liver to Smithsonian, "for their Civil War display." When the nurse suddenly returned, Barrymore alerted her as to exactly who the "insurance man" was. Then he blew a kiss, exclaiming, "If only I were ambulatory, I would spring from this bed of thorns and pay you my praise in the coinage of rapture." The woman left, blushing, and Barrymore raised the bottle of cognac to his friend. "My farewell performance as Don Juan," he toasted. ★

H. L. MENCKEN ONCE DECLARED, "I'm ombibulous: I drink every known alcoholic drink and enjoy them all." A nice sentiment, but John Barrymore put Mencken to shame, such was the breadth of his taste for alcohol. When Barrymore's second wife broke every bottle in their house, he drank all of her perfume. When he embarked on a 1935 boating trip with their daughter and discovered (once at sea) that the ship had been stripped of booze, he siphoned a pint of the engine's coolant. Two wives later, he drank a goblet of boric acid intended to soothe his sunburn.

Perhaps Barrymore mellowed as he aged, though the stories argue otherwise. For the last two years of his life, he was a permanent guest on the radio show of singer Rudy Vallée. And every day at 4 p.m., on his way to the studio, he'd stop at St. Donat's Bar on Sunset and order his favorite drink: a Pimm's Cup. You can't get more civilized.

PIMM'S CUP

· ·

2 OZ. PIMM'S NO. 1

3 OZ. FRESHLY SQUEEZED
   LEMONADE

1 LEMON-LIME SODA SUCH AS
   7UP OR SPRITE

2 CUCUMBER SLICES

1 MINT SPRIG

ASSORTED FRUIT OPTIONAL:
   ORANGE SLICE, APPLE
   SLICE, STRAWBERRIES

Pour Pimm's and then lemonade into a chilled highball glass filled with ice cubes. Top off with soda. Stir. Garnish with cucumber and mint, additional fruit may be added. Serve with straw.

the AMBASSADOR HOTEL

3400 WILSHIRE BLVD.

FIRST OPENING ITS DOORS on New Year's Day 1921, the posh Ambassador Hotel on Wilshire quickly overtook the Alexandria as the ne plus ultra destination for Hollywood elites, visiting dignitaries, and clandestine lovers.

The hotel would host six Academy Awards ceremonies and the first Golden Globes. Marilyn Monroe got her start at the poolside modeling agency, Blue Book, and the jury for the Charles Manson case stayed there during his trial.

So frequently was the hotel used as a set in both films and television, it was nicknamed the "Ambassador Studios." Some titles include: *A Star Is Born, The Graduate, Rocky, Pretty Woman, Hoffa, Apollo 13,* and *Forrest Gump.*

But in real life, the Ambassador's most storied parties took place in the tropically themed supper club and dancehall, the Cocoanut Grove. Decorated by palm trees inherited from the set of the Valentino silent *The Sheik,* the Grove was unique among hotspots because it hosted constant performances. These eventually became de facto auditions. Bing Crosby and Merv Griffin first sang there. Judy Garland recorded her comeback album there. And a host of young female superstars were first discovered dancing there: Carole Lombard, Loretta Young, and Joan Crawford (who won over a hundred dance trophies). Years later, the Rat Pack adopted it as their haunt of choice, and in 1963 Sammy Davis, Jr., even recorded a live album there.

But over time the Ambassador Hotel would earn its place in history more through tragedy than celebration. In 1968 presidential candidate Robert F. Kennedy, fresh from his victory speech in the California primary, was shot in the pantry area of the hotel's kitchen.

The death of Kennedy, along with the deterioration of the surrounding neighborhood, marked the beginning of the end for the hotel. Drugs and gang warfare, already on the rise, would soon flood the area. In 1971 an attempt was made to renovate the Cocoanut Grove, overseen

IT WAS PERHAPS the most glamorous nightclub ever. Beneath the palm trees and coconuts, watched by the mechanical monkeys with their glowing eyes, the world's biggest stars laughed and danced and above all else drank.

There is the story of a young Tallulah Bankhead enamored with a much older John Barrymore. After a night at the Grove and one too many, she sneaked into Barrymore's Ambassador Hotel bungalow and hid under the sheets to wait for him. Back from the club and three sheets himself, upon discovering the naked starlet, Barrymore just groaned "Tallu . . . I'm too drunk and you're too awkward." It was a hell of an offer to turn down. Their cups truly overflowed.

COCOANUT GROVE COCKTAIL

2 OZ. DRY GIN
½ OZ. MARASCHINO LIQUEUR
¼ OZ. FRESH LIME JUICE
¼ OZ. GRENADINE
ORANGE WHEEL
MARASCHINO CHERRY

Pour all of the liquid ingredients into a cocktail shaker filled with ice cubes. Shake well. Strain into a chilled cocktail glass. Garnish with orange wheel and cherry.

by none other than Sammy Davis, Jr., himself, but the effort only led to such seemingly incongruous bookings as the Grateful Dead and Sly Stone. The credits were already rolling.

The Ambassador heaved its final sigh and closed its curtains in 1989, then languished behind weeds and chainlink fences as a movie location for more than a decade longer. In 2006, it was demolished. The only bright note to its unhappy demise was that the Robert F. Kennedy Community Schools rose out of the ashes, a complex of six public schools in downtown L.A. Designed loosely on a modern interpretation of the hotel, a 582-seat school theater now stands in the footprint of the original, a showplace for a new generation of performers. ★

CLARA BOW

1905–1965
ACTRESS AND SEX SYMBOL

• •

"We did as we pleased. We stayed up late. Today, they're sensible and end up with better health. But we had more fun."

C lara Bow was the first celebrity described as the "It Girl" (a phrase from her best-known film, *It*, 1927). Bow's unaffected screen persona as a dancing, singing party girl captivated audiences but led to an undeserved off-screen reputation as a tramp from the slums of Brooklyn. She did in fact grow up in poverty, moving to Hollywood in 1923. Studios thought Bow vulgar and actors thought her talentless, but her sincere and uninhibited performances struck a chord with moviegoers. (F. Scott Fitzgerald said she could "stir up every pulse in the nation.") While her starring roles made tons of money, Bow's harsh Brooklyn accent didn't translate well to sound. And she hated learning lines. After a few mildly successful talkies, Bow retired, in 1933.

———————————— ★ ————————————

IT WAS OCCASIONALLY SAID, but mostly understood, yes, Clara Bow was the most famous actress in the world. And yes, she was always incredibly sweet, professional, and beloved by the film crews she worked with. But she was *not* to be invited to parties. At least the parties of anyone who wished to remain among the respectable Hollywood elite.

This saucy teenager was from (gasp) Brooklyn, her mother was insane, and her father a lecherous hanger-on who was bleeding her dry through a series of failed business ventures. And Bow herself was so licentious that she could shock even jaded old-Hollywood types. As Budd Schulberg, son of Paramount president B. P. Schulberg and later a gifted screenwriter (*On the Waterfront*) recalled, "They all thought she was a low-life and disgrace to the community."

But the truth about Bow was simpler. She was a scared twenty-year-old tomboy with little formal education. Her childhood friends were boys, and as a result, the things she enjoyed doing were almost exclusively reserved for men: drinking, gambling, swearing, and screwing. She was also completely sincere.

A fun-loving innocent, at first Bow behaved no worse than a typical twenty-year-old. Sure, she had parties with USC undergraduates, but they only ended in front-yard wrestling matches, like an eleven-year-old on the streets of Brooklyn. Sure, she kept the back door open so cops could stop by and grab a beer. Who wouldn't?

> **Her childhood friends were boys, and as a result, the things she enjoyed doing were almost exclusively reserved for men: drinking, gambling, swearing, and screwing.**

But Clara Bow had so few friends that she usually played cards with her maid and cook. She ended her multiple affairs with powerful men before they got bored and told her what they really thought. One such powerful man was the elder B. P. Schulberg himself, who—in addition to keeping Bow as a mistress—had her under contract at Paramount.

However much Schulberg enjoyed the pleasure of Clara's company, he needed her to appear less scandalous. In an effort to clean up her image, he made her hire a female secretary/chaperone. The woman promptly eloped with Bow's father. In an attempt to see her through a nervous breakdown, he sent her off to Reno. She returned with $100,000 in gambling debts.

Once, in 1928, Schulberg made the mistake of agreeing to host Bow for dinner. The other prominent guest was Judge Ben Lindsey, a close friend of Schulberg's wife. The judge had recently been kicked off the bench in Denver after championing premarital sex as a way to reduce the exploding divorce rate. That's right, in 1928 premarital sex was a big no-no in most of the United States. Not in Hollywood though. And Judge Lindsey, hoping to revive his career amidst the more forgiving celebrity culture, came out to interview Clara Bow as part of a *Vanity Fair* magazine series called "Impossible Interviews." It'd be perfect—a judge interviewing a law-breaking tramp!

Bow, clearly uncomfortable at the prospect of dinner with her ex-lover and boss, showed up late and tipsy. Her first move was introducing herself to Judge Lindsey with a French kiss, which he pulled away from quickly—probably because his wife was standing next to him. Even so, Clara soon wrangled him into a dance. As the judge awkwardly complied, she deftly unbuttoned his shirt. Then, arriving at his pants, she didn't hesitate and began to unzip them, too.

Suddenly, the permissive judge became a scared teenager and jumped away, putting his arm around his wife. Ushered out of the room, Bow was taken to task by B. P. Schulberg.

Clara was confused by the judge's double standard—"If he likes all that modern stuff," she asked her boss, "how come he's such an old stick-in-the-mud?" ★

MONTMARTRE CAFÉ

6763 HOLLYWOOD BLVD.

A BLOCK AWAY FROM the Hollywood Hotel, the Montmartre Café was Hollywood's first see-and-be-seen nightclub. Catering to the celebrities it fed, it opened in 1923 graced with imported chandeliers and carpets, and Romanesque architecture. (It was actually on the second floor of the building; the first, appropriately, housed a bank.)

Regulars included Mabel Normand, Joan Crawford, Valentino, Gloria Swanson, John Barrymore, and Marion Davies. The maître d', Bruce Cabot, went on to star in *King Kong*. There was dancing, even at lunch; women without partners could take their pick from "the Bachelors' table," reportedly well stocked with handsome men. The wife of airplane manufacturer Jack Maddux started a tradition called "Flying Luncheons," in which she'd take her friends to the Montmartre for lunch, and then into an airplane for an hour or two of cards and conversation while circling the city.

Founder Eddie Brandstatter, hit by the stock-market crash and a series of other bad investments, was forced to sell it in 1932. The building has since run through scores of owners with bad ideas, but managed to preserve its onetime glamour. Today it's part private-party space, part Hollywood nightclub. And the bank below has become a convenience store. ★

LOUISE BROOKS

1906–1985
ACTRESS AND MEMOIRIST

Asked why Hollywood kicked her out: *"I like to drink and fuck too much."*

Louise Brooks was popular but only mildly successful in her day. She appeared in twenty-four films, the best being *Pandora's Box* (1929), *Diary of a Lost Girl* (1929), and *Prix de Beauté* (1930). Brooks didn't help her career by turning down the lead in the Cagney classic *The Public Enemy* to visit her married lover in New York. She claimed she was blacklisted in Hollywood after refusing to sleep with studio head Harry Cohn (Columbia Pictures) and retired from film in 1938. Brooks first moved home to Kansas, then to New York, where she worked as a salesgirl at Saks Fifth Avenue. In 1955, she was unexpectedly championed by new wave filmmakers and became an international cult figure, celebrated for her realistic acting style, her flapper bob haircut ("The Black Helmet"), and her open disdain for Hollywood studios. In 1982, at age seventy-five, Brooks published her critically acclaimed memoir, *Lulu in Hollywood*, about her time in Hollywood, which is still considered one of the best inside accounts of American film.

★

NOW THAT SHE THOUGHT ABOUT IT, of course she would stay. Three days earlier, Louise Brooks and her then-husband, director Eddie Sutherland, had arrived at the Ranch for a getaway weekend.

"The Ranch" was everybody's nickname for San Simeon, the estate of newspaper mogul William Randolph Hearst. The 250,000-acre, ten-home expanse had become a nexus of Hollywood social life, courtesy of actress Marion Davies, Hearst's mistress. Eddie Sutherland declared it all very boring, unless you worshipped opulence or celebrities. But Louise Brooks had found a third object of worship: Pepi Lederer, Davies's seventeen-year-old niece. Pepi lived at San Simeon; she and Brooks became fast friends, and the teenager implored Brooks to stay a day or two longer without her husband. It ended up being three weeks.

Brooks was only twenty-two, but already she'd been notorious for almost a decade. She stood up to studio heads. She turned down choice parts. She had affairs with men and women alike, and spoke frankly about sex. When she was eighteen, she had a two-month fling with Charlie Chaplin, and she loved telling friends the glowing red penis story: Apparently, Chaplin had heard that a drop of iodine on your penis could prevent venereal disease. During a three-day sex bender with Brooks and another couple, he decided to be extra cautious. He emerged from the bathroom naked, with an erection, his storied "eighth wonder of the world" penis completely covered with red iodine. He proceeded to chase the screaming girls around the suite.

Brooks herself drank inconceivable amounts of gin. In fact, her lifelong dedication to a good drink was so unwavering that she actually got kicked out of the Algonquin Hotel during the Round Table years. And during her San Simeon stay, gin was again her biggest problem. Specifically, that she couldn't find any. Famously concerned about his mistress Davies's drinking problem, Hearst had forbidden almost all spirits on estate grounds, rationing one cocktail at meals, some sherry and champagne here and there, or a few bottles at a business meeting. But while the teenage Pepi could get champagne easily by flirting with Hearst's assistant, Brooks preferred gin.

One afternoon, Brooks and Pepi were carousing in the swimming pool, drinking and "fooling around a bit," when word came that a group of Hearst newspaper editors were in one of the outbuildings for a meeting. Brooks knew what that meant: real liquor. *Good* liquor. Within minutes, she, Pepi, and eight teenage girls, all in bathing suits, danced in a line through the meeting-room door. The men were seated at a table, well fortified with booze and cigars. As the parade of flesh shimmied past, startling, distracting, and

> Brooks was only twenty-two, but already she'd been notorious for almost a decade. She stood up to studio heads. She turned down choice parts. She had affairs with men and women alike, and spoke frankly about sex.

entrancing the men, ringleader Brooks snatched a few bottles from the table. Their mission accomplished, the line of girls left as hastily as they had come.

The door closing, one confused newspaper editor turned to a housekeeper. "Does Mr. Hearst know these people are here?" ★

PRIX DE BEAUTÉ (1930)

W hen Italian director Augusto Genina began shooting the French noir film *Prix de Beaute*, he could scarcely believe the daily schedule of Louise Brooks, the American actress who, twenty-five years later, would become history's most revered flapper. Then she was just a stunningly pretty second-tier Hollywood actress with a work method that, had he not already fallen in love with her, Genina would never have tolerated.

This would be Brooks's last European film and first talkie, although since she hardly spoke a word of French, all her dialogue and singing would be dubbed—probably a good thing, given her lifestyle. Brooks woke up at 4 a.m. and drank a bottle of champagne. She'd be asleep again by six. At which time a small crew would enter her hotel room and carry her, asleep, to a car. The car was driven to the lot. She was then carried, still asleep, to the makeup room.

The hair and makeup people did their entire job while Brooks *still* slept. Finally, when a scene was close to rolling, they would somehow rouse her. She would emerge on the set, nail her scene, return to her dressing room to drink gin, and fall back to sleep until the next scene was ready. Brooks was somehow able stay on her feet through a few hours in the late afternoon, only to return to the hotel and fall asleep at around midnight. This pattern continued for the duration of principal photography. Except the last day.

On that final day of production, Brooks didn't show up at all. Desperate to finish the film, after twenty-four hours, Genina had to call in the police. Three days later, they found her holed up in a chateau. Her boyfriend at the time—the bartender from the hotel.

MARION DAVIES

1897–1961
ACTRESS AND SOCIALITE

"Sober citizens should be sent to Siberia."

Marion Davies was perhaps most famous for her real-life role as the mistress of newspaper mogul William Randolph Hearst, whom she nicknamed "droopy drawers." The queen of Hollywood social life in the '20s and '30s, she starred in over fifty films, all but the very first financed by Hearst. Her biggest hit was *When Knighthood Was in Flower* (1922); and her best known film remains *Going Hollywood* (1933) with Bing Crosby. Refusing to act in more than a few films per year, Davies was equally famous for throwing epic, costumed theme parties: Cowboys and Indians, Civil War, a circus-themed party complete with merry-go-round. Although Davies freely admitted to starting her affair with Hearst as a gold-digger, she stayed because she fell in love. In fact, after decades of being lavished with Hearst's money, when his empire started to crumble she wrote him a check for $1 million. Davies was devastated by her caricature in Orson Welles's *Citizen Kane*. It turns out "Rosebud" was not a sled at all, but rather Hearst's nickname for her clitoris.

★

THE GIRLS WANTED DETAILS — immediately. Actress sisters Norma and Constance Talmadge and screenwriter Anita Loos, the founders of a makeshift Tuesday-night girls club, had learned that their newest regular, fun-loving Ziegfeld dancer Marion Davies, had a story to tell.

The previous night, Davies had attended a party hosted by the country's richest mogul, William Randolph Hearst. Correction: She had been *personally invited* to attend a *very small* party hosted by Hearst at one of his many residences. Davies, a goofy winsome blonde with a stutter, entered the party assuming that one of Hearst's friends must have taken a shine to her, or perhaps to her girlfriend. But then Hearst himself approached her. It seems he had seen Davies in a stage show and was very impressed.

In private, Davies had made no secret of her desire to follow her mother's advice and marry a wealthy man. Her most ardent admirer at the time was the millionaire publisher of the *Brooklyn Daily Eagle*. But here, now, flirting with her, was the infinitely more wealthy, more famous (and more married) newspaper publisher. She freaked. She became anxious and awkward, then tried to soothe her frazzled nerves with champagne. The trouble was that no amount of liquor could ease her anxiety, try as she might. And instead of calming her nerves, it unsettled her stomach. She simply became an extremely frazzled girl who needed to throw up. Badly.

> The trouble was that no amount of liquor could ease her anxiety, try as she might. And instead of calming her nerves, it unsettled her stomach. She simply became an extremely frazzled girl who needed to throw up. Badly.

Obviously, Davies couldn't let Hearst know about this. So instead of asking for the bathroom, she snuck into the nearest doorway. It was a study, but Davies didn't have the luxury of choice now. She vomited behind some corner pillows. Mortified, she covered up her gift with the pillows, didn't say a word, and left.

Well, she thought, *so much for ever seeing Hearst again.* ★

THE GRAND DAMES all loved champagne. It was the beverage of choice for generations of leading ladies, from Marion Davies to Ginger Rogers to Elizabeth Taylor. Which is not to say champagne was just for women (after all, Bogart drinks it in *Casablanca*).

If nothing else, the Mimosa provides a ready excuse to drink in the morning. It was Marion Davies's cocktail of choice, perhaps because the orange juice hid the alcohol from her somewhat teetotaling lover, William Randolph Hearst.

The problem is, the Mimosa has been woefully cheapened in recent decades, with restaurants using poor quality orange juice—the most important element in the recipe being "freshly squeezed." And Davies, a woman who once had a bar built in 1560 transported from Surrey, England, to her Santa Monica beach house, would never have skimped on the ingredients.

MIMOSA

. . . .

2 OZ. FRESHLY SQUEEZED ORANGE JUICE

4 OZ. PREMIUM CHAMPAGNE

Combine in a champagne flute or a narrow highball glass.

SAN SIMEON

SAN SIMEON, CALIFORNIA
750 HEARST CASTLE RD.

OPEN!

IF THE HOLLYWOOD PR machine was turning its celebrities into America's new royalty, San Simeon (nicknamed "the Ranch" by its owner) was their palace. William Randolph Hearst built the palatial estate in the early twenties and lived there with his longtime lover, actress Marion Davies, in an open affair for more than three decades—Hearst's wife and kids were in New York.

It is hard to overstate the splendor that was and in some ways still is San Simeon, 250,000 acres along the shimmering coastline between Los Angeles and San Francisco. As Coleridge wrote, "In Xanadu did Kubla Khan / A stately pleasure-dome decree." And San Simeon was indeed a pleasure dome, director Orson Welles in fact changing the estate's name to Xanadu for his film *Citizen Kane,* which was based in part upon Hearst. Characterized by biographer Richard Meryman as a "Medici gone mad," the newspaper tycoon spent twenty-six years building the estate, eventually bankrupting himself. Designed by architect Julia Morgan, the castle is a hybrid of different historical styles (Spanish Revival, Gothic, Greco-Roman), described as a cross between the Palazzo Uffizi and the Hippodrome.

Over a mile of pergola encircles the hill, Hearst desiring the hedges be high enough for a "tall man with a tall hat on a tall horse." This from a man who once spent $12,000 on a planting of daphnes. In addition to a landing strip, stables, and a beach house, the grounds included what was once the world's largest private zoo, complete with zebras, giraffes, and ostriches. In addition, all the produce eaten at the Ranch was farmed and the meat and poultry raised on site.

Hearst's mistress, Marion Davies, made the Ranch a film-industry mecca with her extravagant, often themed costume parties. Guests arrived at nearby San Louis Obispo via Hearst's private train car and were then shuttled to the Ranch in limousines. Each visitor had a dedicated servant. Sometimes a premade costume waited in their room.

The other significant Hollywood estate noted for its parties, the Pickford/Fairbanks home Pickfair, could not come close to approaching the opulence. At San Simeon you could sleep in Napoleon's bed (in a guest room, no less) and wonder if Josephine had graced it before you. There were three main guesthouses, totaling over 10,000 square feet, which could house over seventy-five guests. There were picnics, horse rides, and even campouts, complete with bonfires, sing-alongs, and grand tents pitched over wooden floors where cowboys would sing and Spaniards dance. The indoor pool featured approximately 800,000 gold-leaf tiles, installed over the course of three years. There was a ten-foot high-dive (this is indoors, remember) and a skylight cut into the ceiling (the tennis courts were directly above) to let in sun. The famous Neptune outdoor pool held 345,000 gallons of water and featured marble colonnades with a Greco-Roman temple at one end. No slide; perhaps that seemed excessive.

Over the decades guests would include such international stars as Charlie Chaplin, the Marx Brothers, Bob Hope,

Jimmy Stewart, and Joan Crawford. World leaders would also visit: Calvin Coolidge, Franklin Roosevelt, and Winston Churchill among them. It was a grand time at the Casa Grande (as the main house was called). Hearst was, in fact, not a strict teetotaler. True, he had sworn off hard liquor as a young man at Harvard, but he enjoyed wine quite a bit. His wine cellar stored up to 10,000 bottles, of which 3,000 still remain. He loved beer, too, in particular, German lager and Irish stout.

If there were limits put on liquor, it was out of Hearst's concern for Davies, who by most accounts was a cheerful alcoholic with an adorable stutter. If known drinkers were on the weekend's guest list—and there never seemed to be a shortage (Flynn, Gilbert, Mankiewicz, Grant, Niven, etc.)—Hearst would make sure they had not smuggled in a private stash. But the house itself was not too stingy with booze. Cocktails were served in the Assembly room from 7–9 p.m., an enormous chamber designed to resemble an Italian palazzo hall. During dinner, held in a room Hearst called "the Refectory," only wine was served. The guests were seated at two long seventeenth-century refectory tables with Hearst and Davies in the middle. The tables were only three feet wide, perfect for conversation, and part of being a good guest (and securing a return invitation) was to be engaging.

Certainly, anyone who got embarrassingly drunk would not be invited back. And some say the drinks were watered down and that eventually the cocktail hour was reduced to just ten minutes. But after dinner, guests retreated to the billiard room, men and women alike, Hearst being quite modern in this way. Cigars were lit and after-dinner drinks served. Often a movie would be screened in the private theater, equipped with fifty lodge seats covered in silk damask. Perhaps a new release from Hearst's film company Cosmopolitan Productions, such as *The Patsy* or *Show People,* and likely starring Davies. The original screen was designed to be lowered down through the floor into the basement, to make room for stage performances by celebrity guests. All alcoholic beverages were cut off at 1 a.m., but cold beer remained on tap in the kitchen throughout the night.

Even so, Davies responded to the house rules by hiding bottles of gin in the tanks above various toilets, and visiting girlfriends were expected to spend much of their time in "the Salon"—the downstairs bathroom. Eventually, the sprawling estate somehow became too constricting, and Davies had Hearst build her a palace of her own in Santa Monica.

Called simply "the Beach House," though anything but simple, the property was an enormous thirty-four-bedroom ocean-front Georgian estate also designed by Julia Morgan. It would one day become a hotel.

Unfortunately, independence was not to be sobriety's best advocate. Davies was so devoted a drinker that Dorothy Comingore, who just played a character based on her—Susan Alexander in *Citizen Kane*—went on to become a lifelong alcoholic. Even late in Davies's life, after Hearst had passed away and San Simeon was quieted, Davies's occasional parties still offered a glimpse of lost Hollywood, of true glamour and excess. One of her final blowouts, after Hearst's death and close to her own, involved 700 guests, 40 cases of champagne, 80 pounds of beef tenderloin, 50 pounds of caviar, a roman sarcophagus to chill the champagne, and rosebushes with hundreds of gardenias pinned to them. Why gardenias, nobody knew.

Davies walked downstairs an hour late, wearing $750,000 worth of jewelry. She loved hosting parties, she said, because "then no one can tell me to get out." It was an attitude in keeping with her lover's heirs. Because as time has shown, the Hearst family also has little interest in telling people to get out—at least in regard to San Simeon. The estate was generously donated to the state of California in 1957, not long after Hearst's death. A historic park, it is now open to the public year around, offering daily tours that cater to over one million visitors a year. ★

WILLIAM RANDOLPH HEARST so enjoyed German lager and Irish stout that he kept a cold keg of each on tap in the kitchen of San Simeon at all times. In addition to liking the taste of stout, he believed the beverage offered health benefits, once even recommending it to his architect Julia Morgan when she became ill. There may be something to Hearst's thinking. Guinness long ran advertisements with the slogan, "Guiness Is Good for You." And it may just be true: in recent years, a study by the University of Wisconsin has found that Guiness contains antioxidants.

Legendary carouser Errol Flynn was also a proponent of the medicinal quali-ties of stout (that being perhaps the only belief he shared with Hearst). Flynn's attitude was summed up pithily in his declaration, "Guinness Stout is good for the gonads." After four wives, two statutory rape charges (he was acquitted), and countless starlets, groupies, and prostitutes, at age fifty Flynn would die in the arms of a sixteen-year-old. Turns out, it was a heart attack that killed him (as was the case with Hearst), while his gonads remained intact.

Healing properties aside, the Half and Half is worth a try. Please note: while it is sometimes also called a Black and Tan, the Half and Half is made with lager, not ale.

HALF AND HALF

· ·

8 OZ. CHILLED LAGER
8 OZ. CHILLED GUINNESS STOUT

Pour lager into a chilled pint glass. Pour stout in over the back of a bar spoon so as to make it float.

W. C. FIELDS

1880–1946
ACTOR AND COMEDIAN

*"Back in my rummy days,
I would tremble and shake
for hours upon arising.
It was the only exercise
I got."*

W.C.

Fields was known for his piquant one-liners, his signature top hat, and his loveable-grump persona. Self-conscious about his bulbous nose, he had cartilage removed in an attempt to fix the problem, but that only worsened it. A major star of vaudeville, Broadway, and radio, Fields made a number of silent films but did not become a star until sound arrived—he needed dialogue to translate his act to the screen. Fields's most enduring films are *The Dentist* (1932), *The Man on the Flying Trapeze* (1935), *You Can't Cheat an Honest Man* (1939), and *The Bank Dick* (1940). He died in Pasadena on Christmas Day as his girlfriend sprayed the roof with a hose to approximate his favorite sound, falling rain.

★

SPRING 1941 AND AMERICA WAS ON THE VERGE of war. Take a look at the May 12 issue of *Life* magazine. The cover shows a U.S. Army parachutist, braced for whatever is to come. The world was at war, and America was inching toward declaration. But within the magazine's pages was the real bombshell: the legendary W. C. Fields had started to exercise. At age sixty, the portly actor had apparently abandoned his lifelong disdain for health and good sense—he had even hired a personal trainer.

Then, as now, working out was common in an industry built upon youth and beauty. Never mind that Fields had neither, the real surprise here was that he could walk, let alone jog. Fields drank heavily anytime he was awake. In fact, the *Life* article's first paragraphs were devoted to reminding readers of his status as a first-class "tippler." He would only confess to being drunk one time—it lasted "from the Spanish-American war to the New Deal." The *Life* photographer witnessed Fields drinking straight rum from a "tall glass with a wooden lid, to 'keep out the flies.'" He finished five such drinks in the two hours the photos were taken. While working out.

He had also spent the morning drinking double martinis.

Not in the halls of Seagram's will you find a more staunch advocate of the martini than William Claude Fields, Bill to his friends. Fields started drinking relatively late in life. As a young vaudeville performer, he didn't touch alcohol because he wanted full reflexes for his astounding juggling and stage acts. Eventually, out of boredom, he started drinking whiskey as a means to socialize while on tour. The oft-reported date is 1904, when Fields was twenty-five, but in the W. C. universe no fact was safe from convenient rearrangement. Whatever the case, by the dawn of Prohibition in 1920, he had discovered martinis.

> **Fields started drinking relatively late in life. As a young vaudeville performer, he didn't touch alcohol because he wanted full reflexes for his astounding juggling and stage acts.**

At the time, many people adopted the martini merely because gin was the easiest liquor to bootleg. Fields was not one of those people. He wrote essays about the drink's perfection. It was the object of passion in his only known poem. He decried any nonalcoholic substitute, even water—because he reasoned "fish fuck in it."

By 1941 Fields estimated that he was drinking two quarts of gin a day. How he would survive daily workouts nobody knew, but apparently, this was no joke. An upstairs room and the garage had been converted into gyms. He had a stationary bike with a full bar just in front of it, which his girlfriend, Carlotta Monti, said "provided incentive." And so it was that his trainer, Robert Howard, would show up daily at 4 p.m. Fields would run around his lake while being timed. He lifted weights, rode the exercise bike, and jogged on the roads of Bel Air with either a beer wagon or a starlet running in front of him. Again, "incentive."

The third photo shows Fields, shirtless, taking a drink of rum from that aforementioned tall glass. Fields wrote his own caption: "It is imperative that the right elbow be kept in perfect condition at all times." Apparently no Fields endeavor would be complete without a few jokes, the *Life* article included. He was indeed a master of the one-liner, especially when it came to booze. ★

W. C. FIELDS ON DRINKING

"I like to keep a bottle of whiskey handy in case I see a snake, which I also keep handy."

★

"I cook with wine, sometimes I even add it to the food."

★

"If I had my life to live over, I'd live over a saloon."

★

"I exercise extreme self control; I never drink anything stronger than gin before breakfast."

★

"Some weasel took the cork out of my lunch."

★

"During one of our trips through Afghanistan, we lost our corkscrew. We had to live on food and water for several days!"

★

"I never worry about being driven to drink; I just worry about being driven home."

★

"Who put pineapple juice in my pineapple juice?"

★

"I was in love with a beautiful blonde once, dear. She drove me to drink. That's the one thing I am indebted to her for."

★

"The cost of living has gone up another dollar a quart."

JOHN GILBERT

1897–1936
ACTOR AND MATINEE IDOL

Telegram to the set of John Gilbert's final film:
HURRY UP, THE COSTS ARE STAGGERING.

Reply:
SO IS THE CAST.

J ohn Gilbert was known for his striking looks, rivaling Rudolph Valentino for the mantle of "The Great Lover." At one point the highest-paid actor in Hollywood, Gilbert starred in *The Big Parade* (1925), the second-highest grossing silent film in history. He had affairs with Clara Bow, Lupe Vélez, Marlene Dietrich, and most notably Greta Garbo—who left him standing at the altar. After an MGM underling signed Gilbert to what was then an outrageous $250,000 per movie, the studio pushed poor material his way, hoping Gilbert would leave. At the arrival of sound, Gilbert secretly slipped into a screening of his first talkie only to hear the audience laugh at his squeaky, high-pitched voice. (The high pitch was rumored to have been exaggerated by MGM's sound engineer.) With no movie offers, but still under contract, Gilbert refused to be bought out. He became a $10,000-a-week beach bum.

★

FOR GOODNESS SAKES, WHAT NOW? Adela Rogers St. Johns, a well-known journalist with Hearst and a Hollywood social fixture of the era (who, fifty years later, appeared as herself in *Reds*), was used to the occasional racket from the house next door.

St. Johns covered the entertainment beat, so she knew what to expect when the house was rented by MGM producer Paul Bern. Bern was the trusted confidant of production chief and Hollywood *wunderkind* Irving Thalberg—the inspiration for Monroe Starr, protagonist of Fitzgerald's unfinished novel, *The Last Tycoon*.

Thalberg was forever stopping by the house with the actor John Gilbert. And wherever Gilbert went, loud music, bootleg liquor, and women followed, Gilbert being the reigning matinee idol and MGM's golden boy—golden on-screen, anyway.

Off-screen, he was the opposite. For one thing, MGM president Louis B. Mayer despised Gilbert and by 1928 was refusing to speak to him. Another problem was Gilbert himself. Longtime friend and director King Vidor described the actor as the first in a long line of Hollywood stars who, young and lacking confidence, confused fiction with reality and became the roles they played. Off-screen, he would adopt the mannerisms of each new character until the next role came along. "John was impressionable, not too well established in the role of his own life."

One day Gilbert would be cast as a Russian and hire an entire Russian orchestra to perform at his house over caviar dinners; the next he'd fire the orchestra, dump his caviar and, having played a sailor of some type, buy an extravagant sailboat that he didn't know how to use and would sell a year later.

Gilbert was also dubbed "The Great Lover," and that role, too, he embraced off-screen, to the delight of many Hollywood actresses, models, and extras. His affair with Greta Garbo lasted three years, during which she repeatedly balked at the idea of marriage. After finally agreeing to wed, the story goes that Garbo left Gilbert standing at the altar. After that profound embarrassment and his disastrous attempt to shift to talkies, Gilbert's life and relationships grew increasingly dark. On-screen he was now a failure and, true to form, he became a failure in real life.

> **Gilbert was also dubbed "The Great Lover," and that role, too, he embraced off-screen, to the delight of many Hollywood actresses, models, and extras.**

But none of those things had happened yet in 1926, on the night that Adela Rogers St. Johns claimed to have heard the party at her neighbor's house. At that time, Gilbert was still a handsome, charming movie star who liked women and loved parties. And that was the cause of the ruckus next door. Or so St. Johns thought. But the more she listened, the more it sounded distinctly different from a party. Her curiosity was heightened by the possible presence of Paul Bern's fiancée, the raunchy actress Barbara La Marr ("I take lovers like roses. By the dozen.") St. Johns's reporting instincts took over and she walked next door. What she discovered became legend.

St. Johns entered to find Gilbert and Thalberg crowded into a small bathroom. The producer Paul Bern was on the floor, wearing what looked like a neck brace. He appeared to have been crying, though his friends seemed more on the verge of laughter. Gilbert emerged, poured a drink, and unwound the story for St. Johns.

La Marr had been refusing Bern's proposals for months, and finally she eloped with cowboy star Jack Dougherty. That night, Bern found out. As the friends got more and more drunk, Bern left for the bathroom. Soon thereafter, they heard Bern's histrionics, and rushed in to find Bern beyond hammered with his head inside the toilet. Trying to drown himself.

Containing their laughter, the friends tried to pull him out, but now they had another problem: the older, pudgy Bern had become stuck inside the toilet bowl he was supposed to drown in. He couldn't even get *that* right. Thalberg got a screwdriver and eventually Bern was extracted from his poor-man's noose. Gilbert shared with St. Johns his theory about the attempted suicide. "He has a Magdalene complex," Gilbert said. "Paul does crazy things for whores."

St. Johns laughed, but there was still the question of how a doctor could possibly have had time to drive over, outfit Bern with a neck brace, and leave again. The question was answered easily enough; the thing around his neck was no brace—it was the toilet seat. ★

GARDEN OF ALLAH HOTEL

8152 SUNSET BLVD.

THE GARDEN OF ALLAH was the original *Melrose Place,* except its residents were great writers and actors instead of knuckleheads.

Initially a mansion, the residence was leased by debaucherous silent actress Alla Nazimova in 1918. By 1927, her career fading and in need of a steady retirement income, she remodeled the house as a bungalow hotel, complete with the now-mandatory pool in the center courtyard. She celebrated the occasion by throwing an eighteen-hour party.

At one point or another over the next decade, every important figure of prewar cinema film lived there. Humphrey Bogart, Laurence Olivier, John Barrymore, Vivien Leigh, Charlie Chaplin, Gloria Swanson, Fatty Arbuckle, Clara Bow, the Marx Brothers, Errol Flynn, Greta Garbo, and Lillian Gish—all either lived at the Garden of Allah or partied there so much that it became a second home. Some stayed for days, others for months.

A host of East Coast writers adopted it as their own private oasis from the soulless and unforgiving film industry. A West Coast Algonquin, such famous residents included George S. Kaufman, F. Scott and Zelda Fitzgerald, John Steinbeck, William Faulkner, Alexander Woollcott, Dorothy Parker, and Robert Benchley. As one might imagine of a forty-room apartment complex that houses actors and self-loathing writers, the Garden also became their own private Sodom.

Writer Lucius Beebe described it as the most pronounced example of "concentrated alcoholism and general dementia" since the Harvard-Yale boat races during Prohibition. The tradition of diving into the pool while still decked out in formal regalia was reportedly started by Clara Bow, though the most famous incident involves the time Tallulah Bankhead, the original celebutante, allegedly dove in fully clothed and covered with diamonds. Then there was the evening John Carradine proclaimed he was Jesus Christ and tried to walk across the pool. It was just such antics that supposedly inspired Robert Benchley's famous quip, "Why don't you get out of those wet clothes and into a dry martini," though Benchley insisted that his friend, actor Charles Butterworth, said it first.

As late as 1941, long after Nazimova had sold the place, Sinatra lived at the Garden during his stint at the Cocoanut Grove. Apparently the Ambassador was too stuffy for the Chairman of the Board. When the Garden closed, in late August 1959, its last hurrah was a costume party to which 350 people showed up, many dressed as former denizens.

The complex was torn down, and today the site is home of a strip mall anchored by a McDonald's. ★

D. W. GRIFFITH

1875–1948
DIRECTOR

* * * * * * * * * * * * * * * *

*"The motion pictures
give man a place to go
besides the saloons."*

D.W. Griffith is unanimously considered the greatest American filmmaker of the Silent Era and the first American "auteur." A notorious perfectionist, he began by making silent shorts for Biograph Films in New York City. Griffith soon moved west and became both the first director to shoot a film in Hollywood (*In Old California*, 1910) and the first American director to make a feature-length film (*Judith of Bethulia*, 1914). Credited with pioneering almost every device that now constitutes modern cinematic language, from basics like fades, dissolves, and close-ups to the more complicated techniques of flashbacks and crosscutting. He launched the careers of Lillian Gish, Mary Pickford, Constance Talmadge, and director Raoul Walsh, among others. Griffith's controversial second feature, *The Birth of a Nation* (1915), was the first Hollywood blockbuster, but his follow-up a year later, *Intolerance* (now considered one of the top ten films of all time), was a box office failure that began a steady decline in his output and popularity. When sound arrived, Griffith insisted that it ruined the poetry of filmmaking—and would be a passing fad.

————————— ★ —————————

EVERYTHING HAD BEEN FINE just minutes ago. The party of four were sitting in a discreet booth at the swanky Hollywood restaurant Romanoff's. There was studio mogul Samuel Goldwyn, his wife Frances, the hot new director Billy Wilder, and his fiancée Audrey Young, all laughing and sharing stories. Wilder was fresh off the success of what would become two of his great classics, *Double Indemnity* and that whiskey-soaked horror show *The Lost Weekend*. Goldwyn was eager to produce his next film. The problem was, Wilder had no idea what he wanted to do next.

It was then that Wilder spotted him at the bar—a tall drunk staring them down. The man was dressed like a deposed czar: his clothes regal but frayed, stained with drink. To Wilder's growing consternation, the man started heading toward their table. He walked unsteadily, and everyone could smell gin when he stuck his finger in Goldwyn's face. "Here you are, you son of a bitch," he muttered, "I ought to be making pictures." Although

He had grown to like sound films, which he once predicted would be dead within a decade: "The trouble with the whole industry is that it talked before it thought."

Goldwyn was too stunned to muster a response, his wife Frances did. She told the "silly drunk" to leave them alone immediately. The old man acquiesced and walked away. Immediately, Wilder asked Goldwyn who the hell that was. Goldwyn ordered another drink. "That," he said, "was D. W. Griffith."

There had been rumors that the increasingly reclusive Griffith had been spotted out on the town again. Only a few weeks earlier, journalist Ezra Goodman had heard that Griffith had been holed up at the Knickerbocker Hotel for almost three years, having meals and liquor delivered to his room. Goodman showed up unannounced and tried to interview the great director; his request was declined. A few days later, he showed up with a beautiful young girl, who called alone. Griffith immediately let her in. Quickly, Goodman elbowed his way in after. Unable to kick Goodman out, and after a few drinks, Griffith engaged in an actual interview that would be his last.

He had grown to like sound films, which he once predicted would be dead within a decade. ("The trouble with the whole industry is that it talked before it thought.") He blamed himself for his career problems. He'd grown to dislike *The Birth of a Nation,* which he called a lousy, cheap melodrama. He had lived in the hotel for a few years; before that he had homes in Los Angeles and Kentucky. He had some money and was comfortable. He may have grown to like sound films, but he hated current cinema. Sound wasn't the problem—the lack of good directors was. He liked Sturges, Walsh, and a couple of others. He liked *Gone with the Wind,* saw it twice. He loved *Citizen Kane,* "particularly the ideas Welles took from me." "Ah, the superb egotism of the old man in his hotel room!" Goodman commented in print later.

Eventually, things grew quiet and Goodman took his cue to leave. Griffith had been assuming the girl would stay. When she didn't, Goodman didn't know if Griffith's parting words were about movies or the interview: "We have taken beauty and exchanged it for stilted voices."

Goodman's article was the type of story that has since become an old saw of arts journalism—young fan finds old master living in squalor, brings the forgotten master to public attention, and master has an artistic renaissance. The problem was that in 1948, nobody liked such stories. They contained too much truth. Goodman eventually got it printed in a B-grade gossip rag when Griffith died a few months later from a cerebral hemorrhage.

Nobody paid attention to Goodman's story until he turned it into a book a decade later, but at least one man was profoundly affected by Griffith's final months: Billy Wilder. When Goldwyn told Wilder that he'd just seen the ghost of the man who single-handedly dragged film from vaudeville novelty to genuine art—Griffith being one of Wilder's idols—Wilder was deeply affected. Goldwyn would only understand how much so when he got the script for Wilder's next film some months later. It was titled *Sunset Boulevard*—the definitive elegy for the fading stars of the silent era. ★

A FORGOTTEN PRECURSOR to today's Screwdriver, the near-obsolete Orange Blossom was one of the most popular cocktails of the Silent Era. Fatty Arbuckle's costar, Virginia Rappe, was downing Orange Blossoms at San Francisco's luxurious Hotel St. Francis the night she met her demise. Authorities would charge that she'd been crushed under Fatty's great weight. Louise Brooks and Chaplin were drinking Orange Blossoms the night the little tramp painted his penis red with iodine and chased her around the hotel suite.

But perhaps the most dedicated aficionado was D. W. Griffith. As an old man, living alone at the Knickerbocker Hotel, the silent era's greatest director kept his windows lined with plump oranges, the key ingredient to his favorite cocktail.

ORANGE BLOSSOM

2 OZ. GIN

2 OZ. FRESHLY SQUEEZED ORANGE JUICE

¼ OZ. SIMPLE SYRUP

ORANGE WHEEL

Pour all ingredients into a cocktail shaker filled with ice cubes. Shake well. Strain into a chilled cocktail glass. Garnish with orange wheel.

ALEXANDRIA HOTEL
501 S. SPRING ST.

WHEN IT OPENED, IN 1906, the Alexandria Hotel was immediately crowned the swankiest hotel in Los Angeles; its posh lobby and opulent ballroom (added in 1911 and named the Palm Court) gave it glamour unrivaled by any hotel in the dusty outcroppings of Hollywood or Edendale — or anywhere in town, for that matter.

Presidents held speeches in the ballroom, oilmen and industrial titans closed deals in its restaurant, and soon enough, rich and powerful film industry players would congregate in its bar. In the lobby, between crystal chandeliers and marble floors, lay "the million-dollar carpet," so named because of the many film deals that closed within the walls of the hotel.

Actors would linger in and around the lobby, hoping to be noticed. (Free sandwiches at the hotel bar didn't hurt either.) In 1918 Rudolph Valentino charmed his way into his first lead roles in film here. Chaplin would rent a suite and try out some of his gags in the lobby. Cowboy actor Tom Mix rode his horse through the entrance. Jack Warner lived there, and Gloria Swanson met her first husband there.

The hotel's luster began to fade as Hollywood developed; by the 1960s, the rooms had crumbled into tenements and the ballroom, long neglected, had become a training ring for boxers. Renovations in the 1980s and 2000s led to its reopening, in 2008, as the most fabulous and historic low-income apartments in Southern California. ★

BUSTER KEATON

1895–1966

ACTOR, COMEDIAN,
DIRECTOR, WRITER

"I'll prove I'm your true friend by not letting you get soused alone."

Buster Keaton's talent as a silent film comedian is rated second only to Charlie Chaplin's, and first by many. Nicknamed "Great Stone Face" for his unwavering stoic expression, his other trademarks were a porkpie hat and an astounding gift for physical comedy. Keaton started his own studio in 1920, and his streak of classic comedies from 1920–1929 is still hailed as an unparalleled run of flawless films. He did every one of his own stunts, including the classic chase on top of a train in his best-known film, *The General* (1926), a film considered by many critics to be the best comedy of all time. A move to MGM and the arrival of sound caused an unexpected lull in Keaton's career, but he had a long and fruitful second act as a character actor and television star (*The Buster Keaton Show*).

★

CHRIST, WHERE AM I?" Buster Keaton was getting used to this feeling. A few weeks earlier, on Christmas morning, he had woken up alone somewhere on the MGM lot surrounded by the ruins of a party. He had cuts on his head. It took him a few days to piece together that he'd gone a little overboard at the studio's annual pre-Christmas bash, trying (and failing) to do pratfalls after drinking an entire bottle of whiskey.

But this was a little more confusing. The last thing Keaton remembered was being at home in the Cheviot Hills area of Los Angeles, a few days after Christmas. Now, as the fog cleared, he found himself in a room he couldn't quite place, probably because he'd never been there before. The mystery of his location, however, could be solved just by looking out the window: He was in Mexico.

Keaton usually went to the Agua Caliente resort and casino in Tijuana. During prohibition, Agua Caliente was the day-trip of choice for the Hollywood elite — a resort hotel with a racetrack, spa, golf, tennis, gambling, prostitution, and most important, booze. But Keaton definitely wasn't there now. This, curiously, was the nearby town of Ensenada. A woman slept next to him. Unfortunately, he knew who *she* was: the nurse MGM had hired to keep him sober.

MGM decided to hire a full-time nurse, Mae Scriven, to keep him off the bottle. Clearly, that hadn't worked either. Buster quickly seduced her, and soon enough the pair of them were going on benders together.

For his past few films, MGM had mandated sobriety and would check Keaton into the Keeley Institute before production started. The Keeley method was simple. Upon arrival, you would immediately be put on a rigid liquid-only diet: whiskey, gin, rum, beer, brandy, wine. You'd get a drink every half hour. You'd throw up when necessary to avoid alcohol poisoning. After three days, you left swearing that you'd never touch another drop. It is a practice still in use, now known as aversion therapy.

But when Keaton went through Keeley before the picture he was currently shooting (*What! No Beer?*), the cure didn't stick. He was drinking again within hours. And so MGM decided to hire a full-time nurse, Mae Scriven, to keep him off the bottle. Clearly, that hadn't worked either. Buster quickly seduced her, and soon enough the pair of them were going on benders together. And although he hadn't counted on the charade continuing this long, here they now were — in bed together, in Ensenada, Mexico. Scriven, at least, could remember everything.

Apparently, Keaton had suggested the trip a few days before New Year's. It was now the second week in January. He couldn't care less that he missed the mandatory New Year's party at MGM chief Louis B. Mayer's house. Or that he was holding up production of *What! No Beer?* He'd done that a million times before. If that was all the bad news, he was golden. Turns out it wasn't. Mae Scriven cheerfully informed him that they were now Mr. and Mrs. Buster Keaton. On January 8th, they'd gone before a judge in Ensenada and had made it official.

For the rest of his life, Keaton could not remember a single thing about the wedding day of his "marriage of inconvenience." What was far more likely is that he spent that morning in Ensenada thinking about his last marriage, to Natalie Talmadge, the nonacting sister of Constance and Norma. Or specifically, the fact that they weren't yet divorced. ★

the **BROWN DERBY**

3427 WILSHIRE BLVD.
1628 NORTH VINE ST.

F OR ALMOST HALF A century, the Brown Derby was a Los Angeles institution, the first and finest purveyor of upscale comfort food. Its building, which was literally shaped like a brown derby hat, became an icon of studio-era Hollywood. When it opened in 1926, actors and executives loved its late hours (open until 4 a.m.), its ostentatious policy of delivering phone calls directly to your table, and its semiofficial policy of only hiring attractive women for its waitstaff. The in-crowd sat in VIP booths that circled the room, while fans could occupy tables in the center to catalog their idols' every bite. Charlie Chaplin, W. C. Fields, and John Barrymore were regulars. Co-owner and playwright Wilson Mizner had a standing claim on Booth 50.

A second location opened in 1929 on Vine St. It soon became the hottest lunch spot in Hollywood, decorated with caricatures of the stars that ate there—which were judiciously rotated based on the subject's standing in town. Clark Gable proposed to Carole Lombard in Booth 5. Stars began getting their fan mail delivered there. Predictably, Hearst gossip queen Louella Parsons eventually pitched a tent and became the most powerful careermaker (and -breaker) in American celebrity journalism. Her nemesis, Hedda

Hopper, later took over the other half of the room.

The Derby continued as one of Hollywood's finest restaurants until the late 1980s, by which time both restaurants had closed for good. The original location had a strip mall built around it, and today the signature derby sits incongruously among insurance brokers and cell-phone hawkers. The dome itself houses a Korean bar popular among hipsters. ★

THE GENERALLY ACCEPTED STORY is that late one night Brown Derby president Robert Cobb found himself hastily preparing a meal. Sid Grauman, showman and owner of the famous Chinese Theater, had dropped by, but the restaurant's kitchen was almost bare. Improvising, Cobb tossed together lettuce, bacon, and blue cheese—and the Cobb Salad was born.

As for the Brown Derby Cocktail, its history is a bit murkier. Some say it was absolutely created at the restaurant. Others credit the nearby Vendome Restaurant with inventing the drink and naming it after its neighbor. Still others argue the cocktail just looks like a brown hat. Regardless, both the drink and the restaurant were wildly popular in the 1930s.

BROWN DERBY COCKTAIL

2 OZ. BOURBON

1 OZ. FRESHLY SQUEEZED GRAPEFRUIT JUICE

½ OZ. HONEY

Pour all ingredients into a cocktail shaker filled with ice cubes. Shake well. Strain into a chilled cocktail glass.

FRITZ LANG

1890–1976
DIRECTOR

"Directors who don't drink, the day they drink will be the day they'll make the best film in the world."

Considered one of the all-time masters, in his era, Fritz Lang was rivaled only by Hitchcock and Hawks. Born in Vienna, Lang was seriously wounded while serving in the Austrian army during World War I. Discharged in 1918, he directed his first film, *Harakiri*, one year later. Lang quickly established himself internationally with a unique style that combined German Expressionist visuals with genre storytelling; this later proved to be the primary antecedent of and influence on film noir. His science-fiction epic, *Metropolis* (1927), was one of the most expensive silent films ever made. Lang's first talkie, *M* (1931)—his masterpiece—is considered the progenitor of the "psycho-killer" genre. Supposedly brutal to his actors, legend has it Lang tossed Peter Lorre down a flight of stairs before the final scene of *M* to make him appear properly battered. Lang left Germany in 1933, and over the next twenty years, he toyed with nearly every genre in Hollywood: Westerns, noir, costume dramas, even musicals. Highlights: *Fury* (1936), *Ministry of Fear* (1944), and especially *The Big Heat* (1953). He returned to Germany in late 1950s, making three final films before failing eyesight forced his retirement in 1960. Embraced by new wave filmmakers worldwide, Lang's cinematic swan song was playing a winking version of himself in Jean-Luc Godard's *Contempt* (1963).

★

HERE'S YOUR REAL SCOOP, he insisted: my martinis. In the mid-1970s, American writer Charlotte

Chandler was interviewing director Fritz Lang for her biography of Marlene Dietrich, whom the legendary filmmaker had directed in the Western *Rancho Notorious* and whose company he'd enjoyed, both sexually and otherwise, decades earlier.

Chandler wanted to talk about Dietrich, but Lang kept pushing his damn martinis. He had a unique recipe, he told her conspiratorially: Tanqueray gin, Noilly Prat vermouth — *real* Noilly Prat, he emphasized — and a secret ingredient that, when mixed with the gin and vermouth, caused a chemical reaction that turned the drink a deep shade of blue.

That was the best part: It was a *blue* martini.

Making a blue martini for a woman was, Lang alleged, a foolproof path to seduction. When he fell in love with someone, he'd ask her if she'd ever had a blue martini, and naturally, she would reply that she hadn't. "She would be mystified, intrigued, enchanted, and fall into my arms," he told Chandler.

> **Making a blue martini for a woman was, Lang alleged, a foolproof path to seduction.**

To be clear, like W. C. Fields before him, Lang was a historically staunch advocate of all forms of the martini, blue or otherwise. He'd drink them any time of day. As a young vagabond in Paris, he'd order one at a café (paying for it with money he earned selling postcard-size sketches), down half of it, complain that it wasn't dry enough, then receive another full one for free.

Later, in his Beverly Hills mansion, Lang hung a mural he painted of topless women dancing out of a martini glass. One of the most charming virtues of Gloria Grahame's character in *The Big Heat* is her ability to mix a perfect martini. Many film directors had their own peculiar recipes (Hitchcock: "Five parts gin and a quick glance at a vermouth bottle"), but Lang's blue martini became legendary — mostly because it combined Lang's three greatest loves: martinis, women, and mystery.

Lang once said he didn't consider Don Juan a philanderer so much as a perfectionist. During his time in Hollywood, Lang had affairs with (among others) Miriam Hopkins, Kay Francis, Joan Bennett, and Dietrich, with whom he had an extreme love-hate relationship. Dietrich found him arrogant and impatient (as did most); he found her annoying, particularly her habit on set of invoking "what von Sternberg would do."

Sometime in the late thirties the pair had a brief fling, which lasted about same amount of time it took for Dietrich to reach across the pillow and phone another man. Yet despite his icy demeanor—so cruel, the joke went, that he could only achieve orgasm with the taste of blood in his mouth—Lang had established himself as a ladies' man, and he credited much of his success to his trademark blue martini. "It was the greatest seduction technique," he told Chandler. The third ingredient was classified, he'd often demur, but the American writer dragged the secret chemical out of him at long last. Food coloring.

Upon hearing this, Chandler proposed her own theory about the drink's powers of seduction: perhaps it wasn't the martini or its blueness that was irresistible to these women, but the man mixing them. Perhaps Lang himself was the blue martini. Lang considered this for a long moment, and then responded with a question of his own.

"Would *you* like a blue martini?"★

BLUE MARTINI

2 OZ. TANQUERAY GIN

1 OZ. NOILLY PRAT DRY
VERMOUTH

2 DROPS BLUE FOOD
COLORING

LEMON PEEL

Pour gin and vermouth into a mixing glass filled with ice cubes. Add food coloring and stir well. Strain into a chilled cocktail glass. Garnish with lemon peel.

STAN LAUREL

1890–1965

ACTOR AND COMEDIAN

Ollie: Go ahead and drink your half. *(Stanley drains the entire glass.)* Do you know what you've done? What made you do it? *Stanley:* I couldn't help it. My half was on the bottom.

— "Men O' War" (1929)

Born in England, Stan Laurel started out as a stage actor (once Charlie Chaplin's understudy) but in 1914 moved to Hollywood to pursue film. After many silent shorts, he discovered an onscreen chemistry with a portly funnyman named Oliver Hardy. In 1927, the pair would formally become the famed comic duo Laurel and Hardy. As the thinner, mopier straight man, Laurel starred in no less than 106 films. He is best remembered for *The Music Box* (Academy Award winner, 1932), *Way Out West* (1937), and *Babes in Toyland* (1934)—and for Laurel and Hardy's now evergreen catchphrase: "Well, here's another nice mess you've gotten me into."

★

FANS WERE OFTEN SURPRISED to read that Stan Laurel was the polar opposite of the madcap smarty-pants he played on screen. In interviews, he was a thoughtful, intelligent, soft-spoken man. He would make time for any fan. He did the unheard-of by keeping his phone number listed. He would answer any call, reply to any letter. He seemed a true gentleman.

But when anyone who knew Stan Laurel personally heard this, they would laugh and tell you that that was really his best performance yet. In actuality, Laurel was a total maniac. Especially when it came to women. Laurel was a hard-drinking, chain-smoking reveler, but "impulsive" couldn't begin to describe his adventures in matrimony. He amassed four wives, one of whom he married twice, and the third of which he had to marry on three separate occasions to avoid charges of bigamy. He invited his first wife on his honeymoon with his third—on a private chartered yacht, no less—and divulged that fact to Wife Three only when Wife One showed up at the dock.

It all seems very difficult to keep track of, even more so when you are drinking a ton of whiskey—which Laurel constantly was. By 1938 his vices and sins reached their apex (or nadir, depending) when a perfect storm crossed his path: this in the form of Wife Three, a "Russian opera singer" named Vera Illiana Shuvalova. A twenty-eight-year-old firecracker who somehow managed to make Laurel seem temperate.

The couple had met the year before, when Shuvalova auditioned at a Laurel and Hardy casting call. They were married on New Year's Day, 1938. Within mere months, Shuvalova had racked up two DUIs, a few stints in jail, a reputation as the most belligerent woman in greater Los Angeles, and a disorderly conduct charge for the unusual crime of "loudly discussing the Russian situation with herself."

In actuality, Laurel was total maniac. Especially when it came to women.

Laurel was hardly the steady hand to guide her. He, too, got pulled over for a DUI that year, and apparently he was dead set on one-upping his wife in a campaign of the ridiculous. He told the cops he wasn't drunk, just upset about a fight with his new bride, who had "a terrific temper." Things had gotten so heated that she had assaulted Laurel with the base of a telephone and further threatened to hit him with "a frying pan of potatoes." This account bore a striking resemblance to the plot of an old Laurel and Hardy movie. He was arrested in short order.

At their inevitable divorce hearing later that year, Vera Shuvalova would state the obvious: Stan's frying-pan story was just a desperate attempt to avoid public embarrassment and getting fired by the studio. But if avoiding bad publicity was his goal, Laurel failed in spectacular fashion. Indeed, "another nice mess you've gotten me into."

A bitter Shuvalova would tell the court and the world, "Hell yes, Laurel was drunk." He'd been drinking all day. In fact, not only was he drunk, he had beaten her and threatened to kill her. "And was not just any kind of death, your honor." He dug a grave in their backyard and told her to get in so he could bury her alive.

Naturally, the story made the front page. Stan Laurel's contract would be terminated by the studio within the year. After the whole mess was done, he built a high wall around his house and posted a sign: ALL ATTACKING BLONDES WILL BE REPELLED ON SIGHT. Then he married Wife Two again. ★

THE GOLD RUSH (1925)

A mere decade into his career, Charlie Chaplin's place in the pantheon of film legend was already secure, and he knew it. At the time, most of his films (in fact most films in general) were improvised from a basic idea or a title. Chaplin would simply go through each bit over and over until he found something that inspired him, usually with the camera rolling. But as his fellow directors became more sophisticated, Chaplin felt compelled to keep pace.

Although he'd been directing films since 1914, 1925's *The Gold Rush* was, astonishingly, his first feature with anything resembling an actual written outline. The movie tells the story of the 1896 gold rush at the Klondike pass. Chaplin had originally planned to shoot the film on location (another then-novel idea), and indeed, he arrived in Truckee, California, in early 1924 with every intention of doing so. Director Eddie Sutherland was serving as producer and was charged with rounding up extras for a marching scene that would open the film. A relentless perfectionist, Chaplin insisted that these men be the same homeless drifter types that had struck gold at Klondike twenty years earlier.

Sutherland spent a week in Sacramento corralling as many as he could find. He rounded up five hundred of them.

In order to gain the men's trust (and because Sutherland was something of a boozer), he insisted on drinking with them every night. This gesture the homeless men appreciated, until it became clear the production had not brought nearly enough liquor. Without missing a beat, they were all soon drinking Sterno (Sutherland included), strained through a sock and diluted by water. Sutherland feared he might be dead before they even reached Truckee.

But somehow he survived. The "hobos," as Chaplin called them, cheered their star when he arrived on location in his tramp costume, and very quickly he subsumed their pathos into his character. It was a stunning performance. And Sutherland's near-death bonding experience had been worthwhile. Until a few weeks later.

Hotel employees had been whispering about the sixteen-year-old lead, Lita Grey, going into Chaplin's suite every afternoon for "rehearsals." (Supposedly Grey was the model for *Lolita* thirty years later.) Then she became pregnant. With jail as his alternative, Chaplin was forced to both marry her and replace her in the film. The entire movie would have to be reshot from scratch, with a new lead.

When the cast reconvened, it was on a studio lot in Los Angeles, and only a single shot from the first shoot ended up in the final film. Not that the new location solved anything. Soon enough, Chaplin was schtupping both the replacement lead (Georgia Hale, far more age appropriate at twenty) and Sutherland's girlfriend (eighteen-year-old Louise Brooks). It was a hell of a thank-you.

STANLEY ROSE BOOKSHOP
6661½ HOLLYWOOD BLVD.

O PENING IN 1935, just a few doors down from Musso & Frank, the proprietor was a free-wheeling Texan named Stanley Rose. A first-rate storyteller with a face raked by whiskey, Stanley swore he had never read a book, and yet he owned and operated the best bookstore in Los Angeles. This was a man of appetites: for drinking, gambling, and whoring; for hunting and fishing; and quite possibly for literature and the company of the men and women (but mostly men) who created it. His bookstore serviced all the big studios; every name producer, director,

and star had a charge account and an open ear for Stanley's latest bestseller.

But colorfulness and clout aside, what was talked about most was Stanley's generosity. A disinterested businessman at best, he staked his pals whenever they needed it. Writers not only ran up huge bills at the bookstore, but Stanley would often cover their tabs next door at Musso's, where all they had to do was sign Stanley's name.

Not surprisingly, there was a back room at Stanley's, an art gallery that also served as a clubhouse for Hollywood writers who aspired to be more than hacks: Nathanael West, Budd Schulberg, John Fante, Dalton Trumbo, William Saroyan, Gene Fowler, among others. The gallery featured modernist art, original Picassos and Klees mixed in with local artists like Fletcher Martin. At this home away from home, writers would sit and drink the orange wine Stanley served up by the pitcher. As Budd Schulberg said, "In those pre-hip-expresso-bongo days, Stanley's was the nearest thing to a Left Bank we had out there." They talked about politics, about women, about all that was wrong with movie work. In fact, so writer-friendly was Stanley's back room and the back room next door at Musso's that together they inspired the title of Edmund Wilson's, *The Boys in the Back Room: Notes on California Novelists.*

Sadly, by the time Wilson's book was published, the Stanley Rose Bookshop had already closed. A victim of Stanley's laissez-faire accounting style, it was shut down in 1939, little more than a month after the publication of his good friend Nathanael West's *Day of the Locust*—a masterpiece that not only mentions the bookstore, but captures so well the seamy underside of Hollywood that Stanley Rose adored. ★

IN ADDITION TO BEING an art gallery, the back room of the Stanley Rose Bookstore was a place for writers to talk and to drink. The beverage served was orange wine, poured from a pitcher.

That many of the writers who congregated there shared a fondness for booze is widely accepted, as is their dislike of the film business. Raymond Carver perhaps put it best when he noted, "The very nicest thing Hollywood can think to say to a writer is that he is too good to be only a writer." Not that they were drowning their sorrows, but it isn't hard to imagine a lot of pitchers went down.

Harder to know is exactly what the orange wine was.

Today, there are at least three different types of alcohol that are considered orange wine. The first kind of so-called orange wine has nothing to do with oranges. Essentially white wine, it is made by letting the grape juice ferment *with* the skins after crushing. Also called "skin-contact wine," it has an orange hue. Popular in the U.S. since around 2009, this orange wine can be found at wine shops and on restaurant menus. Many people consider it a pleasant middle ground between a rich white and a light red, others just an annoying trend. There is no recipe, just buy a bottle, take it home, and drink it.

The second kind of orange wine is again white wine, though with the addition of

ORANGE WINE

. . . .

1 BOTTLE OF WHITE WINE (DRY IS PREFERABLE)

1 MEDIUM ORANGE

⅓ CUP OF SUGAR

First, empty out a little of the wine so it doesn't over-flow. Pour it into the sink or into your own wine glass. Then, zest a whole orange, avoiding the bitter white pith. Push the zest into the mouth of the bottle, and pour in the sugar. Recork, then shake by turning the bottle upside down, so as to dissolve the sugar. Refrigerate for one week, being sure to shake once a day. Strain into a pitcher and serve cold.

orange peel—this version has been popularized by culinary personality Laura Calder.

The last kind of orange wine is actually made from the juice of oranges, as opposed to grapes. You can do this with virtually any fruit: blackberries, pears, plums, cherries, pineapples, etc. Somewhat complicated to make, the process can take months. It is hard to know, but easy to imagine, that Stanley Rose and his pals would never have had the patience.

Tom Mix was the first superstar of movie Westerns. The archetypal screen cowboy, he made over three hundred silent films that showcased his rodeo skills. Wisely declining to smoke or drink on camera, he became an idol to a generation of kids playing Cowboys and Indians, and his aura of authenticity—he was an honorary Texas Ranger and a pallbearer at Wyatt Earp's funeral—made him unassailable as any studio's first choice. Mix lost most of his multimillion-dollar fortune in the 1929 stock market crash. He worked into the sound era, but as injuries and age mounted, younger and brighter stars soon dimmed his own. Undaunted, he continued as a headline attraction at rodeos and circuses until his strange death in 1940.

★

CHANGE A FEW DETAILS, and it could've been a Tom Mix movie. The old cowboy, pushing sixty, rides into Tucson early one morning. He's been left for dead multiple times—including by one of his big-city wives after she shot him five times—and he's had a rough couple of years, but he is still the fastest draw in the land, and he has started a campaign to remind everybody.

Which is to say that, on the eve of his 1941 comeback rodeo tour of South America, Tom Mix arrived in Tucson, checked into the old Saint Rita Hotel, and went looking for Ed Echols.

Echols and Mix had been five-star hell-raisers at the 101 Ranch in Oklahoma. Now Echols was Pima County sheriff, and Mix was a Hollywood

TOM MIX

1880–1940
ACTOR AND RODEO STAR

"I don't think a man is under the influence of liquor until he has to hold on to the grass to keep from falling down."

superstar. (In the movie version, one of them would clearly have to be shot by the other upon learning this outcome, though it's hard to predict which guy would take the bullet.)

Mix and Echols headed over to the home of writer Walt Coburn for an afternoon of rolled cigarettes and whiskey. Mix biographer Richard Jensen later tracked down Coburn for an account of the day: The three old friends talked about the 101 Ranch, the Calgary Stampede, and the Alaska Yukon Pacific. Tom hated all his wives (including, apparently, the one he was currently married to) and couldn't stop ringing the hundred-year-old mission bell on Walt's front porch, listening until the ring faded full away. "If you ever take a notion to sell that old bell," Mix told Walt, "I'd like to have it."

Mix stayed too long, drank too much, and slept too late the next morning. Sometime around noon, he pulled onto Highway 79 toward Phoenix in his convertible roadster, a luxury car that did nothing to stain his bona fides as a cowboy. Such was his reputation, even still.

The events that followed are a matter of some conjecture. This can occur when the investigating sheriff has a *nuanced* view of what may or may not be relevant, as Ed Echols surely did. There was talk that Mix had stopped off at the Oracle Junction Inn for a few hands of cards and some whiskey, but nobody came forward to confirm it. Regardless, it's a known fact that, a few hours later, two highway workers witnessed Mix drive around a corner of Highway 79 doing about ninety and, missing a detour, roll his roadster twice, which killed him instantly.

A theory has since emerged that Mix had been carrying a couple of fancy silver suitcases in his backseat, and when he hit the brakes at the detour, one of them had flown up and hit him in the head so hard it broke his neck and killed him on spot. This so-called "Suitcase of Death" is even on display at the Tom Mix museum in Oklahoma.

Here's the thing. Those suitcases are not made of silver (that would be too extravagant, even for Mix). They're made of aluminum. So while the Suitcase of Death is great pulp, Tom Mix probably deserves something a little more simple, like the poetry of the Westerns that he inspired: He died riding too hard. ★

A T SEVEN STORIES, the Hollywood Athletic Club was the tallest building in greater Los Angeles when it opened in 1924. Designed by Meyer and Holler, the architectural firm behind Grauman's Chinese and Egyptian theaters, the 120-room hotel and spa contained an indoor pool, steam rooms, a barbershop, and a gym; it also doubled as a private, all-male health club boasting a thousand-plus members, a good many of them quite prominent in the film business. In addition to sweating off a hangover, members could avail themselves of one of the rooms upstairs, the perfect hideaway for a man on bender or a husband on the outs. Over time, management put a bar in one of the rooms and the Hollywood Atheltic Club shifted even further away from exercise, unless you count twelve-ounce curls. It became such a social hub, in fact, that in the mid-1930s, John Ford, John Wayne, Johnny Weissmuller, and a dozen or so other members (presumably some who were not named John) formed their own club within the

club: The Young Men's Purity Total Abstinence and Snooker Pool Association.

At the time, show business people were barred from the city's more upscale country clubs, and so the members enjoyed poking fun at such snobbery. They held ad hoc meetings that alternated between the steam room and the lounge upstairs. Ford always took minutes, later preserved by his son, and thus surviving as the only copy of the original TYMPTASPA charter.

GOAL: "To promulgate the cause of alcoholism."

SLOGAN: "Jews but no dues."

CLUB PRESIDENT: Buck Buchanan, the "distinguished Afro-American" steam-room monitor.

MEMBERSHIP REQUIREMENT: proof of status as a "career-oriented drunkard, or at least a gutter-oriented one."

NOT A MEMBERSHIP REQUIREMENT BUT HELPFUL: fondness for steam rooms.

At subsequent meetings, members were quick to note that these qualifications alone hardly guaranteed membership. Frequent applications by one Dudley Nichols, screenwriter, provided a nice case study. Nichols had two major strikes against him, as voters saw it. For one, he did not drink with total and complete abandon, bearing an unfortunate tendency to fall on the wagon. And second, his politics were "socially reprehensible," since he believed in justice, fairness, and other radical left-wing fantasies.

Despite his shortcomings, Nichols ultimately became a member in 1937 at the expense of another member: character actor Ward Bond, a TYMPTASPA founder who was "summarily dropped from our rolls for conduct and behavior which is unpleasant to put in print," Ford wrote in the minutes. "Mr. Nichols's first action on becoming a member was a motion changing the name of the association to The Young Workers of the World's Anti-Chauvinistic Total Abstinence League for the Promulgation of Propaganda Contra Fascism. This motion was defeated."

Several months earlier, the group actually *had* approved a name change: The Young Men's Purity Total Abstinence and Yachting Association. When this was later shortened to the Emerald Bay Yacht Club, the group's primary mission became wearing seafaring blazers with far too many insignias sewn on them. At their first annual St. Patrick's Day dinner, the group ventured to conduct its business in public, choosing as its venue the Cocoanut Grove. The meeting ended prematurely when a food fight led to their expulsion. Ford wrote a letter to Cocoanut Grove management the following day. "I neither understand nor condone our behavior at the recent fête," Ford wrote. "Unfortunately, I am not in a position to remember it." ★

The leading lady of Mack Sennett's Keystone Studios, Mabel Normand became the greatest female comic of the silent era. As a teenager, Normand modeled for illustrated postcards and magazines, and in her early films she was cast as a "bathing beauty." But with Sennett, Normand would quickly demonstrate a remarkable gift for comedy. Appearing in almost two hundred films, she was the first actor to execute the signature gag of silent film comedy: throwing a pie in someone's face, on film. She is best known for frequent work with Chaplin and for her "Fatty and Mabel" series with Fatty Arbuckle. Her nickname outside Hollywood was the "Queen of Comedy"; her nickname inside, the "I Don't Care Girl." One of the first women to write, direct, and produce, Normand eventually ran her own eponymous studio.

MABEL NORMAND

1892–1930
ACTRESS AND COMEDIENNE

Asked about her hobbies: *"Just say I like to pinch babies and twist their legs. And get drunk."*

★

YOU COULD SPEND HOURS WAITING outside Irving Thalberg's office. Nicknamed the "Boy Wonder," Thalberg was running production for Universal by the time he was twenty-one. For over a decade, he would produce MGM's most literary and prestigious films, but getting his ear wasn't easy. It became a joke. Didn't matter when you had a meeting or how important it was, and the worst was if you were a writer. Outside the office there was "the million-dollar bench," so named for all the talent that had sat there. An example of this is the time Harpo, Groucho, and Chico Marx were made to wait so long they actually built a small fire outside Thalberg's door. The smell of smoke managed to flush out the young executive.

Director King Vidor recalled one day in particular, in February 1930, when he and the writer Laurence Stallings ran in wearing tennis clothes for a story meeting about their new project, *Billy the Kid*. With a draft in hand, it turned out, they didn't have to wait this time at all. Instead, the secretary hustled them into Mr. Thalberg's limousine. Thalberg was sitting in back talking numbers with MGM exec Eddie Mannix. The limo pulled out and Vidor and his writer just sat and listened. There had yet to be any acknowledgment that they were even in the car. Finally, Thalberg looked over. "Let's hear what you have," Vidor recalls him saying. And with that King Vidor dove headlong into his pitch and paid no attention to where they were driving until the car stopped in a driveway. It was then the director looked up and saw a long line of other limousines, men in gloves, and a large crowd further away, many of them crying. They were at a funeral.

Thalberg got out. Vidor and his writer were a bit self-conscious now—should they know who died? And as they'd come in tennis clothes, how could they explain attending a funeral in white trousers and sweaters? Director Marshall Neilan helped them out of the car. He was crying, too. They had to go in. They were too mortified to ask anyone about the deceased until they were seated next to Mannix. When he told them, Vidor was in shock: It was Mabel Normand.

Chaplin was still lamenting that his only chance to touch her perfect lips was in front of a camera. Samuel Goldwyn once declared her "the most valuable property in Hollywood."

Vidor had fallen in love with Normand when he began working as a ticket-taker in Texas nickelodeons. He wasn't alone; for almost a decade, Hollywood moguls sparred over her. Mack Sennett built a studio and gave it to her. Thirty years later, Chaplin was still lamenting that his only chance to touch her perfect lips was in front of a camera. Samuel Goldwyn once declared her "the most valuable property in Hollywood."

Normand was the icon of a preflapper generation of girls called Sports. The distinction between flappers and sports really just boiled down to the haircut. Sports smoked, drank gin, and talked like sailors. Normand's friends seemed to agree that her fatal mistake was taking the role far too seriously. She drank constantly. She stood aloof and smirked at serious advances from serious men. During a lunch at the Savoy Hotel in New York, she ordered nine martinis, a Baked Alaska, and a hundred Melachrinos (Egyptian cigarettes) to be delivered at once. In time, Mabel started snorting cocaine. The drug had in fact been legal before the war, but now forced her to run with a shadier crowd. She somehow ended up in the vicinity of a couple of murders.

Vidor hadn't read a paper in days, and he hadn't heard much about Normand recently. Still, he did recall something about the scandals. Thalberg leaned over and whispered, "Too many murders." Vidor nodded, "Shame, shame." Then Thalberg leaned over again and added, a bit too loudly, "The audience won't accept it."

Apparently, he was talking about Vidor's project, *Billy the Kid.* ★

TRADER HORN (1931)

If MGM production chief Irving Thalberg could trust anyone to pull this off, it'd be filmmaker Woody Van Dyke. The workmanlike director was nicknamed "one-take Woody" for the speed with which he'd complete a shoot.

A few weeks earlier, Van Dyke had told Thalberg he wanted his next movie to be something different and ambitious. What Thalberg ended up suggesting was more along the lines of flat-out crazy: He wanted to make a film version of the popular book *Trader Horn*, based on the life of explorer Alfred Horn. And he wanted Van Dyke to shoot on location, with a full Hollywood crew—in Africa.

The crazy part? Thalberg would let Van Dyke set sail with an unlimited budget and half-baked script. When the cast and crew landed in Mombasa, they slowly marched inland to their first location—225 people and ninety *tons* of equipment.

Almost every American caught malaria within a week. Lead actress Edwina Booth was particularly besieged by insects due to her skimpy outfit; she also got dysentery, fell out of a tree (almost fracturing her skull), and claimed she was "forced" to sunbathe nude on the ship to get the tan required to make her role believable. (It took her six years to regain her full health, after which she never made another film.) As for the director, Van Dyke figured he could inoculate himself from any parasites by drinking gin and more gin. Which he reportedly did.

After a few days of shooting, Thalberg sent an insane order of his own: Start over, using sound. Nobody cared about silent films anymore, and they'd care even less when this epic finally premiered in a year or two. *Trader Horn* had to be a talkie. Now they needed sound equipment (none of the crew had made a sound picture before), not to mention an actual script. Three weeks later, a huge shipment of sound equipment arrived and was promptly dropped into the ocean by dockworkers. An "accident." It'd be several weeks before a replacement set arrived and made it safely to shore.

With little to do but sweat, the cast and crew followed their director's lead and drank "at least three fingers of whiskey every morning and three more every night." Unsurprisingly, everybody soon dismissed this odd notion of a script. And so, after two months of accomplishing exactly nothing, the *Trader Horn* cast and crew finally descended into the African jungle to make the most ambitious moving picture of all time.

Seven months later, the ragtag crew came stumbling out. One crew member had been eaten by a crocodile. Another was horned to death by a rhino. Everyone was drunk, sick, or both. Van Dyke returned to Hollywood with an astounding 4 million feet of film (around 600 hours)—and announced he needed to shoot more. MGM had already spent $1 million, so Thalberg and studio chief Louis B. Mayer decided they'd better watch some of the dailies before pouring more money into it.

The footage was disastrous. A sauced Van Dyke had shot way too much, but despite that, there was no story, no discipline, no sense. Mayer thought they would have to cut it into shorter travel films. Thalberg insisted on seeing it through. He put his best writers on it. Six months later, they, too, had nothing. Thalberg was growing increasingly resigned to abandoning the film. Then one of the writers had the novel idea to see if the original book (from which the film was adapted) could be of use. This led to Thalberg's fantastic discovery that there wasn't a single copy of the book on the entire lot. He bought one from a bookstore, and the stunned writers found the perfect structure that had previously eluded them. Reshoots began almost immediately.

Despite his frequent inebriation, Van Dyke had had the sense to bring back the African actors who played major roles. The biggest role was Horn's gun bearer, played by Mutia Omoolu. The tribesman agreed to travel to America if a thatch hut was built for him. It was—on Studio Lot Three. Tall, his head shaven, a ring through his nose, Omoolu had sex with prostitutes whenever possible and ended up in the hospital with a veneral disease. During publicity, he declared the MGM lion too fat. Finally, two years later, *Trader Horn* was released. It was MGM's biggest grossing film of 1931, made the studio a million dollars, and was nominated for a best-picture Oscar.

RAMON NOVARRO

1899–1968

ACTOR

"I only had a bourbon and soda, officer. Or maybe three."

Ramon Novarro was the best known of all Hollywood's post-Valentino "Latin Lovers." Born in Mexico to a prominent family, his parents moved to Los Angeles to escape the Mexican revolution. By his teens, Novarro was already working as a singing waiter and a bit player in films. His first hit as a leading man was *Scaramouche* (1923), and two years later he had his greatest success with *Ben-Hur* (1925). Novarro was homosexual and would go to well-known gay bars with female stars as his cover. Throughout his career, his studio, MGM, remained determined to keep his orientation out of the newspaper. Novarro continued to act in MGM films through 1935, then fell off the public's radar. He would not find headlines again until his death, over thirty years later, when he was the victim of one of Los Angeles's most infamous murders. Having invited two young brothers, both hustlers, up to his Laurel Canyon home, Novarro was severely beaten and then asphyxiated.

---------------------★----------------------

IT WAS A DINNER PARTY hosted by actress Una Merkel, and everyone was on pins and needles. The last two guests had just arrived—billionaire eccentric Howard Hughes and his new girlfriend, Ginger Rogers. The problem was Jean Harlow. Rogers hated the libidinous Harlow, a constant star in the Hughes universe and reportedly his onetime lover. It was always a tricky business mixing starlets—and when you poured enough gin on top of that, it became downright dangerous. Still, as everyone sat down to eat, the two women were gracious and perfectly mannered. It was Ramon Novarro who'd become the night's most memorable guest.

This was in 1933, and Novarro was in a bit of a rut. His brother had just died of cancer. His last few movies had been stinkers. He was still a star in the public's eyes, still had a contract, and could still make hearts flutter. But everyone sensed the end was coming soon. His best friend, actress Myrna Loy, chalked it up to the obvious: He had started losing his looks.

Novarro was in his mid-thirties, and the ruthless studios had little use for romantic leads unable to remain handsome into middle age, unless they were gifted character actors, which Novarro wasn't. His contract was up in a year, and there was little hope of renewing it. Added to that was a more devastating truth: Puritanical MGM chief Louis B. Mayer simply hated homosexuals.

Novarro was in his mid-30s, and the ruthless studios had little use for romantic leads unable to remain handsome into middle age, unless they were gifted character actors, which Novarro wasn't.

Never mind that everyone in Hollywood knew about Novarro's sexual orientation. In the 1920s, as long as you didn't end up in a newspaper, MGM was tolerant of homosexuality, which was still illegal and considered deviant in America at large. But if audiences caught wind, then marriages of convenience (what Hollywood called a lavender marriage), terminated contracts, and other such discrimination would ensue.

Novarro had been careful, mostly. Still, for whatever reason, Louis B. Mayer changed his policy in 1933. Something of a tyrant, he decided to rid the studio of any gay actor who wasn't immensely profitable, i.e., everyone except the rumored bisexual Cary Grant. The defiantly open William Haines and Niles Asther were the first to go. And Novarro looked like the odds-on favorite to be next. True, he was far more discreet, but there had been a few hiccups.

In 1926 the studio discovered that Novarro and Haines had visited a male brothel. Mayer was incensed that Novarro, the recent star of "a religious picture" (*Ben-Hur*), would have put the entire film in jeopardy. He wanted Novarro fired on the spot, but the star had powerful backers—namely Irving Thalberg and W. R. Hearst—so instead the two actors were forbidden to see each other.

But by 1933 Thalberg was ill and Hearst was about to leave MGM for Warner Brothers. Mayer called Novarro into his office and tried to persuade him to enter a lavender marriage with Myrna Loy. Novarro deferred, telling his boss he'd think about it. Una Merkel's dinner party was during just this period of introspection. Let it be said that Novarro was far less discreet in his drinking than his carousing. The man had probably accrued more DUIs than any other star in Hollywood, no small feat. And he was not going to face this particular dilemma without a cocktail firmly in hand.

Sometime after dinner, as the table chatted idly in the lull that often falls between dessert and departure, the guests heard a noise. It sounded like someone doing jumping jacks on the second floor, coupled with loud shouts. Figuring that it was some sort of sexual escapade, Hughes told all the women to stay put and went to investigate. What he found wasn't a sex escapade, exactly, though it was equally scandalous. Hughes and a few other men walked into Merkel's bedroom to find Novarro drunk as a monkey and jumping on the actress's bed. He was completely naked, save a bandana wrapped around his head, and he wasn't shouting, but singing: "I'm Queen Victoria on her deathbed! I'm Queen Victoria on her deathbed!"

Apparently, Novarro had made his decision. He would not marry Myrna Loy. And so yes, his contract would expire and his career would soon be over. ★

THE WEDDING MARCH (1928)

Director Erich von Stroheim was known as a perfectionist, intractable, insane. "What we want is better pictures," he would declare, "but restraint will never produce them." In *The Wedding March*, von Stroheim would put that to the test.

Already rumors were swirling that a scene in his previous film, *Merry-Go-Round*, had been excised when the actors got too drunk and a few female extras got too naked. At a time when shooting on real locations was considered radical, von Stroheim was a director known to go even further. He insisted that actors wear authentic costumes, too, and eat real caviar and drink real champagne. But even when he ordered the actress Fay Wray off the set of *The Wedding March* and instructed that the room be boarded up for privacy, no one quite believed it would happen—that he'd shoot a real orgy.

Biographer Richard Koszarski would later sum up the ensuing events as "exactitude bordering on madness." Von Stroheim was a heavy drinker, and he forced the actors to match him drink for drink as they consumed gin and champagne. Some call girls arrived shortly thereafter and joined in.

As von Stroheim was lining up shots, clothes were peeled off. By the time he was rolling, the actors and call girls had partnered up and were screwing beneath carpets. When a few of the actors had, uh, "nailed their parts," the call girls noticed a couple of donkeys wandering around. Encouraged by von Stroheim, they began coaxing erections out of the burros, too. Full-on penetration, lesbian scenes, bestiality—the resulting footage still stands as one of the most graphic scenes ever filmed for a mainstream movie.

Not that it was ever to be included in *The Wedding March* itself. Von Stroheim was fired by Paramount before he finished shooting. His replacement, ironically, was Josef von Sternberg, whose own career would later be destroyed by the exact same kind of insane demands and foolish stubbornness.

For von Stroheim, it was pretty much the end of his career as a director. His antics had pissed off one studio head too many, and within a decade he found himself broke and humbled. But his admirers, including scores of young directors, refused to let the story end tragically. They gave him acting roles and revived his career, most notably Jean Renoir in *Grand Illusion* and Billy Wilder in *Sunset Boulevard*. They even let his characters drink real drinks.

"I wanted a drink so badly, but I was afraid to get up and get it. So I just waited until it was daylight and got two."

M ary Pickford was the biggest star (by far) of the silent era. The first actress dubbed "America's Sweetheart," she was also known as the "Girl with the Golden Curls" and "Little Mary." Hired by D. W. Griffith at Biograph in 1909, Pickford appeared in fifty-one films in the first year alone. By 1919 she had helped create the star system and was the highest-paid film actress ever, eventually earning $1 million per year. Her films *Tess of the Storm Country* (1914) and *Sparrows* (1926) are routinely mentioned as being among the best silent films in history. Pickford married swashbuckling actor Douglas Fairbanks, and the couple built a fifty-six-acre Beverly Hills estate christened Pickfair, the first movie star mansion in Beverly Hills and an epicenter of Hollywood high society. A founding member of the Academy of Motion Picture Arts and Sciences, as well as United Artists, Pickford won an Oscar for her first sound film, *Coquette* (1929) but retired in 1933. Most of her fans would not see her again until her acceptance speech for an honorary Oscar in 1976, at the age of eighty-four.

---- ★ ----

IN 1917 PHOTOPLAY MAGAZINE SAID of Mary Pickford, "If everybody were as pure minded as she, there would be no sin in the world." Pure minded? How about pure nonsense?

The truth was, Pickford, "America's Sweetheart," just wouldn't drink in public (or hold any object that could be taken for a cigarette). Having almost single-handedly launched the culture of celebrity, she was probably the first actor with a public image—and consequently, an image to protect.

But with Mary's siblings, on the other hand, it was a different story. Her younger brother Jack was a B-list actor, but an A-list lush. A womanizer who was loaded most all the time, the women around town called him Mr. Syphilis—this, because he had it. Rumored a heroin addict, too, Jack would marry three times—each wife a Ziegfeld chorus girl. And then there was Mary's younger sister Lottie, a step behind on the drink but a step ahead on the marrying. Lottie was married four times, including once to a bootlegger who posed as an undertaker so as to smuggle hootch in his hearse. She also liked to party naked.

> "Having almost single-handedly launched the culture of celebrity, she was probably first actor with a public image—and consequently, an image to protect."

As for Mary—Mary was the teetotaler, right? Wrong. Director Eddie Sutherland, one-time husband of Louise Brooks and not averse to drink himself, recalls an evening out on the town with Mary's brother, Jack. The pair had been hopping from speakeasy to speakeasy, but now they desperately needed more liquor. Jack suggested a pitstop at Mary's Beverly Hills mansion, Pickfair. *Nonsense,* thought Sutherland. Everyone knew that Mary and her equally famous husband, Douglas Fairbanks, abstained. They constantly hosted parties at their palatial estate, but Mary didn't even drink then. And now that alcohol was illegal, there wouldn't be a drop within shouting distance of the home.

So why the hell are we going there? Sutherland remembers wondering. But Jack assured him that it wouldn't take long. Pulling up to the fabled mansion, Sutherland was shocked to see Jack stride right through the unlocked front door—no knock, no doorbell. Why this was the home of America's sweetheart! Well, the sweetheart was out. And so Jack walked upstairs, through her bedroom and into her bathroom. Sutherland followed sheepishly, knowing that getting caught in Mary Pickford's bathroom, uninvited and bombed, would not place him atop the studios' hiring lists.

Jack pulled out two medicinal items: hydrogen peroxide and Listerine. "Gin or whiskey?" he asked Sutherland. Sutherland didn't want either. Whatever Jack wanted to jokingly call this stuff, Sutherland didn't have the stomach for a prohibition-era adventure in swallowing poison. Jack took a swig from one bottle, and handed the other to Sutherland. After some prodding, Sutherland cautiously smelled it, then took a taste. *Wow. Okay.* It was real liquor. Only then did Sutherland understand. Mary was a closet boozer—or perhaps more accurately, a bathroom boozer. As Buddy Rogers, her third husband would later admit, "The little dickens, she gets to drinking and she just can't stop."

Sutherland and Jack sat down on the tile and began to down the bottles. Did it feel glamorous getting hammered in the bathroom of the world's most famous teetotaler? Did it matter? ★

THE DEADLY GLASS OF BEER
(1916)

S cripts as we know them did not emerge until the sound era; silent films were shot using prose treatments, or even just an idea or a title. The treatment below, the entire shooting script for the two-reel short *The Deadly Glass of Beer*, provides a neat encapsulation of how much and how little Hollywood filmmaking has changed in the past 100 years. (Certainly, it wouldn't be hard to believe that this was perhaps the synopsis for a new Judd Apatow vehicle.)

This scenario (as it was then called) was written by Anita Loos, who wrote several hundred early films. She was paid $25 for this one (about $500 today). Loos later became a star herself with the book and film *Gentlemen Prefer Blondes*, which began as an angry letter to her lifelong crush and "friend" H. L. Mencken.

Henry and Frank are cousins who meet at a lawyer's office to hear their uncle's will read. The will states: "I leave one million dollars to my nephew Frank if by his twenty-first birthday he has remained a strict teetotaler. But if Frank should drink even a single glass of beer, my entire fortune is to go to Henry." Henry, smothering his fury, plots Frank's downfall.

Disguised by false whiskers, Henry trails Frank about town in the hope of catching him taking a drink. One day Frank passes

a saloon, hesitates, looks furtively up and down the street, and ducks in. Henry follows him into the saloon, grabs off his false whiskers, raps Frank on the back, and says, "Aha! I've caught you!" At which Frank turns around and shows his glass to be full of buttermilk.

The day before Frank's twenty-first Birthday, Henry becomes desperate. Aided by cohorts, he kidnaps Frank and takes him to a den on the waterfront. There he is strapped to a table; his mouth is propped open and Henry is about to pour a bottle of beer into Frank when, just as the clock strikes twelve, police break in to arrest Henry for serving liquor without a license.

MUSSO & FRANK GRILL
6667 HOLLYWOOD BLVD.
OPEN!

A FEW BLOCKS EAST OF the Montmartre sits an early-Hollywood institution that not only remains open to this day, but continues to thrive. The Musso & Frank Grill, a no-frills steakhouse and bar was opened in 1919, and has been owned and operated by the same two families since 1927.

Very likely the oldest restaurant in Hollywood, celebrities were originally drawn to its Italian authenticity, New York feel, and no-nonsense menu. Since the Writers Guild was located just opposite and the Stanley Rose Bookshop next door, the place became a lifeboat for writers adrift in the celluloid sea. In 1934 Musso's expanded into a small space behind the neighboring Vogue Theater. A door was punched through the wall of the dining room, and thus the famed "Back Room" was created, expressly for the literary set. Just to mention a few: William Faulkner, F. Scott Fitzgerald, Lillian Hellman, Dashiell Hammett, William Saroyan, Nathanael West, Aldous Huxley, John O'Hara, Dorothy Parker, Ben Hecht, and Ernest Hemingway.

Whether, to paraphrase Irish playwright Brendan Behan, they were writers with drinking problems or drinkers with writing problems, these men and women knew how to bend an elbow. It is widely said that Chandler penned *The Big Sleep* in one of the booths. But, even though he mentions the restaurant in the novel, that seems unlikely. And that F. Scott Fitzgerald proofread his work there is even less likely. More plausible is Jim Thompson, broke and out of print, wandering down late in the afternoon after working on Kubrick's *The Killing* (the director would later cheat him out of his credit). The Back Room after all was not a place to write, but a place to drink, to talk, to miss New York from. As Charles Bukowski put it, "I never actually ate. I just looked at the menu and told them 'Not yet,' and kept ordering drinks."

Of course, Musso's wasn't only for writers; actors loved it, too. Chaplin naturally had a special booth (did the man ever sleep?). He liked their martinis. And Tom Mix sat by the window so his fans could see him. There is the likely apocryphal tale of Valentino and Douglas Fairbanks racing each other on horseback down Hollywood Boulevard to Musso's. But the list moves forward in time, as virtual roll call of Hollywood cultural history: Arthur Miller, R. W. Schindler, Orson Welles, the Rat Pack, on to Sean Penn, Johnny Depp, and Keith Richards.

From John Barrymore to Drew Barrymore, over the last ninety years everyone who was anyone has graced its entrance and sung its praises.

Although the names and faces have changed with the times, the restaurant has remained resolutely the same. Its two large dining rooms and signature red booths are largely unchanged since the last major remodel, in 1937. And while the Vogue Theater did reclaim its space in 1955 and the Back Room closed down, its historic long bar, as well as the chairs and light fixtures, were all moved to the New Room, where they still stand today. ★

MUSSO & FRANK has long been famous for its bone-dry martini. It's stirred, not shaken—that makes it stronger (less dilution from the ice). There's very little Vermouth included—that makes it even stronger. And it contains 2.5 to 3 ounces of gin—which makes it stronger still. Voted Best Martini in America by more than one magazine, the recipe below comes straight from bartender Manny Aguirre, likely the longest-working bartender in Hollywood. Aguirre has fifty-nine years behind the bar, thirty-seven of them spent at Scandia—for decades an upscale Sunset hotspot specializing in (you guessed it) Scandinavian cuisine—and the last twenty-two years at Musso & Frank.

MARTINI

. . . .

3 OZ. GIN

6 DASHES OF NOILLY PRAT DRY
   VERMOUTH

2 OLIVES OR A LEMON TWIST

Pour gin and vermouth into a mixing glass filled with ice cubes. Stir well. Strain into a chilled cocktail glass. Garnish with two olives, each on separate toothpick. (Substitute lemon twist for olives if desired.)

Part Two

THE STUDIO ERA

1930–1945

"The truth is that the coming of sound meant the
end of the all-night parties. With talkies, you couldn't
stay out till sunrise anymore. You had to rush back
from the studios and start learning your lines, ready
for the next day's shooting at 8 a.m."

—LOUISE BROOKS, actress

TALLULAH BANKHEAD

1902–1968
STAGE AND SCREEN ACTRESS

*"My father warned me
about men and alcohol,
but he never said anything
about women and cocaine."*

Famous for outlandish behavior, Tallulah Bankhead was a proponent of cocaine use as far back as her teenage years. She came from an upper-crust Alabama family; the daughter of former Speaker of the House William Brockman Bankhead. Tallulah's childhood battles with croup were responsible for the husky voice that became her trademark. Starring in more than fifty theatrical productions, she won the New York Drama Critics' Circle Award for performances in *The Little Foxes* (1939) and *The Skin of Our Teeth* (1942). Her sporadic Hollywood career hit a high point with the lead in Hitchcock's *Lifeboat* (1944), during the filming of which she apparently declined to wear underwear. Bankhead married just once, to actor John Emery, who divorced her four years later, citing mental cruelty. She said one of her biggest regrets was not seducing Greta Garbo. Bankhead's final words are still the gold standard for the famous-to-be-famous crowd: "Codeine! Bourbon!"

★

PROBABLY, THE BEST PART she ever played was herself. Sure, Tallulah Bankhead occasionally received good notices for her stage and screen performances, but her fame rested almost entirely on the strength of her off-screen self—a hard-drinking, libidinous force of nature. (Bankhead proudly described herself as "pure as the driven slush.") It's likely even her peers could only tell you a handful of the twenty film roles she played, but her alcohol- and cocaine-fueled affairs were legendary. There was the time she threw a dinner party at her estate, Windows, and passed out, face-in-soup-bowl, before the champagne was even poured. Or how she bragged of having bedded over 500 men and women—Bankhead often described herself as "ambisextrous."

And then there was the nudist thing. Bankhead would often answer the door completely naked. This, before the years in which she consumed five packs of cigarettes and two fifths of Old Grand-Dad bourbon a day (she claimed she could drink a bottle in thirty minutes). She took up residence at the Elysée Hotel, nicknamed the "Easy Lay." In Burgess Meredith's memoir, *So Far, So Good,* the actor talks about first meeting Bankhead. He arrived at a party in her suite only to find Bankhead stark naked, passing out cocaine and booze to guests. Having finished her hostess duties, she confided that she was dying of the "Grand Desire" and subsequently pulled Meredith into her bedroom.

Apparently, the moaning and the groaning were "operatic," but just before consummation, Bankhead pushed him aside, saying "For God's sake, don't come *inside* me! I'm engaged to Jock Whitney!" That would be the son of famed businessman Payne Whitney.

Bankhead would forever maintain, "What I do with my bits and pieces is *my* business," and "For every fan that I lose who's stuffy, two more come along who approve of my lifestyle." And indeed, Bankhead's escapades were funnier and more risqué than any film comedy she could have hoped to act in. A legendary such incident occurred the summer of 1933, two years after she returned from a triumphant decade-long stretch in the London theater. In the mood for an extended party, Bankhead did what any in-the-know actress would have done in those days. She showed up, resplendent in a heavily beaded gown and diamonds at the Garden of Allah.

> There was the time she threw a dinner party at her estate and passed out, face-in-soup-bowl, before the champagne was even poured.

She spent most of that evening making eyes at Johnny Weissmuller, the Olympic gold-medal swimmer who had just made his Hollywood debut as Tarzan. But by five in the morning, she had grown tired of simply wondering what lay hidden beneath his loincloth. There are (at least) two different versions of what happened next. One is that Tallulah, having thus far failed in her advances on Weissmuller, decided to pull a damsel-in-distress, fling herself into the pool fully clothed, screaming that she was going to drown if someone didn't save her. Someone like, perhaps, the Olympic swimmer standing nearby. The other version is that she and Weissmuller drunkenly dove in together.

Whatever the beginning, the stories share their most crucial detail: its ending. Once in the water, Tallulah's dress and diamonds found their way to the bottom of the pool, and she found her way into Weissmuller's arms, naked. As he carried her out of the pool, the gathered revelers stared at the spectacle of Tarzan and the Naked Socialite. "Everybody's been dying to see my body," Tallulah told the remaining partiers. "Now you can." ★

POLO LOUNGE
9641 SUNSET BLVD.
OPEN!

IN 1906 A GROUP of investors led by California businessman Burton Green bought 4,500 acres of land west of Los Angeles in the hopes of striking oil. They drilled and drilled and drilled, but found only water. So they decided to build a city. They formed the Rodeo Land & Water Company and built a new subdivision named Beverly Hills—this because Green had just visited a Massachusetts town with a similar name.

When Green announced that parcels were for sale, he got approximately zero takers. After a few months of similar luck, he was truly desperate. So he built a huge pink hotel on the area's only thoroughfare (a dirt-road extension of Hollywood's Sunset Boulevard), hoping to attract visi-

tors. It was called the Beverly Hills Hotel. He hired Margaret Anderson, the manager of the Hollywood Hotel, to run the place. And there it stood for the next several years, empty—a huge pink monument to failure: remote and ridiculous.

Then, at last, Green got lucky. Movie star Douglas Fairbanks and his bride Mary Pickford built their dream estate nearby. Named Pickfair, the mansion quickly became the heart of the Hollywood party circuit, and soon every star wanted to live in Beverly Hills. The population tripled. And the Beverly Hills Hotel's Le Jardin bar became their default nightspot. Each booth had a phone, each table a phone jack. Chaplin always got Table Number One. After every polo game, Will Rogers would hang out there with pals Darryl F. Zanuck and Hal Roach, and this inspired a 1937 name-change to the Polo Lounge. It remained a nexus of power for the entire century.

It is rumored that, in 1932, Johnny Weissmuller landed the title role for

Tarzan when the director saw him jump into the hotel's swimming pool to save a drowning girl. (It seems Weissmuller did this with some frequency.) Howard Hughes lived at the hotel for almost thirty years. Mia Farrow was supposedly banned from the Polo Lounge for wearing pants. Paramount signed itself over to Gulf + Western on a Polo Lounge table.

In 1972, G. Gordon Liddy called John Mitchell at the Polo Lounge the day after the Watergate break-in; their hotel phone records became crucial evidence against them. That same year, the hotel hosted Chaplin once again, returned from exile to receive an honorary Oscar. Elizabeth Taylor spent an astounding six out of eight honeymoons in the hotel's bungalows. Neil Simon's *California Suite* was filmed there, as was *The Way We Were, American Gigolo, Shampoo,* and much of the opening of Lauren Bacall and Gregory Peck's *Designing Women.*

And let's not forget—the Eagles used the hotel on the cover of their 1977 album *Hotel California.* ★

ROBERT BENCHLEY

1889–1945
WRITER, CRITIC, ACTOR

"A great many people have come up to me and asked how I manage to get so much work done and still keep looking so dissipated."

Robert Benchley cut his teeth at *The Harvard Lampoon* and cemented his reputation with his contributions to *Vanity Fair*, *Life*, and the *New Yorker*. Along with Dorothy Parker, he was a founding member of the Algonquin Round Table. His comic routine, "The Treasurer's Report," part of the Round Table theatrical revue was adapted as a short film in 1928, launching Benchley's Hollywood career. He would write and star in nearly fifty shorts over the next fifteen years, including *The Sex Life of the Polyp* (1928) and *How to Sleep* (named Best Short Subject at the eighth annual Academy Awards, in 1935). He penned more than two thousand essays and reviews, in addition to film credits. To celebrated peers like James Thurber, Benchley had no equal.

★

MAYBE IT WAS BECAUSE he got a late start? A fervent Prohibitionist and strict teetotaler, Benchley did not have his first drink until he was thirty-one. This was at Tony Soma's speakeasy, right across from Jack and Charlie's (later renamed the 21 Club). On a side note, Soma was the grandfather of actress Anjelica Huston and, in the days before Rockefeller Center (before television, period), his was a literary joint.

Benchley was in the company of Zelda and F. Scott Fitzgerald and his best pal Dorothy Parker that night. The story goes, he turned to Parker and cracked, "Let's find out what all the fuss is about," then ordered an Orange Blossom. Benchley would make up for lost time.

Like so many East Coast intellectuals, he was soon lured out to Tinseltown by the promise of easy money and . . . well, easy money. He holed up with his great friend Charles Butterworth, and by the 1930s no one was more closely associated with the Garden of Allah than Benchley, the hotel's unofficial master of ceremonies. He once quipped, "Drinking makes such fools of people and people are such fools to begin with, that it's compounding a felony," and yet stories of his own exploits would soon pile up. Like the time he bet Errol Flynn a thousand dollars he could swim all the way to Catalina Island, then dragged everyone within earshot down to Long Beach. Benchley paddled all of twelve feet before calling for a rope. Or the time he phoned for his doctor, complaining of side effects from a new prescription. When the doctor arrived, he pulled up his shirt, revealing a mess of feathers he'd glued to his body.

> He once quipped, "Drinking makes such fools of people and people are such fools to begin with, that it's compounding a felony."

But as pianist Oscar Levant famously said, "Strip away the phony tinsel of Hollywood and you find the real tinsel underneath." And this was true for Benchley, who came to loathe the town. Respected and beloved by his friends, he considered himself a fundamentally lazy man who had wasted his talents—a hack and a sellout. Arriving at a party once, he spied an old buddy from New York, playwright Robert Sherwood. Benchley pointed at Sherwood and exclaimed, "Those eyes—I can't stand those eyes looking at me! He's looking at me, and thinking of how he knew me when I was going to be a great writer."

Years later, at his bungalow at the Garden of Allah, Benchley would convey his feelings about life and booze to his dear friend F. Scott Fitzgerald. Checking his watch, Benchley saw that it was indeed the cocktail hour and, consequently, time for a pitcher of martinis. At this point, Fitzgerald had moved out to Hollywood himself. He was separated from Zelda, dating columnist Sheilah Graham, and trying his hardest to stay on the wagon. Fitzgerald tried to talk Benchley out of it. "Don't you know drinking is a slow death?" he said. To this, Benchley just tasted his martini and replied, "So who's in a hurry?" Apparently, Benchley was lazy even in his despair. ★

IN A TOWN NOT INCLINED toward self-restraint, maybe hangovers at least provided some measure of control—a temporary dam against the raging river of booze. But it was never pretty. As Robert Benchley once declared, "The only cure for a real hangover is death." While that may have worked for John Barrymore, one need not be so extreme. Some other popular hangover cures included:

- Crazy Hotel Mineral Water (from Mineral Wells, Texas): D. W. Griffith
- A bath in ice water: Fatty Arbuckle
- Half an hour in a steam room: Errol Flynn

- Swedish Glogg: Greta Garbo
- Three swigs of gin: Louise Brooks
- An eight ball of cocaine: Mabel Normand
- Thin, slightly green draft beer accompanied by the faint smell of urine: Charles Bukowski

As for Benchley, in his less dramatic moments he swore by the Prairie Oyster. It is actually not a bad concoction, so long as you shoot it back, just like an oyster—allowing for some texture and burn, but not much taste. Writer Lillian Hellman, a friend and colleague of Benchley's, offered her own twist on the recipe—what was more or less just a heavy injection of sherry.

Finally, if you are at all put off by raw egg, try the Bloody Bull. Just use the same recipe as a Bloody Mary (see page 114) and add 1 oz. of beef broth.

PRAIRIE OYSTER

. . . .

1 RAW EGG
1 TSP. WORCESTERSHIRE SAUCE
2 DASHES TABASCO
SALT AND PEPPER

Crack the egg into an Old-Fashioned glass, being careful not to break the yolk (this will give it the appearance of an oyster, sort of). Add Worchestershire and Tabasco, then sprinkle salt and pepper.

Lillian Hellman's Version

6 OZ. SHERRY
1 RAW EGG
2 TSP. WORCESTERSHIRE SAUCE

Pour sherry into a double Old-Fashioned or Collins glass, then make as you would the Prairie Oyster. Be forewarned: The goal of the remedy is to make you vomit but by cocktail hour, you should be fully recovered.

THE LOST WEEKEND (1945)

Easily the studio era's most frank look at the ravages of alcohol, *The Lost Weekend* had everyone concerned when the script arrived. Was the story too bleak and repellant? Who would want to see it? So cowriters Billy Wilder and Charles Brackett made a couple of concessions: for one, they added a love interest; for another, they made Ray Milland, one of Paramount's biggest stars, their first choice, hoping some of his inherent likability would rub off on the film's lead character—Don Birnam, an alcoholic writer from New York.

When Milland first read the book (which his agent sent along with a note that said "Read it. Study it. You're going to play it"), he knew the part could be a game changer for him. But still, he had reservations. He wasn't sure he had the acting chops, for one thing. Mostly, though, the guy just didn't drink very much. His only previous experience with acting and drinking had been on the set of DeMille's *Reap the Wild Wind*.

During that picture, Milland's agent had dragged him to a party where he downed way too much champagne. Early the next morning, Milland's car was found parked out on his front lawn. With the help of his butler, Milland made it to the set on time, but immediately wardrobe shoved him into a diving suit. He had a scuba scene that day.

In desperation, Milland turned to his fellow cast members and asked for their favorite hangover remedies. John Wayne offered him two enormous green pills he said had to be taken with gin. *Ummm, OK, thanks.* An actor named Lynne Overman handed over three black pills that Milland consumed with tomato juice. Finally, Robert Benchley told Milland the only surefire cure was a wine glass full of Worcestershire, mixed with a raw egg. (A Prairie Oyster, to you and me.) And whoa, what do you know, but Benchley happened to have one right there!

The day mercifully ended for Milland around five. When he emerged from the flotation tank, he was mortified to find DeMille waiting for him. The director wanted to give him something. Apparently, in the mid-thirties, DeMille had purchased an entire lot of specially minted half-dollars, which he handed out on rare occasions to anyone he felt had displayed tremendous fortitude or courage in the line of duty. And as wardrobe stripped away Milland's diving suit, DeMille placed one in Milland's hand, saying it was one of the best jobs of acting he'd ever seen.

For Milland, it was like being given an Academy Award. But if he had any hope of winning a real Oscar with *The Lost Weekend*, he knew his research would have to be more methodical. So Milland invited his in-laws to a dinner at his home, explaining that he intended to get very tipsy, then attempt to act out the two scenes in the movie where Don Birnam is at his drunkest. That night they all got ripped on Mammoth Cave whiskey, then convened to Milland's library, where after twenty hilariously inept minutes of acting, Milland raced to the bathroom. It took six months before he felt ready for another drink.

Then, shortly before filming, Milland had another inspired thought. He checked himself into the psychiatric ward at Bellevue Hospital for a night, just to see what it was like for alcoholics to suffer through withdrawal. The staff at Bellevue accommodated him, issuing him the standard hospital robe and assigning him to a bed. But within a couple hours—once patients started screaming and fighting with attendants—Milland decided he'd had enough. Not bothering to change out of the robe or even put on slippers, he slid out the door of the building and was immediately stopped by a policeman, who noticed the Bellevue Hospital stamp on the robe and tossed him right back into the psych ward. The night nurse spent a half-hour convincing the cop it was okay for Milland to leave the building.

It wasn't the last time Milland was mistaken for a drunk on the streets of New York. During filming of the famous scene where Birnam stumbles down Third Avenue looking for a pawnshop, Milland passed an old friend of his wife and another woman—some flirt he'd once asked the management of a hotel in Mexico City to remove from his room. So believable was Milland's appearance and manner (cameras were hidden, so there wasn't an immediate tip-off) that word of his public drunkenness started to filter into the gossip columns.

Back on set at the Paramount lot, shooting was less eventful, if not less amusing. As Milland tells it in his autobiography, interiors Stage Five had been rebuilt into an exact duplicate of the popular New York writers' bar P. J. Clarke's. No detail of Clarke's was spared, from the stools to the bottles to "the dusty stuffed cat on the top of the telephone booth." Every day during shooting, at around five, the stage door would open and a strange man would walk onto the set. Whether film was rolling or not, the man would head to the bar and order a whiskey. The bartender, being played by Howard da Silva, would indulge him by pouring a real bourbon from a real bottle. The man would gaze about the bar and tip back his whiskey, maybe make some banal comment about the weather. He would finish the glass, put down fifty cents and leave. Apparently, Robert Benchley was working at the studio—and he was homesick for New York.

The Lost Weekend was finished in December 1944, only two months after production began, but long enough for Paramount to once again get cold feet. Some say the liquor lobby was offering the studio millions of dollars in an effort to stop its release. It wouldn't see the light of day until the following year; but when it did, it became an instant classic, winning Oscars for Best Picture, Best Director, and Best Writing, as well as for Best Actor. The likeable Milland had succeeded in showing that humanity remains even in our darkest moments.

CHARLES BUTTERWORTH

1899–1946

CHARACTER ACTOR

* *

"Looks like it's going to get drunk out tonight."

Wit and wingman first class, Charles Butterworth rarely received top billing in his films, but his natural charm made him an ideal supporting actor. His best-remembered role: Eddie Dibble in *This Is the Army* (1943), though he's also known for being the inspiration for the voice of Cap'n Crunch as well as the sidekick of writer Robert Benchley. Butterworth studied law at Notre Dame, then worked as a reporter for a time, but soon quit to take up acting. He moved to Hollywood in 1930 and had a fourteen-year, forty-two-film streak of unqualified success. Because of Butterworth's gift for improvising funny dialogue, screenwriters often provided him with fragmentary scenes, expecting him to come up with better lines on his own. (Most famous: "You ought to get out of those wet clothes and into a dry martini," *Every Day's a Holiday*, 1937.) He had only begun to display his marquee talents when he died in a car accident on Sunset Boulevard—six months after Benchley passed away.

★

CHARLIE BUTTERWORTH AND Bob Benchley were inseparable. As in "could not be separated." If you even glanced at the Garden of Allah in the 1930s, you saw Benchley, and if you saw Benchley, you saw Butterworth next to him. They were like a ventriloquist and his doll, always arguing who was the real dummy. And they had a way of making their presence known.

One night, while drifting to sleep in the room beneath Benchley's, screenwriters Albert Hackett and Frances Goodrich could hear the two men drinking and talking upstairs. When they woke up at 8:30 a.m., Benchley and Butterworth were still at it. A typical early morning conversation would go like this: "Look Charlie, we can't have martinis forever. We must have something to sober up with. Let's have three vodkas."

> **A typical early morning conversation would go like this: "Look Charlie, we can't have martinis forever. We must have something to sober up with. Let's have three vodkas."**

Another time, director Elliott Nugent had come to the Garden for a peaceful vacation with his wife and kids. When it was over, Nugent left a note: "When I hear laughter coming from Bungalow 16, I know it's coming from comedian Butterworth and literary wit Benchley. But my children, who have never heard of you, regard you as a couple of drunks."

Benchley had even told his wife that Butterworth was practically living with him. In fact, it was due to their incessant giggling and carrying on — they were "like a couple of pansies," according to singer Kay Thompson — that the rumor spread: *The Garden of Allah is being infiltrated by homosexuals.*

In response, the bar at the hotel instituted a new policy — every male patron had to be accompanied by a woman. A bouncer was put in place to enforce it, a Pinkerton nonetheless. But when Benchley and Butterworth got wind of the rule, they not only knew why it had been instated, but how to get around it: Butterworth simply dressed as a woman. ★

JOHN CARRADINE

1906–1988
ACTOR

"Like every dog, I've had my day."

Renowned eccentric and patriarch of an acting dynasty, John Carradine was nicknamed "Bard of the Boulevard" for his habit of wandering Hollywood Boulevard dressed in a cape and bellowing Shakespeare. He studied art in the Northeast as a youth and later hitched through the South peddling portraits of people he encountered along the way. First major acting job: a New Orleans production of *Camille* (1925). First major movie: DeMille's *Sign of the Cross* (1932). His good standing as a member of John Ford's stock company (see his major roles: *Stagecoach* (1939), *The Grapes of Wrath* (1940), and *The Man Who Shot Liberty Valance* (1962), among others) was nearly overshadowed by late-life status as a B-movie icon. Carradine played Dracula three times, replacing Bela Lugosi in Universal's *House of Frankenstein* (1944) and *House of Dracula* (1945) and reprising the role for a final time (ludicrously) in *Billy the Kid vs. Dracula* (1966). The money from such schlock went to fund his own repertory theater company. Married four times, he had five sons, of whom David, Keith, and Robert became film actors. The exact number of films Carradine appeared in remains in dispute, but most sources put it at close to three hundred.

★

CARRADINE WAS OFFICIALLY IN. John Barrymore, the King of Hollywood Lushes, saw in the young actor all the makings of a Bundy Drive Boy, and he was soon initiated into the club. Carradine was the right blend of brilliant, drunk, and crazy, and on top of that, he openly worshipped

Barrymore, which never hurt . . . well, most of the time. It was definitely *not* cool when the young sycophant, who had taken to publicly reciting Shakespeare (as if Barrymore didn't *own* that trick), drummed up the nerve to reveal to the legend, "I'm told you are very much impressed with me."

"Sure," Barrymore said. "In fact, I know a screen test you'd be *perfect* for."

This could not be happening. Carradine had worshipped Barrymore since he was sixteen, after seeing him in a New York production of *Hamlet*. It was Barrymore's performance—which Carradine attended six times—that sparked the younger man's lifelong love of Shakespeare. When Carradine had landed the role of Richard III in a production at the University of Southern California in 1929, he decided it was time to meet his idol. He drove to Barrymore's estate, rang the house from a telephone at the back gate, and somehow talked his way onto the property. Barrymore met him outside. "Mr. Barrymore," Carradine said, "I'm going to play Richard III." *"Really,"* Barrymore replied with a smirk. "Let's have a drink!"

And so it began, specifically with two Tom Collins cocktails, and thousands more drinks to follow in the coming years. Errol Flynn, who became their Third Musketeer, later recalled that they'd "start out in some bistro at noon, and a week later find ourselves in Mexico or on a yacht off Catalina with a dozen bottles on the floor and a gaggle of whores puking their guts all over the place."

Still, Carradine had to know his place. If he strayed too far from the role of young apprentice, Barrymore might stop calling him "shithead" (Barrymore's highest compliment). And if he got too cocky, Barrymore might teach him a lesson.

Which brings us back to the screen test. Carradine would be auditioning for a supporting role in a movie that Barrymore was set to star in. The screen test required him to dress up "like a fop" and give a long soliloquy at a dinner banquet. Never mind that the soliloquy was a total piece of crap, Carradine played it like Shakespeare—after all, he wanted to make his idol proud.

And proud Barrymore was. So much so that he celebrated by screening the clip to a select group of friends. He introduced the clip by assuring those gathered that it would demonstrate Carradine's "uncanny special talents." But to Carradine's surprise, the test had been drastically edited down and now contained only two scenes: a close-up, in which he wiped his mouth with a napkin and delivered the soliloquy's final line: "Delicious! The best I've ever had!"

Cut to: A shot of Barrymore from the waist down, zipping up his fly. ★

THEY FIRST MET at Bella Vista, John Barrymore's legendary Beverly Hills estate, named after the spectacular view of the city below. A 7,000-square-foot Mediterranean villa built for director King Vidor, the estate included two guest houses, as well as a pool and stone cabana. Pleasant to think of John Carradine and Barrymore each enjoying a Tom Collins. This was 1929, out on the veranda. Barrymore was wearing a blue polka-dot dressing gown, as perhaps one does on one's estate. Carradine sported striped morning pants, spats (to distract from the fact that he had no socks), a wing collar and York puff tie, topped off by a Homburg hat and cane.

A pair of freaks, or master thespians—depending upon your point of view—each with a Tom Collins in hand.

TOM COLLINS

. . . .

2 OZ. GIN

¾ OZ. FRESH LEMON JUICE

¾ OZ. SIMPLE SYRUP

CLUB SODA

ORANGE SLICE

MARASCHINO CHERRY

Pour gin, lemon juice, and simple syrup into a cocktail shaker filled with ice. Shake briefly. Strain into a Collins glass filled with ice cubes. Top with club soda and stir gently. Granish with orange slice and cherry. Serve with two straws.

RASPUTIN AND THE EMPRESS (1932)

Nobody thought it could be done. Teaming the three Barrymore acting siblings—Lionel, Ethel, and John—in one motion picture? No way. Too many ghosts, too much ego. You couldn't cast Ethel as the romantic lead. *Opposite her brothers?* Or as the mother. *Of her siblings?* Not to mention how John's insane alcohol consumption made him dangerously unreliable. Or how Lionel's alleged morphine addiction made him dangerously uninspired. Seriously: Forget it.

Yet one man in Hollywood wouldn't; he alone believed it could work brilliantly. Fortunately, he was John Barrymore himself. "It's like a circus with three white whales," he once declared. (White whales at a circus? Never mind.) If John would do it, MGM's Irving Thalberg knew that the other dominoes would fall. Ethel owed thousands in back taxes, and though she'd made her name on Broadway, she desperately needed a film gig. And Lionel needed money for his morphine habit. Now all they needed was a script. Languishing in MGM's story vault were the rights to Alfred Klabund's 1927 novel *Rasputin*, about the notorious Russian mystic whose sway over Russian Czar Nicholas II and his wife, Alexandra, led in part to the October Revolution. Ethel could be Alexandra; Lionel, Rasputin; and John, Prince Felix Youssoupoff, a triggerman at Rasputin's 1916 assassination. Done.

A demi-script was cobbled together, but only hours into principal photography, the crew began to rue the day that Ethel had ever signed on. She'd never made a sound movie before and was completely lost on set. When a crew member asked aloud if "Grandma was ready" ("Grandma" being the nickname of the sound blimp on the camera), Ethel blew her stack, assuming *she* was Grandma. Ten days later, she personally saw to the firing of director Charles Brabin and to his replacement by Richard Boleslavski, a Stanislavski alumnus.

Lionel had an entirely different issue, and it wasn't even morphine: John was trying to upstage Lionel's own chin-stroking, scenery-eating performance as the villainous Rasputin. Things got so bad that the crew started referring to the movie as *Disputin*. And that was before the real problem emerged—the script.

According to biographer Mark Vieira, everyone had a different take on what film they were making. Screenwriter Charles MacArthur wanted a movie that revealed the true reason Rasputin had succeeded in duping the powerful Romanoffs: because the powerful Romanoffs were dumb. Thankfully, Thalberg vetoed it, though his grounds for doing so had nothing to do with so-called "artistic merit." Rather, the Czarina was the granddaughter of Queen Victoria, and England was a vital market. Nobody complained.

Thalberg had his own solution: There should be a scene, he insisted, in which Princess Natasha, the wife of Prince Paul, gets raped by Rasputin. Okay. But for starters, Princess Irina and Prince Felix (the real-life models for Natasha and Paul) were very much alive, and thus had certain legal rights. There was also the minor issue that such a rape had never occurred. No matter. It had been decreed, so off everybody went to make their movie in which the hero never bathes because he's too busy raping and murdering dumb royals.

Ethel wrapped in mid-October, but the production dragged on until December 12, with MacArthur sometimes turning in scenes the morning they were to be shot. The premiere (an event so ridiculously star-studded that it was lampooned in a 1933 Mickey Mouse cartoon) took place a week and a half later. Reviews were surprisingly favorable and the movie took in $1 million at the box office. And so it ended.

Until 1934, when Princess Irina sued MGM for $700,000 in libel damages because, as it turned out, she didn't want everyone thinking she was raped. MGM argued it was fiction. The royals scoffed. Their evidence? A press release from Thalberg's office, sent to John Barrymore when he first signed onto the film. The release stated that he'd be playing the role of "Youssoupoff"—Prince Felix's real name, not the character's. Case closed.

The loss spooked the studio so badly that you can see its fingerprints on every film and television show made today: "All characters and events portrayed in this film are entirely fictitious. Any resemblance to real persons, either living or dead, is coincidental." The disclaimer was put into use shortly after and as a direct result of *Rasputin*.

T he patron saint of late bloomers, Raymond Chandler lost his job as an oil industry executive at the age of forty-four due to excessive drinking, then launched a new career as a hard-boiled fiction writer—and proceeded to revitalize the genre. His sharp, lyrical prose and dialogue had a lasting influence on writers of all stripes, and his evocative renderings of thirties/forties Los Angeles, his adopted home, are still considered definitive. He eventually completed eight novels, each centered on private detective Philip Marlowe; all but one were turned into films. (Most notable: *The Big Sleep* in 1946, directed by Howard Hawks, starring Humphrey Bogart and Lauren Bacall, with a screenplay by William Faulkner.) Chandler earned two Academy Award nominations as a screenwriter himself, first for *Double Indemnity* (1944), then for *The Blue Dahlia* (1946). He was hired by Hitchcock to adapt Patricia Highsmith's *Strangers on a Train* but was fired after calling the director a "fat bastard." He spent his final years in seclusion at his home in La Jolla, California; he remains one of the most revered architects of classic film noir.

RAYMOND CHANDLER

1888–1959
AUTHOR AND SCREENWRITER

* * *

"Anyone who doesn't like Hollywood is either crazy or sober."

RAYMOND CHANDLER KNEW THERE was no alternative. The novelist and screenwriter sat in producer John Houseman's office, his confidence shattered. The day before, Paramount had offered him a bonus of $5,000 if Chandler delivered the remaining pages of his screenplay *The Blue Dahlia* on schedule. And given that they'd already been shooting for weeks, the phrase "on schedule" was pretty generous.

The truth was, *The Blue Dahlia* had been a rush job from the beginning. In early 1945, actor Alan Ladd had been unexpectedly called up to the army. Paramount wanted to squeeze one more film out of him before he left, but they had nothing in the pipeline that was suitable. So they had exactly three months to write, cast, and shoot a film from scratch—for one of their biggest stars.

Chandler, who was under contract with Paramount at the time, happened to have a half-written novel laying around that he thought might make a better screenplay. He gave the first 120 pages to Houseman. A few weeks later, with only a partially completed script in place, principal photography began. Veronica Lake was to star alongside Alan Ladd (both boozers in their own right). And then Chandler got writer's block.

Production rolled on, eventually getting ahead of the pages, and panic started to set in. And yet, Chandler didn't consider the $5,000 bonus an enticement, he considered it an insult, a bribe that revealed a complete lack of faith. For a man in a crisis, it only made things worse. No, much as it pained Chandler to disappoint Houseman, he didn't see any possible way he could complete the film. *Unless* . . .

It was no secret that Chandler had had problems with alcohol in the past. But before shooting began, he had assured Houseman that he was sober—happily, proudly sober—he had given up booze for good. But drinking empowered Chandler in a way nothing else could, unlocked his creative tumblers. And if Chandler was going to crank out the rest of *The Blue Dahlia,* he was going to have to start drinking again—and twenty-four/seven. This required nothing less than a "continuous alcoholic siege."

Houseman, who had already coaxed *Citizen Kane* out of the impossibly besotted Herman J. Mankiewicz, was not fazed by the pronouncement. To seal the deal, the two men lunched at Perino's, where Chandler downed three double martinis before the meal and three stingers after. Houseman would observe that his mood seemed much improved.

And so for the final eight days of shooting, Chandler wrote from home. As planned, he was utterly ruined with booze every waking second. Because he ate no solid food—none—Paramount provided a doctor to inject glucose into his arm twice daily. He was also given six secretaries, working in three relays of two each, and a direct line both to Houseman's office and the studio switchboard. Limousines were made to wait outside, ready to run pages to the set at a moment's notice.

In the end, the plan actually worked. *The Blue Dahlia* was completed on time. And while it was initially rejected by the Production Code for, among other things, excessive references to alcohol, it went on to earn Chandler an Academy Award nomination for Best Original Screenplay. A real Hollywood ending.

Except this was a noir drama, and so required a final twist. Houseman later discovered that the Chandler hadn't exactly been sober earlier in the shoot, as he'd claimed. In fact, he'd been on a binge since before *The Blue Dahlia* began and was having trouble even driving himself to the production lot. What had seemed like a heroic act of self-sacrifice—Chandler throwing himself off the wagon for the sake of art—was nothing more than an elaborate scam to stay home and get loaded. For Chandler it was all or nothing. Or, to hear one of his characters say it, "I'm an occasional drinker, the kind of guy who goes out for a beer and wakes up in Singapore with a full beard." ★

HARD-BOILED DETECTIVES are a thirsty lot. Nick and Nora Charles of *The Thin Man* were Dashiell Hammett's (and perhaps cinema's) thirstiest. Still they brought a certain sophistication to their intoxication. As Nick famously said, "Always have rhythm in your shaking. Now a Manhattan you shake to fox-trot time, a Bronx to two-step time, and a dry martini you always shake to waltz time." It was martinis they loved most.

For Raymond Chandler, the detective was Philip Marlowe, played first by Humphrey Bogart in *The Big Sleep*, then in later years by Robert Mitchum in *Farewell, My Lovely*, as well as by Elliott Gould in *The Long Goodbye*. In the latter, Marlowe says, "Alcohol is like love. The first kiss is magic, the second is intimate, the third is routine. After that you take the girl's clothes off." As for what kind of drink, Chandler himself tells us straight, "A real Gimlet is half gin and half Rose's Lime Juice and nothing else. It beats martinis hollow."

It should be noted that *The Long Goodbye* (1973), directed by Robert Altman, was set twenty years after the novel was published. And yet Philip Marlowe remained true to form, even in by-then health-conscious Los Angeles: he smokes like a chimney, a cigarette always drooping from his lips; he's a loner, disinterested in the hippies next door eating hash brownies and practicing tantric yoga. Marlowe is every bit the private dick; he even wears

RAYMOND CHANDLER'S GIMLET

. . . .

1½ OZ. GIN

1½ OZ. ROSE'S LIME JUICE

Pour gin and lime juice into a mixing glass filled with ice cubes. Stir well. Strain into a chilled cocktail glass. Can also be served on the rocks in an Old-Fashioned glass.

Chandler's is not a bad recipe and certainly simple enough to make, but if too tart, change the ratio of gin/lime juice to 2/1. And addzzz a lime wedge as garnish.

SEVEN & SEVEN

. . . .

2 OZ. SEAGRAM'S SEVEN WHISKEY

6 - 8 OZ. 7UP SODA

LEMON WEDGE

Pour Seagram's Seven into a Collins glass filled with ice cubes. Fill remainder of glass with 7Up. Stir gently. Garnish with lemon wedge, if you wish.

a jacket and tie and drives a 1948 Lincoln convertible. But Marlowe doesn't drink gimlets. In fact, the one cocktail he orders is a Seven & Seven, truly a cocktail of the times. Easy to drink and impossible to screw up, one sip and you can taste the hard-boil softening.

BACK IN 1925, NOBODY would have predicted that a young waiter named Alexander Perino, fired from his job at the Biltmore Hotel after dropping a tray of tea and crumpets, would become one of Los Angeles's most successful restaurateurs. But in 1932, seven years later, his eatery would open and go on to become one of the city's' finest restaurants for the next half-century.

One of the few Hollywood restaurants specializing in haute cuisine, the swank eatery drew such luminaries as Frank Sinatra, who occasionally played the Steinway in the bar, and Cole Porter, who once wrote a song on the back of a menu. Bette Davis had a booth permanently reserved in her honor; child-star Margaret O'Brien had a Shirley Temple–style cocktail named after her. Bugsy Siegel was a regular during the 1940s, and Richard Nixon celebrated the announcement of his trip to China with crab legs and a bottle of Château Lafite in 1971.

Given Alexander Perino's humble beginnings as a waiter, it should be no surprise that the service was impeccable. There was even a strict policy that dictated no member of the staff was allowed to wait on more than eight diners at a time.

In 1950 the restaurant moved two blocks west, to a larger location designed by renowned architect Paul R. Williams (who also handled the expansion of Chasen's). The result was described by a restaurant critic as "early thirties Grand Hotel." The oval dining room boasted banquettes bathed in peach and pink. One of the chandeliers cost $150,000. Dessert carts were pure silver and dishes were stamped with the restaurant's name on the bottom.

Three decades later, around 1983, newspapers reported growing financial trouble at Perino's. The newest owner in a long line, Frank Esgro had come in with a laundry list of bold ideas that were absolutely unnecessary. Esgro would open and close a lavish second location downtown (a loss of $7.5 million) and did things like advertising a new $12.50 Sunday buffet (the loss of dignity was incalculable.) But when Perino's entered bankruptcy proceedings in January 1986, a court-appointed trustee revealed that he knew the real problem. "Too many waiters," he told the *Los Angeles Times*. ★

JOAN CRAWFORD

1904–1977
ACTRESS

"If they want to see the girl next door, let them go next door."

Joan Crawford's life encompassed several periods of fame/infamy: her early starlet years; her biting, witty cougar period; her brief blue-blood moment as the heir to the Pepsi fortune; and her posthumous reinvention (courtesy of her daughter Christina) as the worst mother in the lower forty-eight. The last phase, sadly, became the most enduring, thanks to camp biopic *Mommie Dearest* (1981) and its signature line: "No more wire *hangers!*" Born Lucille LeSueur in San Antonio, Crawford debuted on Broadway in 1924 and landed a contract with MGM later that year. Her stage name was chosen in a magazine contest sponsored by the studio. A constant presence in dance contests around Los Angeles throughout the late twenties, she would spend much of the next decade as one of the top box-office draws in Hollywood. Her best known early films are *Grand Hotel* (1932) and *The Women* (1939). By the early 1940s, however, she had come to be considered box-office poison. She scored several major comebacks: an Oscar-winning performance in *Mildred Pierce* (1945), the Academy-Award nominated *Possessed* (1947) and *Sudden Fear* (1952), and her unforgettable turn opposite longtime rival Bette Davis in *What Ever Happened to Baby Jane?* (1962). Crawford left Hollywood respected as a tireless professional and, despite a posthumous image as an abusive mother, remains one of the true stars of her time.

★

THERE WOULD BE a few requests forthcoming, but know this: "Miss Crawford is a star in every sense of the word," the document read. "You do not have to make empty gestures to prove to Miss Crawford that she is a star of the first magnitude."

In 1964, Joan Crawford's film career had been sputtering for a couple of years. The brilliant *Whatever Happened to Baby Jane?* was her last major role. She continued to work, but her recent movies had been campy horror thrillers aiming to capitalize on *Baby Jane.* For one strange gig, she actually replaced her daughter Christina, thirty-five years her junior, on four episodes of a soap opera (*The Secret Storm*) while Christina was on sick leave. The event would make it into *Mommie Dearest.*

And so, with her movie career stumbling toward self-parody, Crawford focused on her responsibilities as a global representative and board member of Pepsi Cola, the company at which her late husband, Alfred Steele, had climbed to the rank of CEO before his death in 1959. This meant a lot of traveling. And wherever Crawford went, she took "The Document" with her—a set of instructions sent to hotels in advance that outlined her demands as a privileged guest and her guidelines for hotel staff behavior.

These twenty-eight pieces of luggage contained, among many other things, an ungodly number of shoes, several picnic hampers, a large supply of liquor, and an ax with a three-foot haft.

To wit: Ms. Crawford required a three-bedroom suite: one room for her, one for her personal maid, and one for her wardrobe. She required two rooms for the pilots of the Pepsi corporate jet. She required a uniformed security officer outside her suite twenty-four hours a day, someone "from Pinkerton or a similar organization"; city policemen and hotel detectives were unacceptable. And she required that the staff be prepared to handle twenty-eight pieces of luggage (not twenty-nine, not twenty-seven, but twenty-eight exactly). These twenty-eight pieces of luggage contained, among many other things, an ungodly number of shoes, several picnic hampers, a large supply of liquor, and an ax with a three-foot haft.

Try not to get hung up on the ax; notice instead the part where it says she traveled with her own supply of liquor. Was the idea that, out of discretion, Crawford brought her own booze with her? Apparently not, because "The Document" went on to outline her additional alcohol requirements: "Two fifths of Smirnoff 100-proof vodka. One fifth Old Forester bourbon. One fifth Chivas Regal scotch. One fifth Beefeater gin. And two bottles Moët & Chandon champagne." And she would need a whole new set for each stop of her travels.

After Steele's death—especially during the filming of *Baby Jane,* when drinking was practically part of the production schedule—Crawford's intake had reached new heights. And now it seemed she had figured out a way to put it all on the Pepsi tab. It worked for a solid decade, though not without ever-increasing protests from her husband's replacement, Donald Kendall, whom she playfully nicknamed "Fang."

In 1970, on the exact day that Crawford reached the mandatory retirement age of 65, Fang announced her retirement. She would learn about it in what was an altogether different kind of document, the newspaper—it was the end of a remarkable run. ★

ROMANOFF'S

326 NORTH RODEO DR.
140 SOUTH RODEO DR.
240 SOUTH RODEO DR.

WHEN EMPEROR MICHAEL ROMANOFF first arrived in Los Angeles, his royal bloodline was kept a secret. He was just the lowly grandson of British prime minister William Gladstone. Or so he told people. But at some point, Romanoff admitted the truth: he was, in fact, the nephew of Czar Nicholas II, an emperor by lineage, in hiding under a fake name by necessity.

In short order, Romanoff became a trusted business partner and friend to some of the industry's biggest players. But the peculiar thing about this arrangement was that every single one of his new and powerful friends *also* knew that he was a complete and utter fraud—that the Emperor was, in fact, a two-bit hustler with seventeen (known) aliases. And yet they *still* did business with the guy. It seemed to make no sense. Or did it?

Born Hershel Geguzin (possibly) in Lithuania (or else Brooklyn), the future Michael Romanoff was such a notorious scam artist that the *New Yorker* had already published a five-part feature detailing his numerous schemes and fabrications before he had even arrived in Los Angeles. But everyone who met him in Hollywood found themselves in surprised agreement: Romanoff was a charming and worldly gentleman, never mind who he actually was.

So when Romanoff set his sights on opening a restaurant in the heart of Beverly Hills, investors readily demonstrated their trust in his business savvy. Charlie Chaplin, Robert Benchley, Humphrey

Bogart, James Cagney, Darryl F. Zanuck, John Hay "Jock" Whitney—each ponied up $7,500 to the known con man. And Romanoff rewarded their trust not by absconding with their money, but by actually opening the restaurant, Romanoff's, on Rodeo Drive—and turning it into one of the most successful and renowned eateries of all time.

To discuss the food he served would be to miss the point entirely. Romanoff himself refused to pray at the altar of the celebrity chef or even acknowledge that it existed. "A restaurant," he said, "is only as good as its owner's personality." He wanted people to pray at the altar of *him*. And soon enough, they did.

Romanoff derived his power quite brilliantly—from the building's floor plan. The front room was reserved for his most favored patrons, the best of the best. (Bogart practically took up residence.) And to get anywhere else in the building, you had to walk through this VIP room. Which meant that lesser celebrities (and all civilians) suffered the indignity of marching through the VIP room before being seated in the large, steerage-seeming dining room. It was excruciating. The worst part: If you walked through, you were forced to watch your more successful peers watching *you*. Try turning that into confidence back on set.

The system gave Romanoff a perversely large amount of power in Hollywood. Not a businessman or army-general's type of power, better: He created perceptions of status in an industry *built* on perception. Romanoff had, by force of will, built a tiny kingdom in which he became the *actual emperor*.

And maybe this is what explains the town's genuine affection for the man who's real name was Hershel Geguzin; they understood his con in a deep and primal way. Just like a movie star, Emperor Romanoff was pursuing an exaggerated version of the American Dream, of the idea that a boy from the Ukraine whose highest previous station was pressing men's pants could convince people that he was royalty, that he was an emperor—and then become one. ★

BING CROSBY

1903–1977
SINGER AND ACTOR

"When you can drink champagne from a cooler in your dressing room in the middle of the day, you've reached the pinnacle."

onsidered one of the original "crooners" for his intimate, conversational singing style, Bing Crosby is rivaled only by Sinatra, Elvis, and the Beatles as the most successful pop singer of the twentieth century. He had an unprecedented run of forty-one chart-topping songs, including "White Christmas" (1942), which was for more than fifty years the best-selling single of all time. Crosby was the biggest box-office draw in the world from 1944 to 1948 and seventh highest-grossing movie star ever. He won four Academy Awards for Best Song and one for Best Actor (*Going My Way*, 1944; also nominated for its sequel, *The Bells of St. Mary's*, the following year). The star or featured player of ten different radio series from 1929 to 1958, Crosby's desire to prerecord his weekly *Philco Radio Time* series for ABC led to the development of reel-to-reel tape machines, revolutionizing the entertainment industry. (He was also indirectly responsible for the invention of the laugh track, about which the less said, the better.) Crosby gracefully adopted the role of elder statesman as television and rock and roll rose to prominence in the sixties and even won a Peabody Award for television contributions in 1970. His unlikely duet with David Bowie ("Little Drummer Boy") aired on a Christmas special months after his death.

★

THERE WAS A LOT riding on this, and Bing Crosby knew it. He'd just had a long, fruitless summer in Los Angeles. It was 1929, and Crosby and the other members of the Paul Whiteman Orchestra—twenty-four men in all—had lived comfortably in a specially built lodge on the back lot of Universal Studios, waiting to shoot a musical called *The King of Jazz*. Whiteman had even secured a fleet of Fords for the entire band, each with a spare tire cover emblazoned with the orchestra's logo. Crosby picked a convertible.

The summer was fun, but the script was taking forever, so everyone split in August, having done exactly nothing. Now it was November 16, the Saturday after the first week of principal photography. Crosby went to the UCLA–St. Mary's football game at the Coliseum, which UCLA lost 24–0. But Crosby was a St. Mary's fan, so when the studio threw a party at the lodge that night, nobody had more to celebrate than he did.

It wasn't just the game, either; it was the movie, his career, everything. In addition to the numbers he was playing with his trio, the Rhythm Boys, he'd been given a solo vocal by Whiteman—the tune "Song of the Dawn." His big break had finally come. All the twenty-six-year-old singer had to do was wake up Monday morning and grab the bull by the horns. And since he still had Sunday to recuperate, after the party, he volunteered to take a female guest back to her room at the Roosevelt Hotel.

> Everyone knew Crosby had been drinking too much. He always did; Binge Crosby, they'd call him. Like clockwork, he'd be the most plastered guy after every show.

Everyone knew Crosby had been drinking too much. He always did; "Binge" Crosby, they'd call him. Like clockwork, he'd be the most plastered guy after every show. Later, after he became a household name, his ability to drink in moderation—or abstain altogether—led most to believe he didn't have an alcohol problem. And likely he didn't. But in the late twenties, everybody seemed certain of the opposite.

Crosby and his unknown charge made it to the Roosevelt Hotel, but turning into the driveway, Crosby smashed into another car. Both he and his companion flew over the convertible's windshield and onto the pavement. Crosby emerged shaken but unscathed. Later, he said that the girl just had cuts and scrapes, but several biographers claim that she was actually knocked unconscious. When the cops arrived, Crosby told them that another car had bumped him from behind. The only problem being, there was no other car. He spent the night in jail.

The following week, Crosby arrived in court for a hearing. He had come straight from the golf course, sporting green pants and a loud orange sweater, and the judge was not amused. When Crosby admitted he'd had a couple of drinks prior to the wreck, the judge asked the arrogant kid if he was aware of this thing called the Eighteenth Amendment—the part of the Bill of Rights that enacted Prohibition?

"Yes," Crosby replied. "But no one pays much attention to it."

Crosby was sentenced to sixty days in jail, of which he served forty. By then Whiteman had long since replaced him on "Song of the Dawn" and, citing an unpaid bootlegger's bill and the DUI incident, the bandleader would fire him a few weeks after his release.

Years later, when Crosby told the DUI story himself, he spun the disappointment as a blessing. "My crooning style wouldn't have been very good" for the song in the film, he said. "I might have flopped. I might have been cut out of the picture. I might never have been given another crack at a song in any picture." The fact that he gave up heavy drinking soon thereafter argues that he actually may have felt otherwise. ★

DON THE BEACHCOMBER
1722 N. MCCADDEN PL.

IF EMPEROR MICHAEL ROMANOFF had it right, the more fun the proprietor, the more fun the venue. And, if nothing else, Ernest Raymond Beaumont Gantt sounds like he was fun. As a young man, Gantt spent years knocking around Australia, Papua New Guina, Jamaica, and Tahiti. During his travels he gathered experience, collected cool artifacts and developed a strong taste for rum.

Gantt drifted back to the States at the tail end of Prohibition. In 1934 he rented

an old tailor shop just north of Hollywood Boulevard and opened a bar. Calling it Don's Beachcomber Café, the place was fairly simple: about two dozen seats, Gantt's artifacts scattered about, and the names of cocktails carved into a plank above the bar. It would be America's very first Tiki bar. And if the décor was simple, the cocktails were not.

At the time, everyone pretty much drank gin or whiskey; it was a martini or Manhattan world. Gantt would introduce rum (dark rum, light rum, gold rum, spiced rum) or at least bring it into vogue. In doing so, he would go down in history as the inventor of the tropical drink. Not a bad credit to your name, but then Gantt's name, along with his bar's, was changing. So popular was the tiki craze that in 1937

Don's moved across the street. There, Gantt renamed it Don the Beachcomber and renamed himself Donn Beach. Now you can tell that this guy was fun.

Gantt famously said, "If you can't get to paradise, I'll bring it to you." The expanded new location resembled an island getaway with palm fronds and Polynesian masks; there were Philipino waiters serving "exotic" dishes (really just standard Chinese fare) in dimly lit rooms with names such as the Cannibal Room and the Black Hole of Calcutta. Of course, there were also the wildly inventive tiki drinks, with equally inventive names: Zombie, Missionary's Downfall, Cobra's Fang, and the PiYi, delivered in a miniature pinapple. They were fruity but strong: The Zombie featured three shots of different rums and could make you feel like "the walking dead." So much so, Gantt was soon forced to impose a two-Zombie limit per customer.

Don the Beachcomber fast became a celebrity hotspot, with patrons like Bing Crosby, Humphrey Bogart, Marlene Dietrich, Clark Gable, Joan Crawford, David Niven, Buster Keaton, and Frank Sinatra. Stars were even given personalized ivory chopsticks stored in a special case. The tiki craze would sweep the nation, inspiring hordes of imitators. In 1937, Victor Bergeron returned to the San Francisco Bay area from travels in the South Seas to open the first Trader Vic's. And while Gantt would invent the Zombie, Vic would lay claim to the Mai Tai. It was the beginning of a friendly rivalry.

With the onset of World War II, Gantt went off to fight in Europe. During his time away, his ex-wife Sunny expanded Don the Beachcomber into a chain of Beachcombers. And while none of the original restaurants remain today, at one time there were sixteen. Upon Gantt's return, the couple split up assets, Sunny keeping the mainland U.S. locations and Gantt moving to Hawaii. There he would start over again on the burgeoning Waikiki Beach with his own unaffiliated Don the Beachcomber. For the remainder of his life, Gantt would serve delicious rum concoctions to bikini-clad customers thirsty from the sun. How fun is that? He died with eighty-four cocktail recipes to his name. ★

ZOMBIE

- -

1 OZ. FRESH LEMON JUICE

1 TSP. BROWN SUGAR

1 OZ. GOLD PUERTO RICAN RUM

1 OZ. LIGHT PUERTO RICAN RUM

1 OZ. 151 DEMERARA RUM

1 OZ. UNSWEETENED PINEAPPLE
    JUICE

1 OZ. FRESH LIME JUICE

1 OZ. PASSION-FRUIT
    SYRUP

1 DASH OF ANGOSTURA
    BITTERS

1 MINT SPRIG

Dissolve brown sugar in lemon juice at the bottom of a shaker.
Add ice cubes and pour in remaining liquid ingredients.
Shake well and strain into Collins glass filled with crushed ice.
Garnish with mint. Serve with a straw.

MISSIONARY'S DOWNFALL

- -

1 OZ. LIGHT RUM

½ OZ. PEACH BRANDY

1 OZ. HONEY SYRUP*

½ OZ. FRESH LIME
    JUICE

¼ CUP DICED FRESH
    PINEAPPLE

¼ CUP MINT LEAVES

¼ CUP CRUSHED ICE

1 MINT SPRIG

Put all of the ingredients into the blender and blend at highest
speed for 15–30 seconds. Pour into a goblet or, as substitute, a
Collins glass.

*Honey syrup: The same process as simple syrup, with 1 part honey
to 1 part water.

FRANCES FARMER

1913–1970
ACTRESS

"I put liquor in my milk, in my coffee, and in my orange juice. What do you want me to do, starve to death?"

Beautiful and troubled, Frances Farmer had a career that derailed not long after leaving the station. A precocious girl, she won a national essay contest in high school for a piece titled "God Dies." Farmer provoked further controversy in college with a publicized trip to the Soviet Union in 1935, when she visited the Moscow Art Theatre. Signed by a Paramount talent scout soon after, she despised Hollywood from the start and constantly bucked against the studio. Nonetheless, Farmer managed to get cast opposite major stars such as Bing Crosby, Tyrone Power, and Fred MacMurray; her finest moment was a double role in Howard Hawks's *Come and Get It* (1936); Hawks declared her "the greatest actress I've ever worked with." A failed marriage to actor Leif Erickson and professional frustrations led to increasingly erratic behavior; she was arrested for drunk driving in 1942 and for assault in 1943. The latter resulted in an involuntary commitment to a mental hospital, which led to seven years shuttling in and out of institutions. (Her mother recommitted her in 1945.) The 1982 biopic *Frances* depicts Farmer getting a lobotomy, but the scene was entirely fictional and all records show that she never underwent the procedure. Her final years were spent in Indianapolis, hosting *Frances Farmer Presents*, a weekday movie showcase.

★

HAVE YOU EVER HAD a broken heart?" The stunningly beautiful Frances Farmer was shouting after her recent arrest—her second in four months, to be exact. The first was on a charge of drunk driving; she'd been fined $500 and placed on probation. The second, in January 1943, was a bit messier. For one thing, nobody could say exactly what had happened. Farmer certainly couldn't—she had been drinking far too much. Witnesses alleged she'd started a brawl in a restaurant and then run topless along Sunset Boulevard. Added to that, she hadn't checked in with her probation officer, and the police had been looking for her for the last two weeks. When they finally found her, at the Knickerbocker Hotel, she did not go quietly.

At the police station, when asked her occupation, Farmer answered "cocksucker."

Farmer's six-year marriage to actor Leif Erickson had recently ended, but if her heart was indeed broken, there had been a number of wrecking balls. A few years prior, while playing Lorna Moon in a Group Theatre production of *Golden Boy* in New York, she had an affair with playwright Clifford Odets. Odets would later turn to screenwriting (*Sweet Smell of Success*)

> Witnesses alleged she'd started a brawl in a restaurant and then run topless along Sunset Boulevard. Added to that, she hadn't checked in with her probation officer, and the police had been looking for her for the last two weeks.

and name names before the House Un-American Activities Committee. The thing was, both Farmer and Odets were married to other people at the time, and Odets refused to leave his wife. Eventually, it would be Farmer he left—left feeling used and betrayed. It was then that problems with her temper and alcohol began to spiral out of control.

In a Los Angeles courtroom on the morning after her second arrest, the presiding judge asked Farmer a few basic questions about what had transpired the day before. Had she been fighting? Yes, Farmer replied, she had. "For my country as well as myself." Had she been driving a car (a violation of her parole)? No, Farmer replied. "But only because I couldn't get my hands on one."

After a series of such replies, the judge sentenced Farmer to 180 days in jail, which was commuted to a court-ordered commitment to a mental hospital. She left the courtroom and asked a police matron if she could use a phone. When told she couldn't, Farmer punched the matron. Police had to put her in a straitjacket to get her to a cell. As they dragged her away, both from the courthouse and from Hollywood forever, Farmer tried to explain herself. "Have you ever had a broken heart?" ★

• •

WILLIAM FAULKNER

1897–1962

AUTHOR AND SCREENWRITER

• •

"Isn't anythin' Ah got whiskey won't cure."

onsidered America's preeminent Southern writer (many feel the qualifier could be dropped), William Faulkner was raised in Oxford, Mississippi. As a young man, his neighbors nicknamed him "Count No 'Count" because they reckoned he didn't have a steady job. Setting most of his novels in the surrounding area, his fictional Yoknapatawpha County, between the years of 1928 and 1941 Faulkner would write ten novels—including his masterpieces *The Sound and the Fury, As I Lay Dying, Light in August, Absalom, Absalom!,* and ending with perhaps his last work of distinction, *Go Down, Moses.* It was a feat of astonishing creative output, unmatched in American literature before or since, and made even more astonishing by the fact that, following the publication of Faulkner's fifth novel, *Sanctuary,* he would make intermittent trips to Hollywood, working at first for MGM, then Twentieth Century–Fox and later Warner Bros. Much more important than the studios was his lifelong collaborative friendship with director Howard Hawks. Faulkner's most important films were *To Have and Have Not* (1944) and *The Big Sleep* (1946), both adaptations directed by Hawks and starring Humphrey Bogart. In 1949, after decades of financial instability, Faulkner was awarded the Nobel Prize for Literature and thereafter became an international celebrity.

———————————— ★ ————————————

WILLIAM FAULKNER PUT A good deal of faith in bourbon. In addition to its medicinal benefits, bourbon, he felt, provided creative benefits, too: "I usually write at night. I always keep my whiskey within reach."

Although writers are generally known to knock it back, few of them actually drink *while* they write. Hemingway made it a point to keep his drinking separate, saying "[I] have spent . . . all my life drinking, but since writing is my true love I never get the two mixed up." Eugene O'Neill, who drank everything from wood alcohol to absinthe to his own urine (this on a binge in Provincetown), declared, "I never write a line when I'm not strictly on the wagon." Raymond Carver, who also knew how to bend an elbow, confessed he "never wrote so much as a line that was worth a nickel when I was under the influence."

Faulkner, it seems, was the exception. But then given his feelings about Hollywood and the amount of time he would be forced to spend there (four years total), maybe that was understandable. Hailing from Oxford, Mississippi, he didn't like Los Angeles, "that damned West Coast place." He didn't like the film business, that "place

Picture a small man wearing worn but neatly pressed tweeds with a pipe between his teeth. Faulkner didn't belong on a studio lot and he knew it.

that lacks ideas." And he didn't like screenwriting, "It ain't my racket." But by 1932 sales of his first four novels (including *The Sound and the Fury*) had averaged only two thousand copies each, and so off to Hollywood he went.

Picture a small man wearing worn but neatly pressed tweeds with a pipe between his teeth. Faulkner didn't belong on a studio lot and he knew it. He knew it so clearly that he fled almost immediately upon arriving, running in panic from the MGM offices out into the scorched and desolate wasteland that is Death Valley. (How about that?!) He returned a few days later, but is it any wonder he kept his whiskey close?

What made doing that that much easier was, first, by the time Faulkner arrived in Hollywood his abiding passion for alcohol was already well known and, second, Faulkner didn't care a whit about keeping his drinking a secret. A perfect example is the time Faulkner began work on the screenplay *The Road to Glory* for director Howard Hawks. This was at Twentieth Century–Fox, and one of the producers was the highly respected Nunnally Johnson (*Grapes of Wrath, The Man in the Grey Flannel Suit*). Soon after arriving at Johnson's office for what was to be the very first script meeting,

Faulkner pulled a pint of bourbon from his pocket. Unfortunately, the bottle happened to be sealed with heavy tinfoil and Faulkner, in his eagerness to uncork it, sliced his finger. He started to bleed. Not to be dissuaded, Faulkner began to suck on the wounded finger while he continued to open the bottle. Having accomplished that, Faulkner sat down with one hand dripping blood (some say over a wastebasket, others into his own hat) and the other hand swigging whiskey. Then the work began. It was 1936.

Almost a decade later, Faulkner would find himself back in Hollywood, again writing for Hawks, though now at Warner Bros. This time, taking a page out of W. C. Fields's playbook, Faulkner employed a different strategy for getting through the workday. He hired a male nurse, named Mr. Nielson, to accompany him around the lot. Carrying a bottle in a black doctor's satchel, Mr. Nielson would ration out drinks of whiskey and Faulkner would write. In fact, over the next two years at Warners, he would write *The Big Sleep* and *To Have and Have Not.*

Maybe his faith in bourbon was well placed. ★

LIKE MANY WRITERS, William Faulkner felt little affection for Hollywood. After winning the Nobel Prize for Literature and, consequently, leaving Tinseltown town for good, he would say, "I have never learned how to write movies, nor even to take them seriously."

There is one story about him working for director Howard Hawks and suffering from *mal de Hollywood*. He asked Hawks if he might write from home, as opposed to the studio lot where, in those days, screenwriters actually wrote. Hawks agreed, but after a number of days had passed, the studio called to check on Faulkner. Nobody answered. Apparently, by home, the novelist had meant two-thousand miles away in Mississippi. Faulkner was back in Oxford eating watermelon on the porch and watching the rain.

Still, whenever he was in Hollywood, his favorite watering hole was Musso & Frank's. Known for their martinis, they let Faulkner behind the bar to mix his own beloved Mint Juleps. That recipe, if ever known, has been swallowed up by time. But one can only imagine that to Faulkner, at least, it tasted like home.

MINT JULEP

. . . .

3 OZ. BOURBON
½ OZ. SIMPLE SYRUP
7 MINT SPRIGS

Crush six mint sprigs in the bottom of a chilled Old-Fashioned glass. Pour in simple syrup and bourbon. Fill with crushed ice and stir. Garnish with the remaining mint sprig and serve with two short straws. Add a splash of club soda if you like.

F. SCOTT FITZGERALD

1896–1940
AUTHOR AND SCREENWRITER

"I cannot consider one pint of wine at the day's end as anything but one of the rights of man."

He was the preeminent chronicler of the Jazz Age, a term F. Scott Fitzgerald coined and the period for which he became a symbol. Fitzgerald's debut novel, *This Side of Paradise*, based on a book he had begun at Princeton, made him an instant success. Next came *The Beautiful and the Damned*, followed by his masterpiece, *The Great Gatsby*, considered one of the greatest American novels ever written. The book has been adapted to screen no less than five times, ranging from a 1926 silent film (now lost) to a 2013 3D version. Living in Paris during the 1920s with his wife, Zelda, Fitzgerald was at the heart of the Lost Generation and, even amongst the likes of Ernest Hemingway, Gertrude Stein, and John Dos Passos, the celebrity couple stood out. But Fitzgerald's fourth novel *Tender Is the Night* would take more than eight years to complete. By then, the stock market had crashed and the book was a disappointment to the cash-strapped Fitzgerald. He made several forays into screenwriting, often in the employ of MGM. But despite considerable time and effort, the great American author found little success in Hollywood. Most of Fitzgerald's contributions, including some work on *Gone with the Wind* (1939), did not receive a credit. He would earn only one screenplay credit (shared), for the film *Three Comrades*, in 1938. But Fitzgerald poured his Hollywood experiences into his final novel, *The Last Tycoon*, published posthumously and based on MGM's famed executive Irving Thalberg.

★

FITZGERALD NEVER LOVED HOLLYWOOD, though in truth, the feeling seems to have been mutual—at least where the studios were concerned. Naturally, for any serious East Coast writer, movie work held above all else the allure of easy money. But Fitzgerald, more than most, took a serious interest in the screenwriting craft. His colleague Ben Hecht (the "Shakespeare of Hollywood") once observed, "It's just as hard to make a toilet seat as it is a castle window. But the view is different." And indeed, most of Fitzgerald's time in the California sunshine was marked by struggle.

However decadent or excessive Hollywood might have been in the 1920s, good old Scott, the bard of the Jazz Age, had them beat. That said, for a committed drinker, Fitzgerald was a spectacularly lousy one. The problem being, he got drunk very easily. Fitzgerald's first stint in Hollywood was in 1927, with Zelda along for the ride (as you can imagine, she did little to quiet the storm). They stayed for two months, sharing a bungalow at the Ambassador Hotel with, among others, John Barrymore (no quiet from him either). Fitzgerald had been hired to write a scenario for a comedy titled *Lipstick,* to star Constance Talmadge. But work seemed to be the last thing on the Fitzgeralds' minds.

> For a committed drinker, Fitzgerald was a spectacularly lousy one. The problem being, he got drunk very easily.

The stories from this trip are manifold. That they arrived at a fashionable party dressed only in their pajamas. Or at another gathering, under the pretext of a magic trick, they collected guests' watches and jewelry, then retreated to the kitchen and proceeded to boil the booty in tomato sauce. As Cole Porter sang that very same year, "We're all alone, no chaperone . . . Let's misbehave!" Crashing Samuel Goldwyn's costume party, the couple was found on the doorstep on all fours barking—as if dressed up as dogs. Once inside, Zelda marched upstairs and ran a bath. The party happened to be in honor of none other than Constance Talmadge herself, and she never forgave Scott. His scenario would be rejected, and the Fitzgeralds would soon flee Hollywood. Their final gesture: stacking all their hotel furniture into a pile, the unpaid bill on top.

Years later, Fitzgerald would say he had been overconfident, believing himself "a sort of magician with words." While for her part, Zelda had just found the town boring. "Hollywood is not gay like the magazines say but very quiet," she wrote their daughter, Scottie, swearing that, "If we ever get out of here I will never go near another moving picture theatre or actor again." It would be almost four years before Scott returned to Hollywood, and by then Zelda, very much unwell, was left in the care of her parents in Montgomery, Alabama.

Fitzgerald's second chance at screenwriting was given to him in 1931 by MGM's boy genius, Irving Thalberg. He was hired to write some "smart lines" for the Jean Harlow vehicle *Red-Headed Woman*. Hollywood's attitude toward one of America's great men of letters might have been amusing were it not so sad. Years later Fitzgerald would cross paths with another red-headed woman, Joan Crawford, who famously exhorted him to, "Write hard, Mr. Fitzgerald, write hard!" By most accounts he did write hard. He just played hard, too. And on this trip there was to be another social fiasco—at a tea party held on a Sunday afternoon at the home of his boss Irving Thalberg and Thalberg's movie-star wife, Norma Shearer, after far too much gin, Fitzgerald gathered together the crowd of A-list actors and directors—John Gilbert, Marion Davies, Robert Montgomery, et al—for a parlor trick. He asked Norma Shearer for a small dog and a piano player; he was given a poodle and Ramon Navarro. Clearly soused, with the dog cradled in his arms, Fitzgerald sang a drunken tune he had written years ago at Princeton with his old pal Edmund "Bunny" Wilson. It was a song about dogs. "Larger that a rat! / More faithful than a cat! /Dog! Dog! Dog!" The song was a flop and, despite five weeks of work, the script was, too—Thalberg rejected Fitzgerald's draft and gave the film to Anita Loos.

It would take more than half a decade and the death of Irving Thalberg for Fitzgerald to return to Hollywood. By then, 1937, Zelda was in a sanitarium, and Fitzgerald's life was truly in shambles. He had already written *The Crack-Up* for Esquire, that early masterpiece of self-revelation. But this time he would really give Tinseltown a go, spending three and a half years writing scripts. All told, little of significance ended up on screen. But maybe he and Hollywood were finally warming up to each other. Under contract with the studios, Fitzgerald spent the majority of his time on the wagon. There were of course a few exceptions; most notably a week-long binge with screenwriter Budd Schulberg. But then that took place in New Hampshire during the dead of winter, at Dartmouth, no less—who could blame him? Back West, Fitzgerald was head over heels for columnist Sheilah Graham, which helped, his first truly intimate relationship since Zelda. And he had begun his first novel in nearly a decade, *The Last Tycoon,* a book about Hollywood and about America. All this, and then Fitzgerald went and died of a heart attack at Graham's apartment in Hollywood, age forty-four. But even if the town never really loved him, most would agree, it wasn't what killed him either. ★

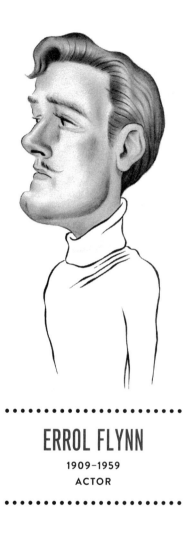

ERROL FLYNN

1909–1959
ACTOR

*"I like my whiskey old
and my women young."*

Errol Flynn became famous for his roles as swashbucklers and chivalrous rogues—costumed adventures that were a precursor to action films. See *Captain Blood* (1935), his first starring role, or *The Adventures of Robin Hood* (1938), the defining portrayal of the folk hero. Onstage, Flynn often did his own stunts. Offstage, he was a gallant hedonist whose antics exceeded those of his screen persona. Nicknamed "Satan's Angel" by Marlene Dietrich, the phrase "In like Flynn" referred to his facility with women. Acquitted on two charges of statutory rape, Flynn once spanked gossip queen Hedda Hopper at a nightclub for a negative story. Although his career slowed in the early fifties, he had a late-life renaissance playing aging alcoholics—most famously *The Sun Also Rises* (1957) and *Too Much, Too Soon* (1958), in which he played old drinking buddy John Barrymore. In regard to his newfound respect as a serious actor, Flynn said, "Why all the fuss? I was only playing myself." He wrote one of the best Hollywood memoirs the year before his death, *My Wicked, Wicked Ways* (he had wanted to call it *In Like Me*). Flynn's debauched lifestyle led to diabetes, paralysis, and, finally, heart failure. His friend David Niven would describe him as "a magnificent specimen of the rampant male." He was buried with six bottles of whiskey in his casket.

———————— ★ ————————

RAOUL WALSH REFUSED TO believe it. Walsh, a respected Hollywood director (*High Sierra, White Heat*), had just completed the brilliant *Objective, Burma!* for Warner Brothers. A week before its release, he was summoned to the office of Jack Warner, who ran the studio. Such a summons rarely portended good news.

But when Warner told Walsh exactly why he had brought him into his office, the reason proved to be more laughable than anything else. Errol Flynn, the star of *Objective, Burma!* was slated to begin a week of press in New York the following day. At the time, Flynn was an international sensation and among the studio's most bankable actors. But to Warner's great consternation, he was also a world-class reveler and loyal member of the Bundy Drive Boys. As the club's own in-house chronicler, screenwriter Gene Fowler (*The Mighty Barnum, Billy the Kid*), noted in his memoir, "These men lived intensely, as do children and poets and jaguars." Flynn was one of Walsh's best friends, having starred in five of the director's previous six films. Flynn loved Walsh and, more important, would listen to him. Thus Walsh had managed to keep the hard-living Flynn sober on most shoot days. ("Sober" being a relative term. In his autobiography, Walsh says that Flynn did have a half-dozen drinks a day, "which to him was total abstention.")

Flynn had just bought his love interest two pedigreed poodles, at $500 each, and again put it on the Warner tab. He even gave his name to the breeding house as "Jack L. Warner." Flynn had a peculiar habit when drunk of buying animals.

So now Jack Warner wanted Walsh to babysit Flynn on the New York press tour—partly to keep Flynn sober during interviews (made sense), and partly because "turning Flynn loose in New York is playing with dynamite. If you don't watch out, he'll bankrupt us." (Wait, what?) True, Flynn was the loosest of cannons. In 1943, when he was on trial for the statutory rape of two seventeen-year-olds, Flynn spent his free time romancing an eighteen-year-old courthouse worker—Nora Eddington, who also happened to be the daughter of a police captain. He was acquitted of the statutory rape charges, but got Nora pregnant and made her his second wife.

Still, Walsh had seen the profligate spending of Warner's brass on even the most minor of films. The idea that his best friend could affect a studio's demise on a mere press tour was ridiculous. But Warner had asked, and so Walsh would go.

The next day in Manhattan, as Flynn and Walsh entered a lavish two-bedroom suite at the Waldorf, Flynn glumly noted that, "It'll have to do, I suppose." He plopped down and phoned room service for scotch, gin, and brandy in bottles and two magnums of champagne on ice. As Flynn himself would readily confess, "I can't reconcile my gross habits with my net income." Walsh held his tongue.

Soon, heavily into the bottles, Flynn announced a new devil to be conquered: he was hungry. Caviar, oysters, and twelve bottles of Guinness Stout arrived forthwith. As they ate, Flynn revealed yet another surprise: "I'm in love." Actually, this was *not* a surprise. Walsh had seen Flynn fall in and out of love an average of twice a week during their time together, so he remained unconcerned, until Flynn picked up the phone and ordered six dozen roses delivered to the woman every day—all on the Warner tab.

He next placed a mysterious call, the subject of which only became clear to Walsh after it was too late: Flynn had just bought his love interest two pedigreed poodles, at $500 each, and again put it on the Warner tab. He even gave his name to the breeding house as "Jack L. Warner." Flynn had a peculiar habit, when drunk, of buying animals. Once, on another bender in Chicago, he bought a female lion cub he named Wellington and promptly abandoned her in the lobby of a hotel. Walsh knew that this would be where the worm turned. He insisted that Flynn cancel the order, and ultimately Flynn acquiesced and promised his dear friend that there would be no poodles.

The poodles arrived the next day. ★

IT WASN'T UNTIL the mid–1940s that Errol Flynn first laid eyes on the Bloody Mary. In his memoir, *My Wicked, Wicked Ways*, he reported, "One day, on the lot, I asked Ann Sheridan what she was drinking. It looked like tomato juice. It was, but it had vodka in it. I took up vodka drinking. Vodka has no odor. Nobody need know you have had it." It was the beginning of a lifelong love affair. Flynn looked into his heart: "Why didn't I tire of it? Why did most things pall on me, but vodka never?"

At this point, by his own admission, Flynn was up to more than a fifth a day. And obviously, when you're drinking like that, discretion is a necessity—even more so if you have Jack Warner to contend with. In fact, when on the studio lot, another one of Errol's tricks was to inject an orange full of vodka. That seems a little complicated. Better to stick with Bloody Marys.

BLOODY MARY

2 OZ. VODKA

4 OZ. TOMATO JUICE

1 OZ. FRESH LEMON JUICE

3 DASHES OF TABASCO

3 DASHES OF WORCESTERSHIRE

½ TSP. WHITE HORSERADISH

1 PINCH OF CRACKED PEPPER

1 PINCH OF SALT

1 PINCH CELERY SALT (OPTIONAL)

CELERY STALK

LIME WEDGE

Combine all ingredients except celery stalk and lime wedge in a highball glass, then carefully pour into another highball glass filled with ice cubes. Stir gently. Garnish with celery stalk and lime wedge.

THE BIG TRAIL (1930)

When Raoul Walsh was tapped to direct *The Big Trail* less than a
year after an on-set accident cost him his right eye, he wasn't
simply being asked to work again; he was being asked to rescue a studio.
Not long after buying out distributor Marcus Loew in 1929, Fox Studio
chief William Fox was injured in a car crash that required a lengthy (and
expensive) rehabilitation. While Fox was still mending, MGM boss Louis
B. Mayer, capitalizing on his friendship with President Herbert Hoover,
suggested the Justice Department launch an antitrust investigation into
the Fox/Loew deal. Then, in October 1929, the stock market crashed.
The Fox Film Corporation, Walsh's longtime employer, was on the brink
of collapse.

Fox was banking on the success of a new widescreen 70 mm film
format the company called Fox Grandeur. To sell the gimmick, the
studio needed a spectacle. So they turned to their most-trusted hand,
Walsh, and put him in charge of an epic Western talkie that would be
shot on location in five states—Arizona, California, Utah, Wyoming,
and Montana—with a budget of $2 million. It was a huge gamble at a
desperate time.

Driving the stakes even higher: *The Big Trail,* a tale of revenge set on
the Oregon Trail in 1842, was saddled with an unknown lead. Walsh had
cast a Fox stagehand named Marion Morrison, who had played football
at USC, after spying him moving furniture on the lot. The studio, need-
less to say, balked. Only after numerous screen tests (and the discovery
that Tom Mix and Gary Cooper were unavailable) did Fox acquiesce, on
the condition that the man change his deeply forgettable name. He did:
Marion Morrison would become known to the world as John Wayne.

Filming began in April 1930 in Yuma, Arizona, and eventually covered more than two thousand miles—a caravan of thirty-five principal cast members, dozens of extras, fourteen cameramen, six assistant
directors, over two hundred other crew members, portable dressing
rooms, equipment trucks, and a portable film lab. Because most theaters in the country weren't equipped with widescreen projectors, the

film had to be shot both in 70 mm and 35 mm, requiring radically different setups for each scene. And to save money on dubbing, the film was simultaneously being filmed in both English and German.

Also: there wasn't really a script.

A screenwriter had been assigned to help Walsh round out a rough outline and write dialogue as they went, but his only real contribution was a large supply of booze he'd bought off a bootlegger in Yuma. It would turn out that Wayne could out-drink everybody. Walsh, who'd seen everything with the Bundy Drive Boys, even joked that the movie should be retitled *The Big Drunk*.

Wayne suffered from such severe dysentery and vomiting that it cost him three weeks shooting time and eighteen pounds. During his first scene back, supporting player Tully Marshall passed him a jug secretly filled with rotgut whiskey, an unpleasant surprise. Wayne's female lead, Marguerite Churchill, would develop a horrible case of acne. The veteran cast complained about conditions on the trail and the early call times, mostly because they had stayed up all night drinking with Walsh. Through it all, the director did impressive work. His finest moment, an impromptu scene shot in the Hurricane Bluffs in Utah, entailed lowering several wagons and some livestock down the side of a canyon to the bottom of a ravine. When the last of the wagons slipped out of its ropes and crashed to the earth, splintering among the rocks, Walsh had the shot he needed.

But there would be no Hollywood ending. When *The Big Trail* was released in the fall of 1930, only two theaters—Grauman's Chinese in Los Angeles and the Roxy in New York—showed the 70 mm version. The rest of the country saw a run-of-the-mill Western. Fox Grandeur was all name, no grandeur. Wayne, who'd banked on *The Big Trail* making his name, floundered as an actor for the next eight years. And Fox lost control of his company and declared bankruptcy.

But the film (thanks to Wayne) is considered one of the most important Westerns in cinema history—it's also pretty good. So there's that.

CLARK GABLE

1901–1960
ACTOR

"When a guy boozes with a friend, he usually lets you know something about what's going on inside his noggin."

The number-one leading man of his generation, Clark Gable is best remembered for his roles in *Gone with the Wind* (1939), *Mutiny on the Bounty* (1935), and *It Happened One Night* (1934). All three garnered Best Actor Oscar nods, but he won for *It Happened One Night.* Considered the epitome of virility and masculinity by women and men alike, this was somewhat ironic, given that Gable was mistakenly labeled a girl on his birth certificate. As a young man, he worked in oil fields and as a lumberjack. Later, he stumbled into acting and struck gold with his rugged good looks and alpha-dog personality. A notorious philanderer, he was married five times. He briefly gave up acting to join the Army Air Force during World War II. Mission: creating propaganda films that would encourage enlistment. (Upon discovering this, Adolf Hitler—a fan—offered a reward to anyone who could capture and deliver Gable to him unscathed.) Gable returned to Hollywood in 1945, and despite his diminishing star-status as the studio system gradually eroded, he went on to make another twenty-two features. Gable's final performance in *The Misfits* (1961)—also Marilyn Monroe's final picture—is still considered among his finest.

———————————————— ★ ————————————————

"SIBERIA" WAS WHAT MGM boss Louis B. Mayer called Columbia Pictures. A rinky-dink studio with no stars of its own. And yet Mayer had agreed to loan them Clark Gable for a movie with "Bus" in the title. *Night Bus.* A crappy title based on a crappy story Columbia had bought from a woman's magazine for just $5,000. Now this was a real slap-in-the-face. Gable needed a drink.

It was clear that the Columbia deal was Gable's comeuppance for the attitude he had copped on his last picture, *Dancing Lady*. Gable had been absent for six weeks of production. Depending on who you talked to, some of this time was for medical reasons (getting his teeth replaced with dentures), and some was for personal reasons (his romance with Joan Crawford—this in the days before his affairs with Carole Lombard, Grace Kelly, and Marilyn Monroe). Regardless, the loss of time cost the studio an additional $150,000, and Mayer was not happy. On top of that, after finally wrapping, Gable had laid into the studio boss: he was tired of playing "gigolos," and from now on, he'd only take parts that he liked.

It is worth noting that Mayer was not a nice guy. Reportedly, Mayer covered up murders and rapes. He ruined people's lives to save money or to just to make a point. He did perverse and unforgivable things like not telling his biggest box-office draw (Marie Dressler) that she had cancer until after her movie had wrapped. But if nothing else, Mayer was consistent in one regard: He did not cave to actors' demands. Especially an actor whose affair with Joan Crawford had been "the affair that nearly burned Hollywood down" (as described by Adela Rogers St. Johns). And thus, Mayer's revenge: the Columbia deal. He'd loan Gable out for a flop and that, in turn, would provide his excuse for dropping Gable from MGM entirely. So it was that Gable found himself heading to Columbia to star in *Night Bus*.

Once at the hospital, the staff would be forced to confiscate Gable's clothes to prevent him from leaving for a nightcap. It was four in the morning.

Before the first script meeting, he would surely have to down some liquid courage. Booze and work had long been intertwined in Gable's life—since way before anyone had even cared to hire him. Back when he was a struggling actor in New York, he ran with a crew of such heroic imbibers as Humphrey Bogart and Spencer Tracy—both unknowns at the time, too. They'd talk shop and knock back a few rounds. This was during Prohibition, but thirty-five cents at the right speakeasy could buy a shot of the "good stuff."

When Gable had made it to the big time, his daily consumption had risen proportionally. Once, after a party celebrating the victory at Iwo Jima, he got so bombed that he demolished his car in a one-car accident on Sunset Boulevard. Apparently, he tried to drive through a roundabout, Bristol Circle, but the trees prevented it. Tossed on a lawn with a massive gash on his head, MGM'S security fixer Howard Strickling managed to get Gable to Cedars of Lebanon Hospital before the police arrived. Once at the hospital, the staff would be forced to confiscate Gable's clothes to prevent him from leaving for a nightcap. It was four in the morning.

So yes, the liquid did provide courage for his arrival at Columbia. Perhaps too much. In the first discussion with his new director, Frank Capra, the sloshed star remarked that he had always wanted to go to Siberia, "but why does it smell so bad?" Capra, having seen it all before, asked Gable if he wanted to go over the script. "Buddy, I don't give a shit what you do with it." Okay then.

Gable's costar, Claudette Colbert, was even less pleasant; she argued ceaselessly and, after the production wrapped, said she had "just finished the worst picture in the world." But Capra knew otherwise. They just had to change the crappy title, *Night Bus,* to something slightly more evocative. *It Happened One Night.*

After the film swept all five major Oscar categories, Gable would return to MGM a superstar. Mayer's plot had backfired, spectacularly. ★

JEAN HARLOW

1911–1937
ACTRESS

"I like to wake up each morning feeling a new man."

Born Harlean Harlow Carpenter, Jean Harlow, sex symbol of the early 1930s, was known as the "Blonde Bombshell" and the "Platinum Blonde." "Discovered" by Fox executives while waiting for a friend at the lot, Harlow claimed to have no initial interest in show business. Soon enough, she was encouraged (forced) by her mother, a failed actress herself, and landed bit parts in several Hal Roach shorts, including three with Laurel and Hardy. Word spread that she never wore underwear and iced her nipples before scenes. She was quickly signed by the breast-obsessed Howard Hughes to a five-year, $100-a-week contract to star in *Hell's Angels* (1930). The following year, Harlow became a superstar after playing opposite Jimmy Cagney in *The Public Enemy* and Clark Gable in *The Secret Six* (the first of a half-dozen movies they'd make together). In 1932 her contract with Hughes was bought out by MGM for $30,000. Pilloried as a terrible actress in her earliest films, Harlow revealed more natural talent for comedy as her career progressed, becoming one of the studio's biggest stars. Her marriage to MGM producer Paul Bern ended in scandal when Bern was found dead in their house, killed by a gunshot wound to the head. Officials ruled it a suicide. Harlow briefly remarried and was later romantically linked to actor William Powell. She died unexpectedly, from complications of kidney failure, at age twenty-six. Her look and style later became the template for Marilyn Monroe and countless other blonde bombshells, and it remains so even today.

★

HOWARD HUGHES'S PUBLICITY TEAM described her hair as "platinum blonde." It was term they had coined. Jean Harlow would always insist it was her natural hair color. Others would insist it was bleached, a harsh mixture of Clorox, ammonia, and the cleaning detergent Lux Flakes. But the truth was, the truth didn't matter—the Blonde Bombshell was that beautiful.

Which brings us to the night of April 7, 1933. A few minutes until midnight and a few minutes until, at long last, the end of Prohibition. Outside the Eastside Brewery just east of the Los Angeles River, traffic was at a standstill. A crowd of hundreds surrounded the building. A convoy of trucks waited, fully stocked with bottles and kegs of soon-to-be-legal beer, ready to roll out as soon as the clock struck twelve. And there at the center of it all was none other than the Blonde Bombshell herself, Jean Harlow. A beer spokesmodel for the ages, resplendent in her low-cut evening gown—never mind that in truth she drank gin.

Graves Gin, to be exact, that was Harlow's brand. Like so many of her contemporaries, she drank gin largely because she thought you could not smell it on her breath. Given her capacity for a bottle a day and, if the stories are true, her predilection for flashing her breasts at dinner parties, it's hard to believe Harlow's breath would be the giveaway. No matter, as long as her mother—the famously controlling Jean Poe Carpenter—didn't find out. To this end, Harlow would go to some lengths to keep her drinking secret. She hid her booze at her friend Dorothy Manners's house. When calling her cousin Don Roberson, another drinking companion (they might use the word *enabler* now), she would announce herself as "Mrs. Graves." It was code that meant Harlow would soon be swinging by his house in her Cadillac, a bottle of Graves in hand.

> Like so many of her contemporaries, she drank gin largely because she thought you could not smell it on her breath. Given her capacity for a bottle a day and, if the stories are true, her predilection for flashing her breasts at dinner parties, it's hard to believe Harlow's breath would be the giveaway.

But now here Harlow was on the night of the repeal, this most public occasion, standing outside a brewery. Did Mother Jean, as Harlow's mother was known (Harlow herself was nicknamed "the Baby"), not count beer as alcohol? Was the Blonde Bombshell, despite her alliengence to gin, so much the beer drinkers' fantasy that the Eastside Brewing Company could find no subsitute?

Again, the truth didn't matter. You see, despite her fame and glamour, Harlow had developed a reputation as that rarest of celebrities: one who was both unpretentious and unspoiled. Production crews loved her, and not just because you could see straight through her dress when the lighting was right. Between takes, she routinely shot dice and smoked cigarettes with the stagehands. She was self-deprecating and self-aware — the perfect match, in fact, for a working-class beer company.

As midnight drew closer, signs bearing the brewery's slogan, "Put Eastside Inside," waved in the air. Actor Walter Huston held court, delivering a speech to the eager crowd. No one cared what he said; nearly eighty years later, the only detail anyone recalls is that Jean Harlow, her platinum hair shining in the moonlight, smashed a full bottle of beer on the first truck off the lot. Then she spent the rest of the night partying with the rowdy blue-collar crowd. The Brewery made a quarter of a million dollars that night. ★

CAFÉ TROCADERO
8610 SUNSET BLVD.

AFTER HIS TRIUMPHANT FORAY into the restaurant business with Vendome, *Hollywood Reporter* publisher Billy Wilkerson felt that the burgeoning nightlife scene should be next. To that end, in mid-1934, he acquired the space recently vacated by La Boheme — an operation plagued by gambling and liquor violations — and reopened it as Café Trocadero. Originally drawn to the building's spacious cellar (he had a large cache of rare libations in need of storage), Wilkerson hired famed designer Harold Grieve to remake the interior in the style of a French café, then persuaded agent Myron Selznick to host an invitation-only grand opening. Attendees included Bing Crosby, Dorothy Parker, William Wellman, Samuel Goldwyn, Fred Astaire, William Powell, Jean Harlow, and Myrna Loy, among others. The party, you'll be not so shocked to discover, was breathlessly reported in the *Hollywood Reporter* the following day.

The Troc, as it was commonly known, opened to the general public a few nights later with a formal dinner. From that very night, it was universally considered the jewel of the Strip and the industry's latest see-and-be-seen destination. Its exclusivity — and patrons' potential for a mention in the *Reporter* — assured that the club was always packed with crowds of the highest caliber. The Troc was David O. Selznick's first choice as a location for the 1937 version of *A Star Is Born*. When Darryl Zanuck celebrated the birth of his son, he threw a stag party at the Troc, with a guest list that included Louis B. Mayer, Wallace Beery, Sid Grauman, Irving Thalberg, Hal Roach, Harry Cohn, and Irving Berlin.

The bar itself was polished copper, serving drinks like the French 75, T.N.T., and the Vendome Special Sling (perhaps a carryover from Wilkerson's first outing). Sunday nights became audition night, where aspiring entertainers were given the chance to perform in front of the giants of Hollywood. It was a huge success, not only because of the talent on display, but because L.A.'s Blue Laws forbade dancing on Sunday (so why not watch the amateurs?). Still, the Troc's

popularity would be short-lived. By 1938, Wilkerson had sold the Trocadero, once again revealing that his attention span for nonpublishing ventures was terminally short. The reins were briefly handed to Felix Young (who later opened Mocambo), but a dispute with the building's landlord drove him away. As the Strip continued to develop through the 1940s, newer, flashier options—including Wilkerson's next endeavor, Ciro's—ultimately rendered the Troc obsolete. In 1947 its doors closed for good. ★

MOST HOTSPOTS EVENTUALLY COOL, and today not much remains of the Café Trocadero other than gossip bites lost in faded newsprint. But since the Troc was started by a newsman, the *Hollywood Reporter*'s Billy Wilkerson, maybe that's at least something. Regarding cocktails, one account in a 1936 issue of *Screen Guide* mentions that "Another daisy is the 'Vendome Special Sling' ($1.00) in which the bartender makes magic out of ginger beer, cherry brandy, gin, and lime juice." It's unclear exactly what the proportions were, or how to conjure up the magic of the Troc's heyday. But after a drink at the Brown Derby's Bamboo Room followed by dinner and dancing at the Grove, you would surely press on to the Troc for one more, always one more—maybe a Vendome Special Sling.

VENDOME SPECIAL SLING

. . . .

1½ OZ. GIN

½ OZ. CHERRY BRANDY

¼ OZ. FRESH LIME JUICE

¼ OZ. SIMPLE SYRUP

TOP WITH GINGER BEER

Fill a Collins glass with ice cubes. Pour in gin, brandy, lime juice, and simple syrup. Top with ginger beer. Stir gently. Serve with straw.

MY LITTLE CHICKADEE (1940)

Meet the most unlikely costars in the history of film (at least until the Sylvester Stallone/Dolly Parton epic *Rhinestone*): teetotaling yapper Mae West and alcoholic grump W. C. Fields. Universal Studios, having done big box office on the unlikely pairing of Marlene Dietrich and Jimmy Stewart—in a western, no less (*Destry Rides Again*)—had arranged this similar marriage on a whim.

By 1939 the Hays Code had effectively emasculated West's career. Not that she didn't make movies, but the flirtation and innuendo and *balls* that had distinguished her early work no longer passed muster with the increasingly prudish Hays office. Fields, meanwhile, had spent a decade building and burning bridges at a pace resembling that of Alec Guinness in *The Bridge on the River Kwai.* And although his track record at turning profits had meant forgiveness, his drinking had become so bad that studios were now afraid to take the chance.

West didn't want to take the chance either. She knew what a disaster he'd become, and she was affiliated with the Moral Re-Armament Movement, a cousin of Alcoholics Anonymous. Then again, she was only getting Z-movie offers now, and here was a studio movie with a legit cast, a funny concept, and a real budget. She had to accept. On one condition: If Fields ever showed up drunk, he was to be removed from the set immediately. And so *My Little Chickadee* sprung to life. Though it would be a painful birthing.

According to biographer Simon Louvish, both Fields and West turned in scripts to Universal for consideration, only to have the studio turn around and hire a third writer, Grover Jones. The straightforward Western that Jones churned out insulted Fields so badly that he proposed a satirical rewrite entitled: *Corn With the Wind, a Cinema 'Epic-Ac' of Long Ago. Based on the novel . . . idea that movie audiences have the minds of 12-year-olds.* Universal then informed Fields he didn't have right of script approval, and that if he refused to get with the program they would be happy to sue him beyond his salary of $100,000.

At this point, Fields turned to West in hopes of finding an ally. He was so desperate not to shoot the Jones script that he agreed to throw his support fully behind hers. West turned in another draft, which Universal put in motion and which formed the basis of the shooting script. *My Little Chickadee* went into production. An uneasy peace.

Though it's generally believed that Fields did not so much as even *think* of going on the wagon, he did keep it simple. Martinis at breakfast, an afternoon drink, perhaps the occasional swig of "pineapple juice" from his canteen. Only once was there any rupture: when Fields stumbled in, having neither shaved, showered, nor stopped drinking since he left the previous day. West said he needed to leave and sober up, and he did. The rest of the film was finished without incident. And though critics were fairly hard on the film, *My Little Chickadee* turned out to be big box office, and for Universal, Fields's highest grossing.

So why, for the rest of her life, did Mae West make it a nonnegotiable condition of interviews that there be "no mention of W. C. Fields" or the film? Why did she refuse to meet Fields's grandson thirty years later on a radio show? Because at some point, Fields, either through his own machinations or the studio's, had magically regained a cowriting credit—with his name right alongside hers.

RITA HAYWORTH

1918–1987
ACTRESS

Reporter: "What do you look like when you wake up in the morning?"

Hayworth: "Darling, I don't wake up till the afternoon."

conic sex symbol of 1940s cinema, Rita Hayworth was nicknamed the "Love Goddess," for her turn as the titular man-eater in *Gilda* (1946) and for her World War II negligee pinup photo in *Life* magazine. She was the first performer to dance with both Gene Kelly and Fred Astaire on film. Born Margarita Carmen Cansino in Brooklyn to a famous Spanish dancer and a Ziegfeld Follies chorus girl, Hayworth was discovered as a teenager while dancing with her father at the Caliente Club in Tijuana. She was signed to a six-month contract by Fox and snatched up soon after by Columbia. Following a long string of B-movies, she dyed her hair red and underwent electrolysis in an effort to look less "exotic," adopting her mother's maiden name for good measure. Fairly quickly, she landed a supporting role in Howard Hawks's *Only Angels Have Wings* (1939) with Cary Grant. Hayworth would spend the next decade as the reigning female sex symbol of Hollywood. But despite box-office draw, she clashed with Columbia head Harry Cohn over her personal life. She was married and divorced five times; among her husbands was Orson Welles (her director on *The Lady from Shanghai*, 1947) and Prince Aly Khan. Supposedly shy and quiet off-screen, Hayworth, late in her life, summed up her romantic entanglements with a quip that might equally describe the final decades of her career, "Most men fall in love with Gilda, but they wake up with me."

★

FOR RITA HAYWORTH, MEN and alcohol did not mix. And yet she loved them both in equal measure.

It was thus she found herself at the Polo Lounge at around midnight entangled with yet another rotten husband (her fourth), the both of them royally smashed. That they were drunk had been obvious from the first mumbled "hello," although playwright Clifford Odets would have assumed it regardless. For one thing, Odets never would have gotten a call from Rita Hayworth and actor/singer Dick Haymes had the couple not been deep in their cups. Especially after what had happened earlier that day.

You see, Odets was in Hollywood working on a film he wrote called *Joseph and His Brethren*. But he and the director had just spent the entire evening at Columbia Pictures waiting for their star, Hayworth, to show up. Eventually they went home, and now Hayworth was calling him from the Polo Lounge to ramble about her frustrations as an artist and actress and so on. Even worse, her meddling "manager" husband, Dick Haymes, equally drunk, was egging her on. Whatever his minor talents as an entertainer, Haymes was primarily known for being a major pain in the ass, a first-class interloper who'd chase successful actresses (he'd end up marrying six times) and then suck them into his own black hole of self-pity and booze.

Hayworth could not have stumbled into Haymes at a less opportune moment. She had just emerged from a disastrous marriage to Prince Aly Khan, which had further alienated Columbia head Harry Cohn (he *owned* her, goddammit), and she hadn't completed a movie in two years. Her sex-symbol status was fading, and her relentless partying was accelerating the aging process. In the year and a half they'd been married, Hayworth and Haymes had fallen into a pattern of staying up till the wee hours drinking and then sleeping until noon.

And Hayworth was not someone who could handle her liquor. Her behavior became erratic, her temper flared. She'd often insist on driving through the Hollywood Hills after drunken arguments with her previous husband Orson Welles, who feared she was intent on killing herself. Years later, her fifth and final husband, James Hill, said he'd seen the look Hayworth acquired when drinking only one other time in his life: "during the war, on a machine gunner carrying a Browning automatic."

As for her then-husband, the Argentine-born Haymes, he could have used a porter for all the baggage he brought to the marriage. Nearly $200,000 in debt (a combination of unpaid taxes, alimony, and child support), he was facing deportation because he'd traveled to Hawaii (not yet an official state) without certifiable proof of American citizenship. (And also because, allegedly, Harry Cohn wanted him out of Hayworth's life.)

But *Joseph and His Brethren* looked to be a turning point for both husband and wife—but more so for Haymes. Hayworth had recently renegotiated the terms of her contract with Columbia to include not only a $50,000 loan for her husband, but also his full access to the studio's lot and an option on his services as a screenwriter. He'd also begun to manage his wife's career. In fact, with the ridiculous notion of costarring alongside his wife in *Joseph,* Haymes had actually grown a beard.

Playing the biblical hero Joseph would have been deliciously ironic for a man that *Confidential* magazine had nicknamed "Mr. Evil," but Haymes soon discovered that Columbia had not only cast a relative unknown in the part, but that Cohn had banned him from the set. Haymes was outraged. And now, at the Polo Lounge, he had a filmmaker's ear one final time.

Grabbing the phone from his wife, Haymes accused Odets of not properly explaining the psychology of Hayworth's part to her and of being in the studio's pocket. He made veiled threats, then he hung up.

Her sex-symbol status was fading, and her relentless partying was accelerating the aging process.

The next morning, Haymes called Columbia and said Hayworth wouldn't be coming in that day. A few days later, her lawyers informed the studio that because the picture hadn't started on time, it was breach of contract, and she was owed her full $150,000 fee. The already-shot footage of *Joseph and His Brethren* went on the shelf. Two years later, Columbia severed its ties with Hayworth for good, replacing her with Kim Novak. Cohn, with his trademark cruelty, is reported to have said, "All you had were those two big things and Harry Cohn. Now you just have those two big things."

Not surprisingly, her marriage to Dick Haymes was by this time long over. The final blow had been an actual blow. At the Cocoanut Grove on a similarly boozy night shortly after the *Joseph* incident, Haymes struck Hayworth in the face. She went home, packed her bags, and never returned. ★

THE COCK 'N BULL

9170 SUNSET BLVD.

THE CLOSEST THING Golden Age Hollywood had to a genuine English pub, the Cock 'n Bull opened on the Sunset Strip in 1937 and outlasted a full half-century's worth of fly-by-night operations around it. Founded by Jack Morgan and managed by his family until 1987, it was adopted by such British expats as Richard Burton, Somerset Maugham, and Alan Mowbray, as well as Americans F. Scott Fitzgerald, Errol Flynn, Sinclair Lewis, John Carradine, and Robert Mitchum. Jessie Wadsworth, Hollywood's first female talent agent, kept an office upstairs and generally ended her days at the bar. On one such occasion, Wadsworth was looking on as actor Sonny Tufts threw a punch at another patron, which accidently caught Wadsworth square on the jaw. Morgan kicked Tufts out and told him never to return. He was back a few weeks later. A real drinking man's place,

so sacrosanct was the Cock 'n Bull that it was where the Bundy Drive Boys gathered to mourn the passing of the great John Barrymore.

But the Cock 'n Bull's greatest contribution to world culture was only tangentially related to its high-profile clientele. The joint served classic pub fare such as prime rib, Yorkshire pudding, and Welsh rarebit, but its signature drink was something of a curveball. (And, as these things often are, a happy accident.) According to head bartender Wes Price, Morgan—who by the 1940s was distributing his own brand of Cock 'n Bull ginger beer—found himself saddled with too many cases of Smirnoff vodka and a surplus of his own brew that would go bad if he couldn't unload it. In a desperate bid to avoid pouring all this beautiful ginger beer down the drain, Price mixed the two ingredients, added lime, and served it up in a copper mug. Tough-guy character actor Broderick Crawford was the first customer to give it a try. He liked it. Had a bit of a kick to it. And with that, the Moscow Mule was born: "The Drink with the Velvet Kick." ★

MOSCOW MULE

. . . .

2 OZ. VODKA

1 HALF A LIME

GINGER BEER

Pour vodka into a copper mug filled with ice, then squeeze in lime juice. Top with ginger beer. Serve with stirring rod. Substitute Collins glass for mug if necessary.

••••••••••••••••••••••••

VERONICA LAKE

1922–1973
ACTRESS

••••••••••••••••••••••••

*"My appetite was my own
and I simply wouldn't
have it any other way."*

V eronica Lake is best known for her trend-setting "peek-a-boo" hairstyle and a decade of signature roles: *I Wanted Wings* (1941) with Ray Milland and William Holden; *Sullivan's Travels* (1941), written and directed by Preston Sturges; and three films noir with Alan Ladd, *The Glass Key* (1942), *This Gun for Hire* (1942), and *The Blue Dahlia* (1946). She was notoriously difficult on set, the result of emotional/psychological problems dating back to her childhood (when, according to her mother, she was diagnosed as schizophrenic). She was strongly disliked by both costars and executives, so much so that when her initial contract with Paramount expired in 1948, the studio decided she wasn't worth the trouble. Lake made two more movies before briefly turning to television and the stage, then disappeared altogether. A *New York Post* reporter found her in the early 1960s at a Manhattan all-women's hotel, working as a barmaid. Her autobiography, in 1970, failed to return the meteoric starlet to the public eye; her memorial the following year was attended by a few strangers and only one of her three children.

———————————— ★ ————————————

THE INVITATION WAS THE first surprise. It was December 1941, and Preston Sturges's *Sullivan's Travels* was to open in New York City in just a few weeks. With the premiere looming, the film's leading lady, Veronica Lake, invited the entire cast and crew to an impromptu reunion on New Year's Eve.

Sturges himself hadn't known about the party before the invitation showed up in his mailbox. Though he'd long since had his fill of Lake's surprises — like when she arrived on set six months pregnant (a previously undisclosed detail that threw the director into a he-had-to-be-restrained-type rage). But this surprise, what looked to be a fun party, was much more pleasant.

In 1941 Lake's private life was a secret to most. She'd had her moments on the nightclub circuit, tossing a few back at Ciro's on the Sunset Strip after it first opened, even though she was only seventeen at the time. But mostly she was an introvert. While shooting *I Wanted Wings,* William Holden repeatedly invited her out for drinks, but each time she insisted that she'd prefer to remain in her hotel room. Holden, like everyone else, assumed that the teenager was too shy or square to hit the booze — or that her husband, art director John Detlie, had forbidden it.

The fact was, Lake simply preferred drinking alone, ordering her drinks through the hotel's front desk. Not even Detlie knew the full extent of her boozing. Sure, by the end of the decade, stories — factual or otherwise — of her drunken exploits and random sexual encounters would be a dime a dozen. But on this New Year's, her private life was still a total mystery. Lake had just given birth to her first daughter, Elaine, and even though her

Wiliam Holden repeatedly invited her out for drinks, but each time she insisted that she'd prefer to remain in her hotel room, Holden, like everyone else, assumed that the teenager was too shy or square to hit the booze.

husband was about to leave for the recently declared war, she appeared to be a wife and mother with a very bright future.

The New Year's Eve bash, it turned out, was where the mystery began to unravel. Though Lake and Detlie had just purchased a house in Mandeville Canyon, the actress had opted to throw the party at her parents' modest home in Beverly Hills. In itself, this wasn't strange — except that Lake's stepfather had been battling tuberculosis for years, and he wasn't doing very well. So there was one rule: no one could enter his room or disturb him in any way.

Lake's parents seemed unconcerned. The guests were adults. They knew how to behave. Lake, however, was still a teenager, and once the party hit full swing, the one rule was quickly broken by Lake herself. It seems she hated her stepfather. According to accounts, the tiny, four-foot-eleven actress had a few cocktails, then a few more, and before long, she decided to lead a procession of revelers through her stepfather's bedroom in a "snake dance," whooping and hollering all the while. Now this was a bit more strange, yet still short of real gossip mag fodder, that is, until Lake reportedly started to strip. In the middle of her New Year's party, Lake performed a striptease for her bedridden stepfather, as several lingering partygoers looked on.

Years later, after Lake wrote her autobiography, the facts of her childhood could explain such events more soberly; but to cast and crew that night, only one thing seemed perfectly clear: Wherever he was, William Holden would be scratching his head. ★

GIRL CRAZY (1943)

To the studio, this movie defined *no-brainer:* Mickey Rooney and Judy Garland, two of MGM's most bankable actors, starring in a remake of the 1930 stage musical *Girl Crazy*, featuring hit music and lyrics by George and Ira Gershwin. Rooney and Garland had already proven themselves a potent onscreen combo in eight previous movies, which included three musicals directed by Busby Berkeley. And Berkeley had signed on to helm. The movie would practically make itself. Or not . . .

Within minutes of shooting, cast and crew noticed that star (Garland) and director (Berkeley) were each *barely* keeping it together. Garland had always drunk booze by the gallon. She was now just days away from ending her marriage to bandleader David Rose and, right before shooting, had begun an affair with actor Tyrone Power. At some point during principal photography, she would call Power to say she was pregnant with his child.

At the same time, the brilliant choreographer Berkeley had the kind of obsessive streak that makes for stunning dance-numbers, but his bedside manner as a director would have made a drill sergeant blush. Garland hated him.

Unbeknownst to anyone but Berkeley himself, he had decided to drastically change the production number "I Got Rhythm." Berkeley's new idea involved hoisting Garland, pregnant, and Rooney into the air by their ankles via stunt-wire with pistols firing all around them.

The sequence, budgeted for five days, took nine and ran nearly $100,000 over budget. The guns and spinning and the help-me-I'm-so-fragile had left Garland such a nervous wreck that her doctor insisted she couldn't dance for another three weeks. And just like that, Berkeley was canned.

Production resumed a month later under the direction of Norman Taurog, who had an Oscar under his belt and had, like Berkeley, previously worked with both stars. Taurog also had ideas about one of the first scheduled scenes—a staged automobile ride in which Garland's character abandons Rooney's on a stretch of road outside Palm Springs. Taurog declared it would be shot in Palm Springs itself, not the cost-effective MGM lot—and not for creative or continuity reasons either. Taurog did it because Rooney simply wanted to hang out in Palm Springs.

Thus was the entire production relocated to Palm Springs for a weeklong shoot that was further delayed by equipment failures, sandstorms, and the sudden disappearance of Garland, who was later found in Los Angeles in hot pursuit of Power.

Eventually five and a half months after filming began, *Girl Crazy* wrapped, at a total cost of $1.4 million, more than $300,000 over budget. MGM seemed unusually blasé about it all, but then clearly they'd already guessed the final outcome: *Girl Crazy* was the hit MGM expected all along, earning almost $4 million at the box office.

••••••••••••••••••••••••

CAROLE LOMBARD

1908–1942
ACTRESS

••••••••••••••••••••••••

*"I couldn't settle down;
it would kill me!"*

Throughout the 1930s, Carole Lombard was the undisputed "queen of screwball." Her best known film, *My Man Godfrey* (1936), garnered a Best Actress nomination. The highest paid star in Hollywood at the time of her death, she was also legendary as a party hostess, and much beloved by her peers. Lombard was only twelve when she got her first film role, as a tomboy in *A Perfect Crime* (1921). She was reportedly discovered by the film's director, Allan Dwan, while playing baseball in the street near her mother's Los Angeles home. After cutting her teeth in Mack Sennett shorts, she arrived as a leading lady during the early years of sound. Lombard starred opposite her first husband, William Powell, in *Man of the World* (1931) and her future second husband, Clark Gable, in *No Man of Her Own* (1932). (She and Gable didn't marry until 1939.) Lombard's breakout role came as Mildred Plotka in *Twentieth Century* (1934), directed by Howard Hawks. She turned down the opportunity to costar with Gable again in Frank Capra's *It Happened One Night* to take a starring role in *Bolero* (1934); then she received top billing in Hitchcock's lone American comedy, *Mr. & Mrs. Smith* (1941). Her final film, *To Be or Not to Be* (1942), was criticized for its satirical treatment of Nazis at the time of release but is now considered a classic. Lombard died tragically young, at age thirty-three, in a plane crash while traveling to appear at a rally for war bonds.

★

PUTTING CAROLE LOMBARD IN charge of the Mayfair Ball seemed to many an odd decision. For one thing, the actress had a reputation for being more than a little wild. Not out of control necessarily, just unpredictable. There were the funny pranks: She once threw a party where the guests, to their surprise, were greeted by nurses and interns who took away their clothes and issued hospital gowns in their place. There were the funny comments: The first time she rode a horse, she observed, "I don't know why the hell everybody thinks this is so great. It's like a dry fuck."

None of this recommended her for hostess of the Mayfair—an exclusive ball, held annually, to which only the brightest stars in Hollywood's constellation were invited. It was always an exquisite affair, and Lombard took it as a point of pride that this one—held at Victor Hugo's on January 26, 1936—would be no different. Her theme for the evening was white: white gowns for ladies, tailcoats and white ties for men. The guests, more than three hundred of them, complied. All except one: Norma Shearer, the wife of MGM producer Irving Thalberg (and one of the Mayfair's sponsors), decided to wear a vibrant red dress. Her reason being something along the lines of "because I can." Lombard's reaction was even less circumspect. "Who the fuck does Norma think she is?" Lombard did not whisper. "The House Madam?" Lombard wanted to punch her. She wanted to kick her ass out. But then this was the Mayfair Ball and Lombard was the hostess, so instead she just went to the bathroom and cried.

With that, they started to dance. It soon dawned on Gable that Lombard wasn't wearing anything under her elegant white dress. It soon dawned on Lombard that there was evidence of growing excitement under Gable's elegant white tuxedo.

Clark Gable, who had watched the whole thing unfold, knew a damsel in distress when he saw one. He and Lombard had worked together a few years prior on *No Man of Her Own*. After a rocky first few days, which began with Lombard ripping a Herbert Hoover button off of Gable's lapel, the two had become close. She had been married during the film's production, as was he, and for the first time in Hollywood history, this actually seemed to matter. The only thing she gave to Gable was a gift at the wrap party: a ham with his photo attached. But now Lombard was divorced. And he was . . . separated? Maybe. It was always hard to tell with Gable.

As Lombard emerged from the bathroom, Gable sauntered over and said his favorite line from *No Man of Her Own:* "I go for you, Ma." She considered him for a moment, then said "I go for you, too, Pa." With that, they started to dance. It soon dawned on Gable that Lombard wasn't wearing anything under her elegant white dress. It soon dawned on Lombard that there was evidence of growing excitement under Gable's elegant white tuxedo. Wanting fresh air, they left and hopped into his swank new Duesenberg convertible for a few trips around the block. When Gable invited the hostess back to his room, her response was: "Who do you think you are, Clark Gable?" It wouldn't happen that night. But as the story goes, the next morning Gable awoke to find two white doves flying around his hotel room. (That can't help a hangover.) There happened to be a note tied to one of the doves' legs: "How about it? Carole." ★

CHATEAU MARMONT

8221 SUNSET BLVD.

OPEN!

IF YOU MUST GET in trouble," Columbia Pictures chief Harry Cohn once said, "do it at the Marmont." Famed for its luxurious bungalows, discrete staff, and rich history, the Chateau Marmont has been Los Angeles's celebrity inn of choice since the 1930s.

Modeled after the Château d'Amboise in France's Loire Valley, the Marmont was originally opened as an apartment building in February 1929, but high rents and the Great Depression forced owners to turn it into a hotel. One of the Chateau's earliest long-term residents was Lloyd Bacon, director of *The Singing Fool* (Al Jolson's follow-up to *The Jazz Singer*). He lived in one of the hotel's two penthouses, and his

parties eventually became one of the hottest invites in town. Clark Gable turned up with new flame Carole Lombard in tow. Stan Laurel—who, according to one account, was "barely tolerated" at such affairs—often had to be carried back to his suite. Robert Benchley, famously terrified of the traffic on Sunset, hailed cabs to drive him from the Chateau back home to the Garden of Allah—which was directly across the street.

More notorious residents would soon follow: William Holden and Glenn Ford checked in. Not that they were paying; Harry Cohn had rented the suite as an insurance policy against the foolish whims of his actors and, after receiving Columbia's keys to Suite 54, it quickly became their crash pad of choice. David Niven lived there for a time. Bogart and Flynn both hid out there after volatile fights with their wives. Same went for John Barrymore, by then on his fourth marriage and a shell of his former self, sipping drinks on the terrace dressed in nothing but a robe and socks, giving the young actors advice on how to do Shakespeare. *Don't.*

Not everyone came to the Chateau to swing from the chandeliers. Greta Garbo and Howard Hughes, famous recluses both, loved its quiet solitude. (Garbo used to say it was the one hotel in America where birds sang to her from her window-sill.) When Montgomery Clift needed a secret place to convalesce from his disfiguring car accident in 1956, there wouldn't even be a discussion about any place else. And during preproduction of *Rebel Without a Cause,* Nicholas Ray turned his bungalow into an informal production office, a setup that allowed him to screw Natalie Wood (then sixteen), Jayne Mansfield, and Shelley Winters in some kind of discreet rotation. Advice to any ingénue: Beware directors who work out of hotels.

As the hotel fell into disrepair in the 1960s and stars migrated to the infinitely more private Hotel Bel Air (or to Palm Springs), the Marmont found new life as L.A.'s answer to the Chelsea Hotel: its faint shadow of glamour, untouched by ruinous nostalgia, appealed to a new generation of actors, writers, and muscians. Jim Morrison, for whatever reason, attempted to swing from a drainpipe into his room via the window and fell onto the roof of a nearby shed. Led Zeppelin once rode motorcycles through the lobby. (Not again . . .) John Belushi experimented with speedballs in one of the bungalows, to tragic effect. *L.A. Weekly* journalist Robert Wilonsky interviewed former Red Hot Chili Pepper John Frusciante as he shot up in his room; the guitarist was on a five-year heroin jag. (Soon after, his former bandmates got him into rehab and, once he was clean, asked him to rejoin the band.)

Purchased by hotelier André Balazs in 1998 and spruced up just enough, the Chateau has been a constant for nearly a century. In 1984 *Bright Lights, Big City* author Jay McInerney—one of several early eighties writers, young and talented, whose epic partying often threatened to overshadow their work—stayed there while adapting his book for the screen. The studio he was writing for: Columbia Pictures. ★

HERMAN J. MANKIEWICZ

1897–1953
SCREENWRITER

"It's all right," Mankiewicz once said, after puking in the middle of a formal dinner. *"The white wine came up with the fish."*

Herman Mankiewicz is generally acknowledged to be the creator and master of the pithy, rapid-fire dialogue that characterized 1930s comedy and 1940s film noir and is best known for cowriting *Citizen Kane* (1941), for which he won an Academy Award. A noted member of the Algonquin Round Table, Mank began his career as the drama critic for the *New York Times* and the *New Yorker.* Brought to Hollywood by Paramount and put in charge of writer recruitment, Mank was responsible for bringing out a number of East Coast literary talents. He had an often unseen hand in an extraordinary number of what are now considered classic films. Mank's uncredited script contributions include three Marx Brothers comedies, *Monkey Business* (1931), *Horse Feathers* (1932), and *Duck Soup* (1933), as well as *The Wizard of Oz* (1939). In 1942 he received his second Oscar nomination, for the Lou Gehrig biopic *The Pride of the Yankees*, but spent the rest of his career fighting to overcome his alcoholism, gambling debts, and obstinate personality.

★

HERMAN J. MANKIEWICZ WAS less than a mile from his house. What could possibly go wrong? It was the afternoon of March 11, 1943, and he'd stopped by Romanoff's for a drink or two. Driving the short distance home would be a cakewalk.

But then Mank stayed longer than he intended and drank more than he should have. It was quite dark by the time he found himself driving along North Beverly Drive in Benedict Canyon. Carelessly, he drifted into the oncoming lane and slammed virtually head-on into another car. No one was seriously hurt. The police knew Mank was drunk, and he knew there was a night in jail ahead of him, but all in all, it could have been worse.

Unfortunately, Mank had a knack for worse. He always had. Impossible to intimidate, Mank rankled under all forms of authority. Upon hearing Columbia studio head Harry Cohn's boast that he could feel how good a movie was by the sensation in his rear, Mank had quipped, "Imagine, the whole world wired to Harry Cohn's ass." He was fired. Louis B. Mayer once advanced Mank money to pay back some gambling debts, but Mank just gambled the loan away—and on the MGM lot, no less. He was fired. While working on the Marx Brothers film *Monkey Business,* Harpo Marx asked Mank for an early look at the script—"I want to find out what my character is." Mank replied sourly, "You're a middle-aged Jew who picks up spit because he thinks it's a quarter." He was soon fired. Picking fights in bars, passing out in hotels and waking up with obscene writing all over his body (Ben Hecht's signature prank)—if there was a secret compartment beneath rock bottom, Mank would find it. As a friend once observed, "To know Mank was to like him. Not to know him was to love him."

As a friend once observed, "To know Mank was to like him. Not to know him was to love him."

The Beverly Drive accident would prove to be another such disaster. It wasn't just that he'd drunkenly crashed his car. It was that he'd drunkenly crashed it outside Marion Davies's Beverly Hills house. A house paid for by Davies's lover, William Randolph Hearst. A house that Hearst was—at that very moment—inside. Once upon a time, Mank and Hearst had been quite friendly. There had been many invitations to San Simeon, Hearst's castle up the coast. But while Hearst was trying to keep his mistress, Davies, sober, Mank had been trying to do the opposite. And so, eventually, Mank was banned from all of their parties and from ever seeing Davies again.

It was a feud that, even on the scale of Hollywood spats, soon went nuclear. Mank set out for revenge by writing *Citizen Kane,* a most unflattering biopic based on the newspaper mogul. He used privileged information in stunning ways—like, say, building the entire film around Hearst's nickname for Davies's clitoris, Rosebud. Cowriter and director Orson Welles later mixed in elements of his own life, toning down and subtly misdirecting Mank's poison arrow. But he failed to properly notice the one part that would ensure return fire.

Hearst didn't much care about being hated or mocked, but the *Citizen Kane* character Susan Alexander (generally believed to be a brutally unforgiving portrait of Davies) was where the rubber hit the road. When *How Green Was My Valley* upstaged the considerably better *Citizen Kane* at the 1942 Oscars, there were more-than-slight suspicions that Hearst had used his considerable influence to turn voters against Welles as an act of revenge.

But to get back at Mank was more difficult. After all, Mank had friends. He was an insider. There were rules, codes, lines not to be crossed. And then there was the dotted yellow line—and the Beverly Drive car crash. Now this was legitimate news—and as such, it deserved a place on the front page of every Hearst newspaper across the country. There were quotes from police officers describing Mank as "insulting, sarcastic, impolite." There were descriptions of him kicking the bars of his cell until his shoes were finally taken away. There were photomontages. It was Hearst at his muckraking best.

"I was promoted," Mank said, "from a middle-aged, flat-footed writer into Cary Grant, who, with a tank, had just drunkenly plowed into a baby carriage occupied by the Dionne quintuplets, the Duchess of Kent, Mrs. Franklin D. Roosevelt, and the favorite niece of the Pope." He should have just walked home. ★

LOUELLA PARSONS

1881–1972
GOSSIP COLUMNIST

"The doctor had cautioned me not to drink anything. But doctors are notorious killjoys."

Along with her younger nemesis, Hedda Hopper, Louella Parsons was one of the most feared figures in early Hollywood. She single-handedly established the celebrity journalism industry, and could single-handedly make (Marion Davies) or break (Orson Welles) a career if she set her mind to it. The Illinois native wrote scripts for Essanay Studios in Chicago before launching a column for *Chicago Record Herald*. Picked up by *New York Morning Telegraph* but signed away by W. R. Hearst in 1923, Parsons relocated to the drier climate of Los Angeles after developing tuberculosis and being told she had six months left to live. (She ended up living nearly another fifty years.) Her flagship column for the *Los Angeles Examiner* was subsequently syndicated to hundreds of newspapers with a readership approaching 20 million. Fiercely loyal to Hearst, and a close friend of his mistress Marion Davies, Parsons would work for Hearst enterprises throughout the remainder of her career. She launched a weekly radio show in the late twenties—a precursor to modern late-night talk shows, with stars plugging their current projects and airing audio clips. Parsons faced competition when her former source Hopper premiered her own gossip column for the *Los Angeles Times* in 1938. A heated rivalry between the two persisted until Parsons retired, at the age of eighty-one.

———————————— ★ ————————————

DOCKY WAS DOWN FOR THE COUNT—again. By now, the ridiculous had become commonplace. Dr. Harry Martin—VD specialist to the stars, Hollywood's leading urologist, and Louella Parsons's husband—had taken to ending his evenings out on the town by passing out on his hosts' floors. On this particular evening, the host was Carole Lombard and the occasion was a toga party. Docky had passed out in front of everyone, the fabric of his outfit arranged in such a way that left little mystery. Lombard pointed in shock: "What is *that*?" "*That*," another guest cracked, "is Louella's column."

Louella and Docky ("Docky" was her nickname for him) were big on drinking, big on gambling, big on everything. She'd been part of the party circuit since the 1920s. The Cocoanut Grove, the Brown Derby, Montmartre, Pickfair, Marion Davies's beach house in Santa Monica—Louella frequented them all. As for Docky, he was famous for breaking his neck on a drunken dive into the shallow pool at the Bimini Baths bathhouse, and then holding his spine in place as he walked to the hospital. That's not nothing.

The couple were regulars at the Santa Anita racetrack and the Agua Caliente casino in Tijuana. They held parties at their home in Beverly Hills almost every week, with sometimes as many as three hundred guests. It wasn't that they were terrific fun. People came mostly out of fear of what Louella might write about them if they *didn't* show up.

The unspoken but obvious undercurrent was that Hollywood despised the gossip columnist and her clownish husband—and not just because she had the power to make and break careers, marriages, and friendships. Part of their contempt stemmed from the couple's hypocrisy. Docky was an avowed Catholic who'd converted Louella when they married in 1930; yet it was a not-so-carefully guarded secret that he was house doctor at Lee Francis's Hollywood brothel and the doctor that Fox Studios called whenever an actress needed an abortion. In her column, Louella would shamelessly moralize when a marriage ended in divorce, yet Docky was her third husband. When the story of Clara Bow's gambling addiction broke, Louella wrote that she was sorry Bow hadn't grown up; this from the woman who would bet on eight horses at a time and lose thousands in a weekend.

Thus did the couple's moments of public humiliation become cherished and oft-told tales. Sometimes Louella joined in the mockery of the ever-misbehaving Docky, perhaps because her reputation was more important to her than her husband's dignity. On the night that Docky lay on Lombard's floor with his "column" exposed for any passerby to see, two guests decided to help him to his feet. But Louella, having finally noticed the extent to which her husband was embarrassing himself, interceded.

"Let him sleep," she said. "He needs to operate in the morning." ★

THE EMBASSY CLUB
6767 HOLLYWOOD BLVD.

THE MEMBERS-ONLY EMBASSY CLUB was opened in 1929 by restaurateur Eddie Brandstatter in the space next to his hugely successful Montmartre Café, and for about twenty minutes, it was the most exclusive hangout in Los Angeles. Designed by architect Carl Weyl at a cost of $300,000, combining Spanish and Byzantine styles and featuring a glass-enclosed rooftop promenade and lounge, the Embassy Club was limited to three hundred members at any given time. How exactly one became a member was a mystery, but it was generally understood to be by invitation only. On the board of directors sat Marion Davies, Gloria Swanson, Norma Talmadge, King Vidor, Sid Grauman, and Evelyn Brent. Members included Charlie Chaplin (of course); Tod Browning; Paul Bern; Carl Laemmle, Jr.; Harold Lloyd; and Mervyn LeRoy.

Very quickly, however, Brandstatter realized that the Embassy was a very exclusive mistake, with three hundred hand-selected albatrosses to expedite its failure. A crucial component of any see-and-be-seen establishment, it turns out, is the ability to actually *be seen*.

Sure, it was flattering to be asked to join the Embassy, but once you were in, there was no adoring public like the one that flocked to the Montmartre for a glimpse of your curly locks. Even more damaging, stars who were *not* invited to join the Embassy stopped going to the Montmartre, too, either in protest or out of embarrassment. Which meant that soon, fans *also* stopped going to Montmartre—because they wanted to see stars, not to eat. All of this resulted in Brandstatter declaring bankruptcy within three years and being forced to open the Embassy Club to the general public, at which point Brandstatter learned another important lesson: Once anyone could join, no one wanted to. ★

NOT A YEAR AFTER Brandstatter's debacle, the Clover Club opened on Sunset to attempt the exact same stunt, except it had one attraction the Embassy Club didn't: gambling. Opened by Eddy Neales, with mobster Milton "Farmer" Page as his silent partner, the Clover was, on the surface, nothing more than a fancy nightclub. But one-way mirrors and secret panels obscured roulette wheels where VIPs could lose $100,000 a sitting and gambling tables could quickly be flipped over and disguised.

As it happens, a few gambling tables are all that is needed to turn a bad idea into a profitable one. That, and Mob protection. Because even after all the greased palms and shakedowns, the Clover still minted money. Heavy hitters like Carl Laemmle, Jr.; Howard Hughes; Irving Berlin; Samuel Goldwyn; Douglas Fairbanks; Harpo Marx; Louis B. Mayer; Harry Cohn; and MGM security fixer Howard Strickling played there. By 1937 Neales was allegedly handling $10 million a year in bets.

On January 14 of that year, a private investigator and former cop named Harry Raymond was nearly killed when a bomb blew up his car. Raymond had been investigating city hall corruption and underworld ties, and was about to testify to a grand jury that had been convened for the same reason. The bombing investigation led to the conviction of powerful L.A.P.D. captain Earl Kynette, a known city-hall insider, and the public had finally had enough.

The ensuing outcry began a chain of events—citizens voting to recall the city's mayor; a full-scale Mob turf war; the election of a new anticorruption mayor; and finally the arrival of the FBI, which would shutter the Clover for good. By the 1940s, prominent L.A. underworld figures such as Page, Bugsy Siegel, and Mickey Cohen had relocated to Las Vegas, because who needed this crap when you could build the Flamingo? By then, the Clover Club had reopened as Club Seville, and replaced craps with carp, literally— they installed a glass-bottom dance floor atop an aquarium filled with fish. ★

PRESTON STURGES

1898–1959
DIRECTOR AND SCREENWRITER

"I gave up not drinking and not smoking, and have not been troubled with pneumonia since."

An all-time great of film comedy, on the family tree of wits, Preston Sturges is routinely named as the branch between Oscar Wilde and Woody Allen. After Sturges's second play, *Strictly Dishonorable*, was a tremendous hit on Broadway, he moved to Los Angeles in pursuit of money. The deal for his first original screenplay, *The Power and the Glory* (1933), included a percentage of profits—an unheard of arrangement for screenwriters of the time. But Sturges grew increasingly frustrated with the quality of films made from his scripts. He sold what became *The Great McGinty* (1940) to Paramount for the sum of ten dollars in exchange for the right to direct and, in doing so, became the first established screenwriter to direct his own material. The film went on to win an Oscar for Best Original Screenplay. He followed with a string of critical and commercial hits over the next five years: *Christmas in July* (1940), *The Lady Eve* and *Sullivan's Travels* (both 1941), *The Palm Beach Story* (1942), and finally, *Hail the Conquering Hero* and *The Miracle of Morgan's Creek* (both nominated for screenwriting Oscars in 1945). Sturges left Paramount after repeatedly tussling with studio heads and entered into a partnership with Howard Hughes that disintegrated after just one picture (*The Sin of Harold Diddlebock*, 1947). His next two movies for Fox proved to be flops, and Sturges's career never recovered.

★

STURGES FOUND CURIOSITY TO be overrated, but maybe that was because it nearly killed him.

From his earliest days as Hollywood's most successful screenwriter through his creative peak as its foremost writer-director, Preston Sturges had maintained the same steady schedule: a late riser, he'd putz around at home throughout the morning, then venture off to his studio office, where he'd sip tea spiked with applejack and maybe take a nap. Afternoon activities varied, but one thing they didn't include was work. Evenings began at the fights and were capped off with dinner and drinks, typically at the Brown Derby or, when Sturges opened it in 1940, his own place, the Players Club. When the bars finally closed, he returned home, where he'd bang out pages until the sun came up.

Unconventional as it may have been, this routine had made Sturges one of the richest men in the business. But pressure has a way of making even the most skilled professionals question themselves, and in Sturges's case, when the pressure mounted on his directorial debut, *The Great McGinty,* he endeavored to change his ways. Gone were the late nights, the drinking and the smoking. "After I started shooting," he wrote in his memoir (*Preston Sturges by Preston Sturges*), "I had a masseur waiting for me every night and I had dinner in bed. I saved my strength. I treated myself like an egg." And for this newfound discipline he was promptly rewarded, during the second week of shooting, with a nasty case of pneumonia.

Sturges had actually developed pneumonia once before, while living in Paris with his mother at the age of three. Based on his own personal history, Sturges feared he would be laid up for six weeks while the sickness ran its course—a major problem, given the clause in his contract that allowed Paramount to replace him should he be "unable to fulfill his duties."

Funny thing is, during his first bout with pneumonia in Paris, the one remedy that had pulled him through was booze. Though only a toddler, he was spoonfed champagne, which Preston's mother credited with bringing down his fever. This in mind, Sturges must have been tempted to start drinking again, just a little. But then fortune smiled on him: Paramount executives, thrilled with what they'd seen of his rushes so far, assured him he could take the time to recover. Ten days later, he was back on set. From then on, he would drink as much as wanted, turning his back on sobriety forever. ★

APPLEJACK, NICKNAMED "JERSEY LIGHTNING," is a strong but sweet spirit distilled from apples that tastes not unlike Calvados (a French brandy). Until recently, there was only one brand produced in America—Laird's. The oldest licensed distillery in the country, Laird's originated in New Jersey and dates back to the American Revolution. Apparently, George Washington once requested some.

Fancy pedigree aside, Applejack provided Preston Sturges with the necessary energy to get through his workday—which is another way of saying, it helped him nap.

TEA & APPLEJACK

. . . .

1½ OZ. APPLEJACK

1 CUP OF BLACK TEA

1 TSP. SUGAR

¼ OZ. DRY CURAÇAO (OPTIONAL)

Pour Applejack into a steaming cup of tea, then stir in teaspoon of sugar. Add Curaçao if desired.

THE PLAYERS CLUB

8225 SUNSET BLVD.

WHEN WRITER-DIRECTOR PRESTON STURGES opened this three-story complex in 1940, he was one of the wealthiest men in Hollywood. With two films already in release and a third (*The Lady Eve*) on the way, plus a stake in a promising engineering company specializing in diesel engines, he was flush. Or so it seemed.

From the start, Sturges ran the Players less like a business and more like his own personal clubhouse. Named after the New York theatrical club, it attracted both the East Coast and the Hollywood set. Among the regulars were Humphrey Bogart, Ernst Lubitsch, Orson Welles, Howard Hughes, William Faulkner, and Robert Benchley. According to Billy Wilder, dinners often ended with Sturges offering a complimentary shot of yellow or green Chartreuse (his favorite liqueur) to his guests, while he himself polished off another bourbon Old-Fashioned. Rarely did a night pass when he wasn't on hand to shut the place down. Sometimes, he even shut down early, closing the doors to the public so he could entertain his pals. This couldn't be good business, but then money wasn't Sturges's principal concern—drinking was.

Half the time, Sturges was happy to run a tab, which more often than not meant he simply picked up the check. And when Sturges did charge, he was so determined to keep prices in line with those at the Brown Derby (despite having way more overhead) that he ended the competition by effecting his own demise. In 1944 the Players grossed more than $650,000; its actual profit was just under $26,000. With such an unconcerned management style, it's surprising Sturges turned a profit at all. And soon enough he no longer would.

By the early 1950s, the club's debts and taxes were enormous, and the mounting pressure had sucked so much life out of Sturges that his film career was floundering. Now he was doubly screwed. Sturges's solution? To add an expensive dinner theater, complete with orchestra pit and a retractable dance floor. He was an artist after all.

Two years later, he sold the property to his main creditor. ★

WHATEVER THE BENEFITS of Sturges's Tea & Applejack, they do not compare to those of his Old-Fashioned. Sturges's cocktail of choice, the Old-Fashioned enabled him to talk late into the night and to write into the early morning.

In making the cocktail, there is a great deal of debate surrounding the fruit—some say to muddle it, others to just add as garnish. It's unknown how Sturges took his, but hard to believe he would bother to muddle—even if he had a whole staff of bartenders he was paying to do exactly that.

BOURBON OLD-FASHIONED

1 CUBE OF SUGAR

3 DASHES ANGOSTURA BITTERS

2½ OZ. BOURBON

1 ORANGE SLICE

1 MARASCHINO CHERRY

LEMON TWIST

Place a sugar cube at the bottom of an Old-Fashioned glass. Add bitters, and muddle into cube. Pour in bourbon. Fill the glass with ice cubes, and stir well. Garnish with orange slice, cherry and lemon twist. Add a splash of club soda if desired.

Note that others (though apparently not Sturges) might substitute rye or blended whiskey for bourbon.

SPENCER TRACY

1900–1967

ACTOR

"Hell, I used to take two-week lunch hours."

K nown for quiet confidence and effort-less presence, Spencer Tracy was one of MGM's top leading men, and indeed one of the top leading men of all time. Tracy studied drama in New York and spent several years making ends meet in summer stock and repertory productions. His performance in the Broadway crime drama *The Last Mile* (1930) caught the eye of director John Ford, who cast him opposite Humphrey Bogart in *Up the River* later that year. Tracy appeared in twenty-five films for Fox between 1930 and 1935, primarily in tough-guy roles. One notable exception was *The Power and the Glory*, written by Preston Sturges; Tracy's performance was praised, but it didn't translate at the box office, and Fox slowly soured on him. He switched to MGM in 1935, and his career took off. He won Best Actor Oscars two years in a row—the first actor ever to do so—for *Captains Courageous* (1937) and *Boys Town* (1938). He was nominated another seven times during his career for such iconic roles as *Father of the Bride* (1950), *Inherit the Wind* (1960), and *Guess Who's Coming to Dinner?* (1967). (Tracy is tied with Sir Laurence Olivier for the most Best Actor nominations of all time.) While filming *Woman of the Year* (1942), Tracy began an affair with costar Katharine Hepburn that lasted the rest of their lives, though it was never acknowledged publicly. Tracy suffered from both diabetes and emphysema. He died of a heart attack just seventeen days after completing *Guess Who's Coming to Dinner.*

★

THE PHONE RANG. Not his office phone; the special one. As MGM's Vice President of Publicity and its resident fixer, Howard Strickling figured that almost any call to his office would be a new mess to clean up, but when this specific phone rang, he *knew* it was a mess. It was, more or less, a dedicated line. Dedicated to Spencer Tracy.

Strickling picked up and, sure enough, the Trocadero nightclub was calling to say that Strickling "might want to know" Spencer Tracy was at the club. That was it—no shouting, no fisticuffs. Tracy was simply present. Strickling hung up and called MGM's chief of security, Whitey Hendry. Hendry was the former chief of police of Culver City and his instructions were simple: "Assemble the Tracy Squad."

Spencer Tracy had been part of MGM's roster for less than a year. His films at Fox had fared so poorly, and his tendency to go on drinking binges was so troublesome, that the studio had let him go in April 1935. But MGM's Irving Thalberg knew talent when he saw it, and he signed Tracy the very day Fox severed ties with him. Thalberg's boss, Louis Mayer, was hesitant; he didn't need "another drunken Wallace Beery."

Thalberg managed to sway his boss, but in truth, Beery was a model citizen compared to the unique mess that was Spencer Tracy. Tracy wasn't just a drunk—he was a self-flagellating, self-immolating, utterly filthy drunk. Sure, Tracy understood the value of public image and so yes, his binges were kept very private. Tracy rarely drank in public and, other than a few exceptions, was the consummate professional when working. That said, privacy did nothing to dilute the extremity of his habits.

Tracy's most common binge technique was locking himself in a room at the St. George Hotel in Brooklyn for weeks at a time, downing bottle after bottle of whiskey while sitting naked in the bathtub. It was a peculiar routine. Afraid of airplanes, he would take the train to New York (a four-day ride) just to drink in that tub—rising not even to use the toilet. Maybe Tracy knew that he would sit there forever if he didn't make it so unfathomably disgusting that he'd rather quit drinking than remain one minute longer. Or maybe he enjoyed it. Nobody knows anything, except that after a few weeks of marinating in his own waste, Tracy would emerge and act like a human again.

Unfortunately, Tracy sometimes slipped in public. Like the night he was hauled off to jail in handcuffs and leg straps for resisting arrest, this when Tracy was still working for Fox. The cops had caught him on Sunset Boulevard driving erratically. (What star didn't drive drunk on Sunset?) It seemed the Clover Club (an illegal casino) was located next to Lee Francis's (a brothel the studios used for visiting VIPs). Tracy had been found drunk in a borrowed car trying unsuccessfully to navigate the driveway that separated the two. This would not look good.

Louis B. Mayer was not about to let such a incident happen again. Tracy was what the MGM fixer Strickling called a "multiproblem person," and multiproblem people needed multiperson solutions. So Strickling had assembled the Tracy Squad: an ambulance driver, a doctor, and four security guards dressed as paramedics, all of whom served no function at MGM other than picking up inebriated stars. As further protection, every drinking establishment within twenty-five miles of the MGM lot had been given the number of that private, direct line to Strickling and instructed to call the moment Tracy walked in. It seemed a good strategy, but it also hadn't been put to the test until now.

By the time the Tracy Squad pulled up at the Trocadero, there'd already been an incident, apparently with director William Wellman. Wellman had uttered some unflattering remarks about the actress Loretta Young, who he directed in *The Call of the Wild* and with whom Tracy had been in a much-publicized affair. In defense of Young's honor, Tracy had taken a swing. Some said the punch hit Wellman in the gut; others said it missed altogether. What no one disputed was that Wellman's counterpunch landed nicely. Tracy flew over a nearby table. That was when the Squad arrived. They grabbed Tracy, put him in the back of the ambulance, and drove him home, where security stood guard until he sobered up. It could've been worse. Still, the Tracy Squad would have to work on their response time. ★

LANA TURNER

1921–1995
ACTRESS

"My life has been a series of emergencies."

With a busty figure that earned her the nickname the "Sweater Girl," Lana Turner was signed by MGM six months after the unexpected death of Jean Harlow. She quickly became the studio's go-to sexpot. Turner was discovered as a teenager in a diner (not, as legend has it, in Schwab's Pharmacy), while she was skipping class at Hollywood High, and was given a small role in Mervyn LeRoy's *They Won't Forget* (1937). Her acclaimed performance in *The Postman Always Rings Twice* (1946) marked her arrival among critics as a serious actress. But her private life was constant tabloid fodder, alternately fueling and overshadowing her professional success. She was married eight times (beating Rita Hayworth by three), including to musician Artie Shaw and actors Stephen Crane and Lex Barker. Her abusive relationship with mob bodyguard Johnny Stompanato ended when Turner's teenage daughter, Cheryl Crane, stabbed him to death (ruled "justifiable homicide" during the subsequent trial). Turner was fired from MGM in the mid-1950s as her box-office numbers headed south, but she bounced back with *Peyton Place* (1957), for which she received an Oscar nomination, and the Douglas Sirk melodrama *Imitation of Life* (1959), the biggest commercial hit of her career. Turner's final starring role was *Madame X* (1966), although she appeared on several episodes of the soap opera *Falcon Crest* during the eighties.

★

SURE, HE WAS A millionaire, but nobody would ever accuse him of being a gentleman. And certainly not after "the left hook that unhooked Lana Turner from Bob Topping."

Sometimes called the "nightclub queen," Lana Turner always seemed to have a different man on her arm. *Confidential* declared her "the jilted-est girl in Hollywood," with an "uncontrolled urge for high living, liquor, love, and late hours." If a relationship failed, they wrote, it wouldn't be long before her "glands got to working again." Habitually married, eight times to seven different men, Turner once said, "My goal was to have one husband and seven children, but it turned out to be the other way around."

Soon enough, even "respectable" publications got in on the act. In 1948 *Life* ran an article on Turner's impending wedding to East Coast playboy Henry "Bob" Topping—the headline, LANA TURNER'S FOURTH AND POSITIVELY LAST TIME. The article went on to say Topping was considered a talented man in Hollywood and New York because "he inherited $7 million and plays a fine game of golf."

Turner was fresh off a breakup with actor Tyrone Power, and Topping had just left his previous wife, actress Arline Judge—who, the press also gleefully noted, had previously been married to Topping's older brother Dan (owner of the New York Yankees). Supposedly, Topping proposed to Turner by dropping a diamond ring into her martini. There were more to come—both diamonds and martinis—and soon she lost interest in acting. Mostly, Turner just partied. It wasn't uncommon for the couple to have a hundred people at their house on any given weekend.

So it was that sometime in 1951 that Turner and Topping found themselves on a pub crawl with group of friends from the East Coast. They wound up at the Mocambo, where singer Billy Daniels (best known for his hit recording of "That Old Black Magic") was performing. Turner ate his performance up, and when the show was over, Topping invited Daniels over to their table for a cocktail. When the Mocambo closed, he invited him back to the couple's Holmby Hills mansion for a few more. There they sat around the fire drinking, Daniels serenading Turner all the while.

Eventually, Topping grew tired and stumbled off to bed. His friends followed. Apparently, that left Turner and Daniels alone together in the living room for almost enough time to have sex. Because just minutes after he left, Topping wandered back in, wearing his pajamas—and found the pair in a compromised position. Allegedly, Topping belted Turner first, with a left hook to the jaw, and then turned on Daniels. Hearing all the commotion, the friends returned and broke it up.

At least, that's the story that appeared in *Confidential*. Turner's biographers are split in regard to whether it actually happened or not. As for the celebrity gossips who hounded her, to them Turner's personal life was little more than an ongoing joke anyway. Besides, soon enough they would find gangster Johnny Stompanato, stabbed to death in Turner's bedroom—and by her daughter no less. ★

CHASEN'S

9039 BEVERLY BLVD.

LIKE SO MANY STARRY-EYED men and women before him, comedian Dave Chasen took the plunge in 1930: He went all in on an acting career. Relocating from New York to Los Angeles, he was leaving behind a mildly successful career in vaudeville. But there was a difference between Chasen and most other aspiring actors: pragmatic self-awareness. So it only took him five years, as opposed to the requisite twenty, to conclude that it wasn't really working out, and probably never would.

Chasen threw in the towel on acting, and then took an equally big risk in opening his own restaurant—a move based exclusively on the raves he drew from friends when he'd cook dinner for them. When he mentioned the idea to one of

those friends, *New Yorker* editor Harold Ross, Ross advised him that 97 percent of restaurant owners went bankrupt. "But three percent didn't," Chasen shot back.

With investments from Frank Capra (the director of his first film) and the now-convinced Ross, Chasen opened the Southern Pit Barbecue on Beverly in 1936. Originally limited to six tables and little more than a dozen stools, its menu revolved around chili and ribs. The place proved so popular that within a year he greatly expanded, with a full waitstaff serving thirty-five different items to two dozen tabletops. He also renamed it Chasen's.

A boisterous saloon-type atmosphere, the food was hearty and the drinks were strong. But what Chasen's lacked in elegance, it more than made up for with an insider, clubhouse mystique. It was where Jimmy Stewart, at a party celebrating his marriage to Gloria Hatrick, was served a main course of two "midgets" in diapers atop a silver platter. It was where Bob Hope claimed to have showed up for a meal on a horse that he rode straight into the dining room. *Sure he did.*

Chasen's was where Ronald Reagan, at his favorite booth, proposed to Nancy Davis, his favorite girlfriend. Elizabeth Taylor craved the chili so badly she had it flown to her on the set of *Cleopatra,* in Rome. Alfred Hitchcock was such a valued customer that a fish entree was named after him. Little Shirley Temple, out dining with her parents, requested a nonalcoholic cocktail and, voilà, the Shirley Temple was born. At its peak, Chasen's served three hundred a night, and eventually augmented this with a booming business catering parties and banquets.

As with all things, age and the whims of taste eventually shuttered the iconic restaurant, but it didn't go down without a fight. It managed to stay in business sixty-five years, until 1995 — and again as with all things, its greatness was soon reborn as nostalgia: Orhan Arli, a twenty-year veteran of Chasen's kitchen, has kept many of its signature dishes (including the chili) alive, offering them as options in his own catering business. ★

SHIRLEY TEMPLE

. . . .

¼ OZ. GRENADINE

8–10 OZ. GINGER ALE

MARASCHINO CHERRY

Fill a Collins glass with ice cubes. Add grenadine, then fill to top with ginger ale. Stir gently. Garnish with cherry and serve with a straw.

ORSON WELLES

1915–1985

DIRECTOR, ACTOR, WRITER, PRODUCER

"There are three intolerable things in life—cold coffee, lukewarm champagne, and overexcited women."

Orson Welles is considered by many critics and historians to be the greatest director of all time. His first feature, *Citizen Kane* (1941), is also widely considered the greatest film ever. Still, Welles fell far short of industry expectations. As he would himself admit, "I started at the top and worked my way down." In 1937, Welles formed the Mercury Theatre with John Houseman, thereby establishing a stable of performers he'd return to again and again in years to come. His *Julius Caesar* (1937) set in fascist Italy was wildly successful. His sensational Halloween radio broadcast of *The War of the Worlds* (1938) drew the attention of Hollywood. Welles teamed with writer Herman J. Mankiewicz on the story that would become RKO's *Citizen Kane,* which was nominated for nine Oscars and won for Best Original Screenplay. His brilliant second feature, *The Magnificent Ambersons* (1942), was significantly altered while Welles was in South America shooting his third directorial effort, the documentary *It's All True.* He directed three movies as a freelancer, with mixed box-office results but great artistry: *The Stranger* (1946); *The Lady from Shanghai* (1947), starring his wife at the time, Rita Hayworth; and *Macbeth* (1948). Welles left for Europe in 1947 and remained there for the majority of the next twenty years, hiring himself out as an actor—most notably in *The Third Man* (1949)—as a means of financing his own projects. But most of these projects failed to match the director's vision, either due to editorial interference (*Mr. Arkadian, Touch of Evil*) or Welles's self-sabotaging perfectionism

(*Don Quixote*, *The Other Side of the Wind*). His last completed work, the cinematic essay *F for Fake* (1973), turned out to be a final artistic triumph to a newer generation who knew him best as the Paul Masson wine spokesman.

★

AN EFFECTIVE BIT OF THEATER, that's all it was. In December 1939 Orson Welles was the toast of Hollywood, a boy genius from New York hard at work on his first masterpiece. John Houseman from Welles's point of view, was just his producer, along for the ride. For the last hour they'd been at each other's throats in the private dining room at Chasen's, surrounded by six members of the Mercury Players who weren't really sure how to diffuse the situation.

Welles was pretty lit. He'd been drinking since they sat down and getting more and more agitated, but he wasn't a violent man. He simply wanted nothing more to do with Houseman. And soon enough, Houseman also wanted little to do with Welles. Then, *thunk*.

A flaming can of Sterno flew past Houseman's head (wide left), struck the wall, and landed on the carpet. Houseman turned toward Welles. *Thunk*. Another Sterno, wide right this time—and now the curtains were on fire.

The argument had been concerning some developments earlier in the day: RKO president George Schaefer had informed the Mercury players that, in less than two weeks, they would no longer receive salaries from the studio. The original deal Welles had signed (the famous nobody-ever-gets-this-kind-of-freedom-and-nobody-ever-will-again *Citizen Kane* deal) stipulated that he complete the first of his three pictures by January 1, 1940. Now it was almost Christmas, 1939, and Welles still didn't have anything ready to shoot.

Despite such dire straits, Welles assured everyone he would continue paying them with income from the Mercury's weekly radio show. But Houseman knew the money wasn't there. And he knew Welles knew it. That's when things blew up.

The tension between Welles and Houseman had been building for some time. (This would prove to be something of a pattern between Welles and his collaborators.) Though he and Houseman had been successful partners for years—first on the WPA productions, then with the Mercury Theater—their dynamic shifted after *War of the Worlds*. If you asked Welles, it was a matter of jealousy. Houseman had become more of an employee than a collaborator and he resented it. If you asked Houseman, the problem was ego—Welles's ego. He'd bought into the hype about his genius, at the cost of his creative integrity. As his cowriter on *Citizen Kane* Herman Mankiewicz would say of him, "There, but for the grace of God, goes God." Welles was also drinking excessively—one or two bottles of either brandy or whiskey a day—and his sexual dalliances were running him even more ragged.

In later years, when asked why he threw the Sterno, Welles claimed it was a calculated move. He couldn't just fire Houseman—Welles was in a delicate position with the Mercury players as it was, and didn't want to appear disloyal. Better to make Houseman quit. Which is exactly what happened. Three days after the fight, Houseman sent Welles a letter of resignation and returned to New York. But within a few months, Houseman was back in the fold. Welles needed someone to keep Mankiewicz sober while Mank hammered away on the first draft of *Kane*. By offering the job to Houseman, Welles could appear both gracious and loyal, while avoiding any substantive contact with his once-trusted producer.

Welles was also drinking excessively—one or two bottles of either brandy or whiskey a day—and his sexual dalliances were running him even more ragged.

Houseman had the last laugh, though. He and Mankiewicz spent the next three months together writing, and at some point the Chasen's incident was mentioned. Of course, Mankiewicz felt he just had to put that into the script; it became Kane's furniture-smashing fit, the scene after his wife walks out on him. Ironically, many consider it Welles's finest performance in the film—but he scarcely had to act at all. ★

ANNA MAY WONG

1905–1961
ACTRESS

"Whatever you're about to ask, it's not true."

The first Chinese-American movie star, Anna May Wong was a vocal critic of Hollywood's portrayal of Asian characters. Raised in the Chinatown section of Los Angeles, Wong dropped out of high school to pursue an acting career. Critically praised for her lead role in *The Toll of the Sea* (1922), she rose to prominence after appearing in Raoul Walsh's *The Thief of Baghdad* (1924). Wong quickly developed a level of craft that Hollywood was unprepared to accommodate. Frustrated by repeated typecasting, Wong left for Europe in 1928. Her performance in *Piccadilly* (1929)—her last silent picture and a British production—is regarded as one of her finest. But the lure of top billing and more challenging roles led her back to Hollywood to sign with Paramount in 1930. Her high point within the studio system was Josef von Sternberg's *Shanghai Express* (1932), opposite Marlene Dietrich. (Onscreen chemistry between the two led to rumors of a lesbian relationship.) But institutional racism—MGM considered her "too Chinese to play Chinese"—kept her from moving beyond supporting-player status. Wong's biggest disappointment came in 1935 when the Chinese lead in *The Good Earth*—a part she'd longed to play—was given to German actress Luise Rainer. The following year, Wong embarked on an extended tour of China, during which she wrote dispatches for a number of American newspapers. She rarely acted in the years that followed, devoting herself instead to promotion of the Chinese struggle against Japan.

★

In Europe, they had a word for Chinese-American Anna May Wong: *superstar*. In America, specifically her hometown of Los Angeles, they had dozens of words—but most of them had only four letters.

To be fair, these vulgarians were hardly alone. From 1882 to 1943, Federal Law forbade the Chinese from emigrating to or entering the United States—ever. In fact, any Chinese-American citizen could be stopped by police just for "looking Chinese" and made to show their passport. In effect, these Chinese-Americans were stuck with either hating the Chinese or hating the Americans—neither of which could have felt very good.

As for Anna May Wong, she started drinking.

A third-generation Chinese-American, her family had been in the United States since the Civil War era. But such a pedigree changed nothing. She was forbidden by law from owning land, from working in the public sector, and even from testifying in court. It was also illegal for her to kiss a white man, much less on screen—a restriction that severely hampered her career.

> **Returning home, Wong grew even more outspoken and fearless—and, not surprisingly, began to drink even more. She drifted in and out of film, never losing her elegance and grace.**

Wong was a fairly successful actress in Hollywood but was always passed over, even for female leads written as Chinese (in favor of, say, Myrna Loy). This, because of the kissing issue. Instead, Wong got pigeonholed in stereotypical roles that offended Chinese audiences, most of whom weren't sure what to make of her modern, Americanized image in the first place—after all, she did the Charleston.

Over time, much of her community would feel Wong had betrayed her roots and pandered to her oppressors by accepting racist film roles. (A few of her character names: China Mary, Lotus Flower, Mongol Slave, and Zahrat.) When she visited China for the first time, she was met at the dock by a protester chanting down with the "stooge who disgraces China." Others reportedly tried to block her boat from docking.

At this point, Anna May Wong started drinking more.

Hated by many and disallowed by law from doing her job to the best of her ability, she decided to take an extended trip to Germany in 1928; she immediately became a media sensation. This was partially due, no doubt, to her choice of party-circuit companion: Marlene Dietrich, "the busiest and most passionate bisexual in theatrical Berlin." One particular snapshot of the two, by famed photographer Alfred Eisenstaedt, shows Wong pouring liquor into Dietrich's mouth, neatly capturing in a single frame everything that made her a beloved European superstar: her beauty, her wit, her fearlessness, not to mention her fashion sense.

Returning home, Wong grew even more outspoken and fearless—and, not surprisingly, began to drink even more. She drifted in and out of the world of film, never losing her elegance and grace. By the 1950s, when she could finally fully display her talents without fear of an FBI raid, Wong could no longer do so—she was already suffering from liver disease. This, the result of too many years doing the only thing U.S. law allowed her to do freely. ★

DRAGON'S DEN
510 LOS ANGELES ST.

IN 1935, WITH THE Depression crippling his family's Chinatown antique shop, twenty-nine-year-old Eddy See asked himself a very basic question: What is the one thing people will continue to spend money on, no matter how poor they may be? The answer, he decided, was food. And so, in 1935, See converted the basement of the store, F. Suie One, into one of Los Angeles's first family-style Chinese restaurants. At a time when all Chinese cuisine was condescendingly called chop suey, Dragon's Den served up authentic, inexpensive dishes that, though now de rigueur, were considered novel, even exotic: almond duck, sweet-and-sour pork, egg foo yong, fried shrimp. The cost of an entire six-course meal? As little as fifty cents.

Capitalizing on his connections to the Asian American art world (the antique shop had a tiny gallery in its mezzanine), See enlisted Tyrus Wong and Benji Okubo to decorate the space, which was a basement in every sense of the word, complete with exposed beams and pipes. On the inside walls they painted murals of Buddha, the Eight Immortals, and a warrior fighting a dragon; on the outside, the restaurant's name, in both Chinese and English. With its bohemian aesthetic, Dragon's Den attracted scores of Hollywood set and costume designers (who already frequented F. Suie One for props and wardrobe), as well as actors Peter Lorre and Sydney Greenstreet, the Marx Brothers, Walt Disney, and of course, the Chinese-American movie star, Anna May Wong.

Though Wong was almost universally

despised in Chinatown, See adored her; they discovered they were kindred spirits. Their favorite pastime was telling each other jokes. Decades later, writer Lisa See could still remember her grandfather's favorite. "One day, a fisherman throws out his line," Wong began. "He catches a beautiful mermaid with long blonde hair. He reels her in. The fisherman picks her up, examines every detail of her gorgeous face and body, and then unceremoniously tosses her back in to the sea. His friend, having observed all of this silently, looks at the fisherman in shock."

"Why?" the friend finally asks.

The first fisherman's response: "How?"

The Dragon's Den only lasted through World War II, but the influence of its style and menu remain visible in every Chinese restaurant in Los Angeles. And the antique shop? It moved to Pasadena, where it remains open; now owned by Lisa See and her cousin Leslee Long. ★

Part Three

POSTWAR ERA

1946–1959

"If the Hollywood Party was excessive,
it was only because Hollywood had always
been excessive, a speeded-up, larger-than-life
reflection of the American way."
—BUDD SCHULBERG, screenwriter

Humphrey Bogart is best known for his onscreen persona—a brooding, cynical, self-reliant antihero; see private detectives Philip Marlowe in *The Big Sleep* (1946) and Sam Spade in *The Maltese Falcon* (1941) or nightclub owner Rick Blaine in *Casablanca* (1942). Bogart came up through New York theater—first as an office hand, then as a stage manager—before transitioning to acting. He went to Hollywood after the 1929 stock market crash, but initially found film roles bland and dissatisfying. Bogart played murderer Duke Mantee in Robert Sherwood's *The Petrified Forest* on Broadway in 1934 and reprised the role for Warner Brothers in 1936, sparking an early career as a heavy in B-movie gangster pictures. He worked like crazy, appearing in twenty-eight movies over the next four years. He was cast as the lead in *High Sierra* (1941), written by John Huston, which finally established him as a top-tier star. He went on to appear in six films Huston directed, including *The Maltese Falcon* (1941), *The Treasure of the Sierra Madre* (1947), *Key Largo* (1948), and *The African Queen* (1951). *Casablanca* garnered the first of Bogart's three Best Actor Oscar nominations. He won for *The African Queen* and was nominated a final time for *The Caine Mutiny* (1954). Bogart's last words, "I should never have switched from scotch to martinis."

------------------------------ ★ ------------------------------

IT WASN'T A JOKE, but it damn well should have been. Certainly it began like one: *So Humphrey Bogart walks into a bar with two stuffed pandas.*

HUMPHREY BOGART

1899–1957

ACTOR

"*The whole world is about three drinks behind.*"

Bogart was, by then—September 1949—the biggest movie star in the world, and he was out in New York with an old drinking buddy named Bill Seeman. They'd been carousing since early, the two of them and Bogey's wife, Lauren Bacall, but she'd gone back to the hotel hours ago.

After Mrs. Bogart left, the men found themselves in need of a stand-in that might scare off would-be home wreckers and drunks. Somehow it emerged that a nearby delicatessen sold a historically random nonfood item, as delicatessens have a way of doing: stuffed pandas. Not just any stuffed pandas, mind you. Each of these weighed in at more than twenty pounds, and set you back twenty-five bucks a pop. *Perfect.*

Bogart and Seeman bought a couple and hopped a cab to El Morocco, where they requested a table for four: two seats for them, two for their dates. They were seated, and that was supposed to be the end of it: getting seated with two pandas. Unfortunately for Bogart, the real end would take four days to arrive, and it wouldn't be over drinks with his friends—it'd be in court.

After Mrs. Bogart left, the men found themselves in need of a stand-in that might scare off would-be home wreckers and drunks. Somehow it emerged that a nearby delicatessen sold a historically random nonfood item, as delicatessens have a way of doing— stuffed pandas.

Here's the thing: Bogart was a gregarious man with a keen sense of humor, but he was only comfortable among friends—and his social circle was tight-knit. The Rat Pack, later so closely associated with Frank Sinatra, was in fact Bogart's creation, with Bogart at the center. The mission of the group, Bogart said, was the "relief of boredom and the perpetuation of independence." Bacall was a member, of course. So was Sinatra. Judy Garland, Spencer Tracy, talent agent Irving Lazar, writer Nathaniel Benchley (son of Bogart's old friend Robert Benchley)—they were all part of the original Holmby Hills Rat Pack. You might see them out at Romanoff's or on rare occasions in Las Vegas, drinking and carrying on, but if you weren't part of the Pack, you were an outsider and you weren't welcome.

Which brings us back to the pandas. If you were to spy Bogart at a nightclub in the wee hours of the morning, propping up an oversized stuffed animal, you might think that it was a not-so-subtle message about the company he preferred to keep. And if you knew anything about Bogart—which you might, since he was more or less the biggest star in the world—you wouldn't consider yourself in on the joke. But a young model named Robin Roberts thought she was special—as young models often do. She approached Bogart's table on her way out, laughed, and picked up one of the pandas. And Bogart, given the number of drinks he had put away by this point, happened to be feeling very protective of this panda. So he naturally pulled the panda close to him and told Ms. Roberts to leave him alone, for he was a married man. And then the woman fell over. She said he shoved her. He said she lost her balance. Four days later, he was in a Manhattan courtroom facing legal action.

The panda fiasco immediately hit the tabloids, with Bogart protesting his innocence every step of the way. One reporter asked him if he'd struck Ms. Roberts. He said he would never hit a woman, "they're too dangerous." Another reporter asked if he was drunk at the time of the incident. He replied, "Isn't everybody at four a.m.?" Fortunately for Bogart, the judge presiding over the case found it as ridiculous as he did, throwing it out after the first hearing. It turns out, being left alone, when you're the biggest star in the world, requires a lot of people. ★

NEW YEARS EVE was the one night of the year Humphrey Bogart wouldn't get drunk—for the simple fact that everybody else would. Still, that did not hold true for other celebrations. At the Bel-Air wedding to his third wife, actress Mayo Methot, described as "a blend of Zelda Fitzgerald and Tugboat Annie," they served Black Velvets. The A-list event quickly degenerated into a drunken free-for-all, ending with the newlyweds, soon to be christened the Battling Bogarts, spending their wedding night in different beds—in different countries in fact. Drunk and angry, Bogart had driven off with pals to Tijuana.

There is an amusing Easter Day story as well. Bogart was to speak at the Easter service being held at the Hollywood Bowl. The night before, however, turned out to be a real humdinger, Bogie tossing back scotch until well past four in the morning—around which time he was expected to show up at the amphitheater. He walked onto the stage still tight and launched into a remarkably powerful recitation of the Lord's Prayer. The crowd at the Bowl was brought to tears, rushing the star afterward, as he could only stammer, "I need to puke."

As for Christmas—which happened to be Bogart's birthday, too—that was truly a "make mine a double" affair. Bourbon Milk Punch was the cocktail of choice. Why? A yuletide tradition in the Holmby Hills home he shared with his fourth and last wife, Lauren Bacall, the Bourbon Milk Punch helped with Bogie's hangovers—that throbbing, queasy, altogether uncomfortable hour that would come after he'd stopped celebrating Christmas and before his birthday party had begun.

BOURBON MILK PUNCH

16 OZ. BOURBON

1 QUART OF HALF & HALF

2¼ TBSP. VANILLA EXTRACT

¾ CUP CONFECTIONERS'
   (POWDERED) SUGAR

FRESHLY GRATED NUTMEG

Pour ingredients (except nutmeg) into a large pitcher and stir until sugar is dissolved. Cover with tinfoil and let sit in refrigerator for a couple of hours. Stir again to recombine ingredients and serve in an Old-Fashioned glass (ice optional). Sprinkle freshly grated nutmeg on top. Pitcher should provide for about ten cocktails.

LON CHANEY, JR.

1906–1973

ACTOR

Director: "You cannot drink on the set."

Lon Chaney, Jr: "Then I cannot work on the set."

A ctor and son of silent film legend Lon Chaney, Sr. (*The Hunchback of Notre Dame* and *The Phantom of the Opera*). Lon Chaney, Jr.'s father discouraged him from show business and pushed him to attend business school. It wasn't until the great man passed away in 1930 that his son started acting. Chaney, Jr.'s career would go on to span five decades and mostly consist of horror movies and Westerns. Although he first gained notice for his portrayal of Lennie in *Of Mice and Men* (1939), his breakout role was as the titular star of his best-known film, Universal's *The Wolf Man* (1941). Chaney, Jr., is the only actor to play all of the studio's trademark monsters: the Wolf Man, the Mummy, Frankenstein's Monster, and Dracula. (Technically he only played the son of Dracula, but close enough.) Despite some commendable work as a supporting actor in a few A-list films—*High Noon* (1952), *The Defiant Ones* (1958)—he never rose above typecasting or cult status. Somewhat fittingly, Chaney's final picture was *Frankenstein vs. Dracula* (1971). He was cast not as a monster, but rather Frankenstein's mute henchman—a silent role of which his father would likely still have disapproved.

★

HE THOUGHT HE'D TAKE it easy this time. This was Lon Chaney's third go-round as Frankenstein's Monster. The last time, a year earlier, he'd done a goofy spin on the character for NBC's *The Colgate Comedy Hour* with Dean Martin and Jerry Lewis. Now he was playing a more traditional version for the ABC sci-fi anthology series *Tales of Tomorrow*. By "traditional version," it meant he was supposed to break things: smash windows, bust chairs, shatter mirrors—monster stuff. But Chaney worried he'd been a little too overzealous during previous rehearsals, tearing apart the set when cameras weren't actually rolling, and driving the prop masters crazy. So he figured, this run-through, he'd hold back—take it easy—just go through the motions.

Directors who worked with Chaney applied an informal rule: No changes could be made after lunch. Chaney drank steadily throughout the day, the costumed six-nine, 284-pound brute sipping from a flask between takes, so that by afternoon he sometimes had no idea what he was doing. Word around town was: *Get what you could from him in the morning.*

The first time he played Frankenstein's Monster, in *Ghost of Frankenstein*, the tipsy terror had gotten lost in the labyrinthine set, and even with the entire crew shouting instructions from nearby, it was ten minutes before he staggered out. In *The Mummy's Tomb*, he'd banged his costar Elyse Knox's head against a stone column while carrying her through a cemetery gate. In *The Mummy's Ghost*, he'd nearly choked seventy-year-old actor Frank Reicher to death during a strangulation scene (Reicher in fact passed out), then punched his hand through a window he'd specifically been told did not yet have breakaway glass.

> Chaney drank steadily throughout the day, the giant six-nine, 284 pound brute sipping from a flask between takes, so that by afternoon, he sometimes had no idea what he was doing.

At least now, on *Tales of Tomorrow*, he had realized he only needed to use brute strength when the cameras were rolling. So for the next run-through, in the scene in the dining room of Dr. Frankenstein's castle where the monster knocks the maid and butler to the ground, then rips apart the furniture, Chaney went ahead and knocked the two down, but when it came time to throw a chair, he hesitated, then gently set it back down. Two scenes later, same thing: chair was lifted, chair was gently set back down. For good measure, Chaney threw in a pantomime of what he planned to do with the chair when it really counted, pretending to hurtle it to the ground with the full force of his massive frame. Sure, it looked ridiculous, but he'd nail it live. Problem was, this "run-through" *was* live—the actual broadcast going out live on network television. And Chaney had no idea. ★

MONTGOMERY CLIFT

1920–1966
ACTOR

"We drink to suppress
our panic."

M ontgomery Clift was one of the original members of the Actors Studio and an early proponent of the Method. Noted for his portrayal of moody young men, at the height of his career he was rivaled only by Marlon Brando. He first appeared on Broadway at age fourteen. His Hollywood debut more than ten years later was *Red River* (1948), opposite John Wayne. Clift received three Best Actor Oscar nominations over the next five years, for *The Search* (1948), *A Place in the Sun* (1951), and *From Here to Eternity* (1953). A disfiguring car accident while shooting *Raintree County* (1957) caused him constant pain for the remainder of his career. Although he continued to work—appearing alongside Brando in *The Young Lions* (1958), Elizabeth Taylor in *Suddenly, Last Summer* (1959), and Marilyn Monroe and Clark Gable in *The Misfits* (1961)—his health and physical appearance were noticeably on the decline. Clift received his fourth and final Oscar nomination (Best Supporting Actor) for *Judgment at Nuremberg* (1961). He completed one last picture, *The Defector* (1966), before suffering a fatal heart attack in his New York City townhouse.

★

MONTGOMERY CLIFT WAS DRIVING TOO FAST. But then what proper leading man didn't drive too fast? From Ramon Navarro to Clark Gable right on through to Steve McQueen, isn't the history of Hollywood awash with tales of drunken drag racing? Only thing, Clift wasn't drunk—at least that's what everyone said. Later, when going over the circumstances of the car crash, Clift's friends seemed at pains to stress his temperance that night — *a glass of wine, if that* — as if erecting a barrier against the rushing tide of scandal.

According to the other guests, Clift had been withdrawn and sullen at Elizabeth Taylor's dinner party; then he'd decided to leave early. His good friend Kevin McCarthy, the respected character actor, offered to lead him down the winding Benedict Canyon road back to Beverly Hills, and a relieved Clift accepted. With McCarthy leading the way, the two men set off into the night.

This was during production of an MGM film titled *Raintree County*. Heading down that winding road in June 1956, Clift's image was still frozen in the amber of stardom; he was the dashing lead of *A Place in the Sun* and *From Here to Eternity*, the sexy brooder whom audiences had come to adore. Only those closest to Clift knew that his taste for good whiskey had become an endless thirst. His best friend, Elizabeth Taylor, and his one-time companion, Jack Larson — they knew that during a dinner at Treetops, the 110-acre Connecticut estate owned by torch singer Libby Holman, Clift's face kept falling into the soup. Or that after just a few cocktails, Clift might drop to all fours and begin barking like a dog. Kevin McCarthy, driving ahead, he knew all these things, too. In fact, McCarthy no longer even let Clift in his house after Clift drunkenly dropped his son Flip on the floor.

So when, some distance down the hill, McCarthy looked in his rearview mirror to see Clift driving too fast, he sped up, thinking that it was either a hopped-up prank or the beginning of a blackout. Either way, McCarthy wanted no part of it. A few seconds later, Clift swerved out of control and smashed into a telephone pole.

Biographer Patricia Bosworth described the scene: McCarthy ran back to Clift's car but didn't see Clift anywhere. After pointing his headlights at the accident, he realized that Clift was crumpled on the floor beneath the dash, his nose broken, the bones of his jaw shattered, his face (as McCarthy described) "torn away." Afraid to touch him, McCarthy thought Clift wouldn't survive until the ambulance arrived.

He drove back to Taylor's to get her then-husband, English actor Michael Wilding, but Taylor insisted on going down to the accident. The front door was jammed shut, but Taylor, unstoppable, went into the back and climbed over the front seat. She cradled Clift's head — he was choking. Then she reached her fingers down into Clift's mouth and pulled two teeth out of his throat. When the paparazzi arrived, she was heard to scream, "You bastards! If you dare take one photograph of him like this, I'll never let another one of you near me again!" (You go, Elizabeth Taylor.)

MGM was forced to shut down production of *Raintree County* while Clift recovered. He was hospitalized for two weeks, his face reconstructed, then moved to a convalescent home. Taylor, who was also starring in the film, visited him almost daily, as did Kevin McCarthy. With his jaw wired shut, Clift couldn't eat solid food, but he was able to drink martinis through a straw. Although his face would never look the same again, after more than two months, he was ready to go back to work.

This time, MGM assigned Clift a chaperone, what is a modern-day sober coach, to help him control his alcohol and drug intake. But Clift didn't much like the idea. En route to the location, while laid over in New Orleans, Clift disembarked from the plane absolutely loaded to the gills. A phalanx of reporters were waiting in the terminal and so Clift took off sprinting. He sprinted through the airport with the newsmen, as well as his chaperone, nipping at his heels, until finally Clift managed to lose them. Then he went and found a bar. ★

FROM HERE TO ETERNITY (1953)

"Harry Cohn's Folly." That's what people were calling it. Cohn, the president of Columbia Pictures, had paid $82,000 for the rights to the James Jones novel *From Here to Eternity*, but the odds of it ever being produced looked slim. The story of a group of soldiers stationed in Hawaii in the months leading up to the attack on Pearl Harbor, the book's less-than-flattering portrayal of Army life, sure to draw the ire of the military were it ever to be depicted on film (and don't forget this was the McCarthy era), seemed like an insurmountable obstacle.

But the entire production of *From Here to Eternity*, it turned out, was a series of long shots that delivered. The cooperation of the Army, for instance, was happily granted (thanks in part to the connections of producer Buddy Adler, who'd been a Lieutenant-Colonel during World War II) on two conditions: that the stockade would never be shown, and that Captain Holmes, the film's villain, would be given an unhappy ending. (In the book, he's promoted to major.)

Adler's choice of director, Fred Zinnemann, landed the job despite the objections of Cohn, who considered him too "art house" for the project. (Zinnemann's breakthrough, *High Noon*, had yet to be re-leased.) Donna Reed, of all people, was picked to play a prostitute; Deborah Kerr, a sex maniac. Frank Sinatra campaigned relentlessly for the part of Private Maggio, an event fictionalized in *The Godfather* when producer Jack Woltz wakes up with a severed horse head in his bed. In truth, Sinatra was cast in the role only after Eli Wallach fell out—and even then, Sinatra had to agree to a meager salary of $1,000 a week.

Filming began in March 1953 and lasted eight weeks. While on loca-tion in Hawaii, Sinatra, Kerr, Zinnemann, Burt Lancaster (playing First Sergeant Warden), and Montgomery Clift (playing Private Prewitt) had dinner together most nights. Afterward, Sinatra and Clift—who'd taken Sinatra under his wing as an acting protégé—would slink off to Sinatra's hotel room, where they passed ungodly amounts of time calling Nairobi (where Mrs. Sinatra, Ava Gardner, was shooting *Mogambo* and appar-ently boinking the entire continent) and getting absolutely trashed. It was messy stuff. They'd throw beer cans out the window, stumble through the lobby shouting obscenities. One night Sinatra threatened to commit suicide over the problems he was having with Gardner. (Clift talked him out of it.) Many nights, Lancaster and Kerr had to physically put each of them in bed.

This all came to a head the final night of shooting in Hawaii, when both men showed up for a scene together drunk. Sinatra decided he wasn't happy with the blocking, which required the actors to stand up. Sinatra wanted to sit down, as the drunk frequently do. Zinnemann insisted he stand and Clift agreed. Sinatra's response: slapping Clift in the face, then unleashing a torrent of expletives at Zinnemann. The situation grew so volatile that Adler called Cohn (who was dining with an Air Force general) and insisted he get to the set. Cohn showed up, chauffeured in an Air Force limousine, and threatened to shut the entire picture down if Sinatra didn't pull it together.

Apparently Sinatra did. *From Here to Eternity* went on to become one of the biggest successes in Columbia's history, nominated for thirteen Academy Awards and winning eight, including Oscars for Zinnemann and Sinatra. The film would reignite Sinatra's acting career.

JOHN FORD

1894–1973
DIRECTOR

"I didn't show up to collect any of my first three Oscars. Once I went fishing, another time there was a war on, and on the third, I was suddenly taken drunk."

A rguably the most influential American filmmaker in the history of cinema. John Ford's career spanned six decades and nearly 150 pictures, including more than 60 in the silent era. (First film: *The Tornado*, 1917; last: *Chesty*, 1976). In between, Ford won a record four Academy Awards for Best Director: *The Informer* (1935), *The Grapes of Wrath* (1940), *How Green Was My Valley* (1941), and *The Quiet Man* (1952). He had a unique visual style characterized by long shots and vast landscapes. Ford worked in all manner of genres—war films, period pieces, comedies—but is most closely associated with Westerns, of which his *The Searchers* (1956) is considered defining. He established a stock company of actors, including such heavy hitters as Jimmy Stewart and Henry Fonda, and was instrumental in the development of John Wayne's character and career, directing him in over twenty features. Repeated use of Monument Valley as a location earned the region the nickname of "Ford Country." Legendarily efficient, he was known for shooting a bare minimum of footage, often in sequence (especially impressive, as he didn't utilize storyboards). Despite his reputation as a tough and abusive taskmaster on set, Ford was hugely respected by his actors, particularly by Wayne. Film scholars, auteur theorists, and fellow directors consider him a master to this day.

★

THIS DID NOT RESEMBLE a John Ford production. Having already directed literally dozens of films, *Mister Roberts* was to be an adaptation of a popular stage play, starring Henry Fonda, James

Cagney, William Powell, and Jack Lemmon. It was a big project, partially shot on location in Hawaii, but Ford—in contrast to his normal demeanor on set—was treating it much like a vacation. First of all, he was drinking. Second, he was drinking a lot. This had rarely ever happened on the job. Yes, there was that time on *Arrowsmith* when he went on a bender to Catalina and got canned, but that was more than twenty years ago, and had proven to be an anomaly.

Ford's immigrant Irish father had been a saloonkeeper, so it is not altogether surprising that Ford developed the drinking habit. That his binges were severe and prolonged wasn't a secret. But like, say, Spencer Tracy, they typically only happened between films. During Prohibition, as soon as a picture wrapped, Ford would give his wife, Mary, two thousand dollars for booze. If the bootlegger couldn't handle the order, they'd call in some friends from the Navy, who'd provide some of the 180-proof grain alcohol used to power torpedo motors. The stuff had a poisonous additive that made it unsuitable to drink, but if you were savvy enough, you could figure out how to remove most of it. Ford would mix up big batches of "torpedo juice"—grain alcohol and pineapple juice—in the tub. It might still make you sick, but it was better than nothing.

When in production, however, Ford was a consummate professional. Which is why it was so strange for him to be waddling out to the pool at the Niumalu Hotel, a towel wrapped around his waist, clearly schnockered. Betsy Palmer, the movie's female lead, was sunning herself at the time, the straps of her bathing suit pulled down off her shoulders. Ford asked if she was getting tan. But before she could answer, he pulled her top away, looked down at her breasts, and confirmed that yes, she was indeed getting a tan. He then climbed to the top of the diving board, dropped his towel, and revealed that he wasn't wearing a thing beneath—he was, in cowboy speak, unshucked.

Turned out Ford was having a bit of a breakdown. Fonda, who'd originated the part of Lieutenant Roberts in the stage production, had taken umbrage with Ford's freewheeling approach to the material, his encouraging improvisation and veering off script. Specifically, Fonda had told Ford what he was doing was "shit." Ford responded by throwing a punch. To further aggravate, Leland Hayward, who'd produced the play, was also giving Ford grief, continuously expressing his displeasure with the direction.

Ford, in turn, seemed to have decided "screw it."

It worked: A few weeks later, Ford was in the hospital with his abdomen grossly distended, having his gallbladder removed; Mervyn LeRoy had taken over direction of the film, and Ford's next film, *The Searchers,* would be considered the greatest Western of all time. ★

THIS TAKE ON John Ford's Torpedo Juice is not for the faint of heart, but not so lethal as to blow anyone out of the water. For one thing, the grain alcohol is Everclear. While it is 190-proof (about 10 proof higher than Ford's), Everclear is not used to power torpedo motors and does not contain any poisonous additives. There are a few other alterations, too, that might just keep you from sinking.

TORPEDO JUICE

1¼ OZ. EVERCLEAR 190-PROOF
   GRAIN ALCOHOL

1 OZ. UNSWEETENED PINEAPPLE
   JUICE

¼ OZ. SIMPLE SYRUP

¼ OZ. LIME JUICE

Pour all of the ingredients into a cocktail shaker filled with ice cubes. Shake well. Strain into a rocks glass filled with ice.

AVA GARDNER

1922–1990
ACTRESS

· · · · · · · · · · · · · · · · · · · ·

"A party isn't a party
without a drunken bitch
lying in a pool of tears."

Ava Gardner is best known for the sultry femmes fatales she played during the late film-noir period. Signature role: *The Barefoot Contessa* (1954). Born to a poor farming family in North Carolina, she signed a standard contract with MGM after her photographer brother-in-law submitted her portrait to the studio. With no acting experience, she immediately received voice and diction training to get rid of her Southern accent. Gardner spent years playing bit parts before landing the breakthrough role of Kitty Collins in *The Killers* (1946), with Burt Lancaster. She received her one and only Academy Award nomination for her lead role in John Ford's *Mogambo* and became Hollywood's requisite "love goddess" for a time, as Rita Hayworth's career went into decline. Gardner enjoyed a high-profile romantic life: she dated Howard Hughes, then married Mickey Rooney, Artie Shaw, and most famously, Frank Sinatra, who reportedly cried when their relationship finally ended. She had a second career in 1970s disaster movies.

---------------------- ★ ----------------------

WE HAD A WONDERFUL TIME, that was all she would say. Ava Gardner and Frank Sinatra had met before. Years ago, at Mocambo, back when she was still married to Mickey Rooney. Sinatra had led with a soft open, something to the effect of wishing he'd gotten to her first. Gardner found him charming. They'd bumped into each other a few times since, at various nightclubs, and there was the time she agreed to be a cheerleader for his charity baseball team, the Swooners. There'd even been a dinner date once, after she'd left Artie Shaw. They'd kissed a bit at the end of the evening, but he was still married to Nancy, and had kids, so she hadn't let it get too far.

This time, though, was different. They were at Darryl Zanuck's house in Palm Springs for a party. It was fall 1949. Sinatra, as usual, was flirting with her like crazy. She put up with it for a while, then reminded him once he got too pushy that he was still married. No, he insisted, he and Nancy were finished. For good. And seeing as he was now available, would she be interested in going for a drive?

Gardner grabbed a fifth of whatever for the road. While Sinatra, quite famously, had a predilection for Jack Daniel's, to Gardner the type of booze hardly mattered—it all tasted like hell to her anyway. So bottle in hand, she climbed into Sinatra's Cadillac convertible and the two of them sped off into the desert night, swigging all the way. By the time they came to a stop in the little town of Indio, the streets were deserted. Sinatra pulled her close. They kissed. And kissed. And at some point during their escalating passion, Sinatra reached into his glove compartment and pulled out a gun. Scratch that—he pulled out two guns. Both Smith & Wesson .38s. Naturally, they began to shoot up the streetlights. A hardware store window. Several rounds that ended up who knows where. Sinatra hit the accelerator and they kept on shooting, all the way back to the highway.

It was a few hours later when Sinatra's publicist, Jack Keller, received a phone call from the Indio police station. They had a story that hadn't yet reached the press—not just a story about Frank Sinatra's drunken arrest, but a story of his drunken arrest while out with a famous actress who wasn't his wife—and if Keller wanted to keep it under wraps, he would need to get to Indio fast. (The police back then were so much more amenable.). Keller immediately called a friend who managed the Hollywood Knickerbocker Hotel, borrowed $30,000, and took a charter flight out of Burbank. By early morning, he'd paid off anyone who might be inclined to talk: the cops, the hardware store owner, some poor drunk schmuck who'd been grazed by one of the bullets. Sinatra and Gardner were released without further incident.

Gardner, for her part, denied any of this ever happened. When she returned to the house she was renting in Palm Springs and her older sister Bappie asked how her night with Sinatra had been, all she said was, *We had a wonderful time.* ★

FOR A NOTORIOUSLY fierce drinker, Ava Gardner never much enjoyed alcohol. There were years in which she would wander parties two-fisted, a glass of liquor in one hand and a bottle of Coke to drown it out in the other. But however bad it may have tasted to her, what Gardner did enjoy was being drunk—in fact she loved it.

Forget wine and beer, they were way too slow. Even cocktails were too diluted. No, Gardner was a gal who liked to get hammered and get hammered fast. Her drink of choice was a concoction of her own invention that she called Mommy's Little Mixture.

MOMMY'S LITTLE MIXTURE

· ·

The recipe (which comes out different every time) is simple: dump every type of liquor you can find into a jug or pitcher or punch bowl and suck it down.

THE SUN ALSO RISES (1957)

Everybody behaves badly. Give them the proper chance," says Jake Barnes in Ernest Hemingway's acclaimed novel *The Sun Also Rises*. It's an observation that would prove true not only for the characters in the book, but also for the actors hired to play them some thirty years later.

It was 1957 and Twentieth Century–Fox, headed by Daryl F. Zanuck, arguably the last of the movie moguls, was mounting an adaptation. The story centered around disillusioned American and British expatriates adrift in post-WWI Europe. The action, such as there was, involved a booze-fueled trip from Paris to the Festival of San Fermín in Pamplona, Spain, to see the bullfights—in contemporary parlance, something of a road movie.

In the novel, folks drank and talked and sometimes wandered off together. They clung to each other and got on each other's nerves—and somewhere along the way realized the things that were supposed to be important weren't important and that they were all, as it turned out, a lost generation. During the production, everybody behaved much the same.

The script was written by old Hollywood hand Peter Viertel (*Beat the Devil, White Hunter Black Heart*), who was also a personal friend of Hemingway's. It was Viertel's idea to cast Ava Gardner as the female lead, Lady Brett, but then no good deed goes unpunished. According to Viertel, at first she loathed his screenplay. So much so that, to his annoyance, she took it to Hemingway, with whom she also was friends. Gardner had met Hemingway a couple of years earlier in Madrid. At the time of their meeting, though still married to Frank Sinatra, she was engaged in a passionate affair with the legendary Spanish bullfighter Luis Miguel Dominguín, as well as having just recovered from a tussle with some kidney stones. She and the great writer instantly became pals. Hemingway called her Daughter, she called him Papa. There was even a visit to Cuba.

Now Gardner was asking Hemingway what he thought about this latest adaptation of his work. She had, after all, already starred in two others, *The Killers* (which made her a star) and *The Snows of Kilimanjaro*. But Papa was not at one of his high points. Suffering from liver disease and told to stop drinking, he was pounding it back nonetheless—drunk and depressed and certain that all the other screen portrayals had been crap. Still, he eventually supported the script. Regarding Gardner as Lady Brett, "I guess you'll do. You've got some vestiges of class."

It was a less than enthusiastic endorsement. Even more so, considering that Gardner had drunk daiquiris with him at El Floridita and swum naked in his pool at Finca Vigía. Hemingway had even asked her for an expelled kidney stone, apparently for good luck. Her confidence in the role now shaken, Gardner would need some convincing. Certainly, Lady

Brett's promiscuity should not have been unfamiliar terrain. Gardner by this time was separated from Sinatra and dating Italian movie star Walter Chiari, but there would be others—with Ava, there were always others.

In fact, cast alongside her were Tyrone Power in the lead role of Jake Barnes and Errol Flynn as a besotted Mike Campbell. Both were former friends of Gardner, more than friends even, though time had not been kind to them. Power, after having finally fulfilled his contract with Twentieth Century, had been talked into this one last studio picture. Still, he claimed to be done with Hollywood, done with silly costumed adventures—he would be dead within two years.

As for Flynn, he, too, was done, maybe finished is more accurate. Overweight, his looks wrecked by decades of dissipation, he had lost his fortune and was a tax exile, more or less living aboard his yacht *Zaca*. Like Hemingway, his liver was shot, but he was committed to soldiering on. Flynn, too, would be dead within two years. Perhaps Fox should have called it *The Sun Also Sets*.

The film was to be shot in Morelia, Mexico, not Pamplona, Spain. The only newcomer, picked for the role of sexy young matador Pedro Romero, was twenty-seven-year-old Robert Evans. Naturally, most of the cast hated him. Zanuck himself had chosen Evans after watching him dance the tango at New York's El Morocco. Never mind that he was a Jewish American, the son of a dentist, and had never seen a bull. Zanuck had cast him against the wishes of Hemingway and the film's director, Henry King. After arriving at the hotel in Morelia, where it was a hundred-plus in the shade, Evans was introduced to the film's screenwriter, Viertel. Opening the door to his hotel room, Viertel took one look at Evans and said, "You play Pedro Romero? Uh-uh, not in my film." Then slammed it shut.

Before Evans had even shot a scene, a cable was sent to Darryl Zanuck, "WITH ROBERT EVANS PLAYING PEDRO ROMERO, *THE SUN ALSO RISES* WILL BE A DISASTER" It was signed by all the principal actors, as well as King and Viertel. Only Flynn had refused to add his name. Though given the fact that he was smashed by two every afternoon, his support only meant so much. Still, the two men would strike up a friendship, which for Errol at that period in his life meant someone to go drinking and whoring with. And that they did.

Not so surprisingly, when handed the role of a bankrupt drunk, Flynn succeeded in nailing the part. It was to be his best performance in years, some say ever. Power predicted, "Flynn is likely to walk off with an Academy Award for his work in this picture." Sadly, he was not even nominated, though he received some of the best reviews of his career.

While the young Evans and the older Flynn were out tearing up Morelia, Gardner was suffering from loneliness (Walter Chiari was not in town) and had begun insisting that Viertel sleep in her bedroom. There was nothing romantic about it, no sex involved, more that she needed something of a teddy bear to help her through the night. As Jake Barnes points out in the novel, "It is awfully easy to be hard-boiled about everything in the daytime, but at night it is another thing." Given the arrangement, it is difficult to know whether or not Viertel should be envied.

But soon enough Zanuck arrived on location to help quell all the unrest. After a few minutes of watching Evans with red cape aswirl pivoting about the bullfighting ring, Zanuck grabbed his bullhorn and shouted, "The kid stays in the picture." Almost forty years later, that line would become the title of Evans's best-selling autobiography. According to Evans, at a party later that night, he walked over to Zanuck's table and, without asking, led Gardner out onto the dance floor. They danced together for the next forty minutes, not a word between them, a defining moment that won over the entire cast. Apparently, Evans was a hell of a dancer. The requisite love affair with Gardner would soon follow.

And yet, despite having seduced another rising young actor, Gardner remained lonely and in her own strange funk. Like Power and Flynn, it seemed she, too, had become old or at least believed herself so. Another famous line of Hemingway's:

"How did you go bankrupt?" Bill asked.

"Two ways," Mike said. "Gradually, and then suddenly."

To Gardner, she had aged in a similar manner—and it was on the set of *The Sun Also Rises* that she suddenly felt old. Her wrinkles appeared to be deepening, there were rings under her eyes, hangovers hurt more than they used to. For sure the tequila wasn't helping, Gardner still knocking it back at night, creating riots in restaurants, bedding Mexican playboys, staging mock bullfights at nightclubs with famous matadors. She demanded that all roving photographers be barred from photographing her on set, while all the time peering uneasily in mirrors. She was, after all, thirty-four—the best years, it seemed, were behind her.

In this at least, Gardner was pretty much right. Regarding her fate, decades later and nearing the end, she would sum it up quite succinctly, "A lot of booze has flowed under the bridgework." Within a month after production had wrapped, she was finally granted a divorce from Sinatra.

As for the film itself, *The Sun Also Rises* no longer really holds up. In truth, it never held up—though Evans's performance was actually viewed very favorably. Maybe bullfighting is like dancing—certainly, Zanuck was one hell of a producer. In fact, witnessing Zanuck's power on set, Evans was inspired to leave acting and become a producer himself. He would go on to run Paramount (the first and only actor to head a major studio). During a legendary twenty-five-year run, he produced, among other films, *Rosemary's Baby, Chinatown,* and *The Godfather.* He became one of the defining producers of New Hollywood—picture a very tan man with sweeping hair and oversized sunglasses stepping out of a bathroom with white powder on his shirt. Prone to all manner of excess, Evans would blow through seven wives, never mind the countless actresses, models, hookers and . . . well, hookers.

But back in 1957, he was just a kid with a picture out. Later that same year, during game seven of the World Series, he spotted Ernest Hemingway in the stadium stands. Given Evans's positive reviews, he confidently strode over to say hello. Reminiscent of Viertel, Papa only offered up a quick look, then without a word turned back to Mickey Mantle at the plate. "Everybody behaves badly."

ORIGINALLY OPENED IN 1925 as the Red Spot, the Formosa Café was at first a single red trolley car. It wasn't until some twenty years later that the café hit its stride. In 1945 Lem Quon, who started out as a cook, became part owner and gave it the Chinese-American cuisine and laid-back vibe—red booths, Chinese lanterns—for which it is still known.

The old adage, "Location, location, location," rings true for the Formosa. It was located just east of what was initially "the Lot" studio but became the original United Artists Studios, then later Goldwyn Studios, then later Warner Bros. This prime placement made it a de facto backup commissary, and the procession of stars it drew during each successive ownership is astounding, as can be seen in the endless black-and-white photos that line the Formosa's walls.

Due to its longevity and studio proximity, the Formosa can boast a list of celebrity patrons that dwarfs most any joint east of the Polo Lounge: John Wayne, Marlon Brando, Marilyn Monroe, Bugsy Siegel, Sinatra, Elvis, James Dean, Ava Gardner, Clark Gable, Bogart, and Warren Beatty were proud patrons, as are more recent recruits like Johnny Depp, Nicholas Cage, and Brad Pitt.

In addition to numerous other films, the Formosa was used as a location in *L.A. Confidential*—the scene in which gangster Johnny Stompanato is out dining with the "real" Lana Turner. Vince Jung, Lem Quon's grandson, still runs the place, and unlike most other Hollywood landmarks, the Formosa has defeated numerous attempts to have it shut down or razed. ★

JUDY GARLAND

1922–1969
ACTRESS AND SINGER

"Hollywood is a strange place if you're in trouble. Everybody thinks it's contagious."

F orever an icon for her turn as Dorothy in *The Wizard of Oz*, Judy Garland was born into a vaudeville family, and performed in a trio with her two older sisters until she was a teenager. She was signed by MGM at age thirteen and soon paired up with Mickey Rooney, with whom she'd star in an eventual eight pictures (most notably 1938's *Love Finds Andy Hardy*). She was cast as Dorothy Gale in *The Wizard of Oz* (1939) when Twentieth Century–Fox refused to loan out MGM's first choice, Shirley Temple. The part helped earn Garland a special Academy Award for Performance by a Juvenile and transformed her into a major star of such films as *For Me and My Gal* (1942), which featured the big-screen debut of Gene Kelly, and *Meet Me in St. Louis* (1944). Overwhelming insecurities about her appearance led Garland to a nervous breakdown and suicide attempt in 1947. She came back with a record-breaking Broadway show in 1951, then returned to Hollywood for an Oscar-nominated performance in *A Star Is Born* (1954). There were a few more films in the years that followed, and a final Oscar nomination for Best Supporting Actress in *Judgment at Nuremberg* (1961), but increasingly Garland turned her attention to television specials and live shows in London, Las Vegas, and New York.

———————————— ★ ————————————

JUDY GARLAND WAS BOX-OFFICE GOLD. She *had* to be. When Dore Schary took over as head of production at MGM in July 1948, the studio was coming off its worst year since the Depression: just $4.2 million in profits, buoyed only by a still-strong musical division and its top star, Judy Garland. She was a valuable asset, Schary knew, but also a major headache, troubled and self-destructive. He got his first real taste of what to expect early in his tenure, when word leaked of her drunken tryst with another MGM talent, Mario Lanza.

Lanza had signed with MGM the previous year, after Louis B. Mayer had seen him perform at the Hollywood Bowl. Lanza had yet to release a picture with the studio—his first, *That Midnight Kiss*, wouldn't come out until 1949—but that didn't stop him from taking full advantage of all the benefits his new Hollywood status granted. Specifically, Lanza was bedding every woman in sight, with little regard for privacy. Sometimes he didn't even bother shutting the door to his dressing room, boasting that anyone fortunate enough to catch him in the act couldn't help but learn a thing or two. (Oh, and he was married.)

Whereas Lanza was flush with the promise of impending success, Garland was falling apart from the pressures of actually having achieved it. She'd just returned from a suspension for excessive absences during production of *The Barkleys of Broadway*. She'd self-medicate with booze and pills every morning, and even though she and Lanza weren't working on a film together, the math of their tryst was simple: fragile starlet + confident womanizer + excessive alcohol = trouble. It started on the lot, though at least it didn't move into his dressing room. Instead, they found a driver to chauffeur them into the Hollywood Hills, where they proceeded to get acquainted in the backseat.

Even though she and Lanza weren't working on a film together, the math of their tryst was simple: fragile starlet + confident womanizer + excessive alcohol = trouble.

Schary was livid when he heard the news, but again, Garland was gold, something MGM was desperate for. But the question soon became, how desperate? Garland's next project was supposed to be *Annie Get Your Gun*, yet once again she was suspended due to excessive absences. Then the same thing happened a year later, during the production of *Royal Wedding*. MGM ended its affiliation with Garland for good in 1950. Lanza didn't last much longer: MGM fired him for insubordination despite the fact that his picture, *The Great Caruso*, was the top-grossing film of 1951.

Unfortunately, for this and too many other transgressions to enumerate, Garland had gone from box office gold to perhaps tarnished silver. ★

JUDY GARLAND'S FAVORITE drink was vodka and grapefruit juice, what is essentially a Greyhound. It's not just a perfect eye-opener; when on tour her assistant kept two thermoses at the ready—one filled with pre-mixed vodka and grapefruit juice, the other with ice. Garland even kept a thermos on hand while working on *A Star Is Born*, drinking right up through the film's premiere. For that occasion, she had her dress designer fashion a hand muff large enough to hide a bottle.

GREYHOUND

. . . .

2 OZ. VODKA

5 OZ. FRESH GRAPEFRUIT JUICE

Pour vodka and grapefruit juice into a highball glass filled with ice cubes. Stir gently.

MOCAMBO

8588 SUNSET BLVD.

FORMER TALENT AGENT Charlie Morrison had no training in the nightclub arts when he created Mocambo, the legendary club that opened on January 3, 1941. Leave it to an agent to think that experience wouldn't matter—and get away with it. Well, sort of. He *did* have a partner, entrepreneur Felix Young, but for the next eleven years, Morrison was the face of the hottest spot on the Strip. Mocambo guests walked into a setting once described as a mix of "Imperial Rome, Salvador Dalí, and a birdcage." It was one of the most striking nightclubs in town. Strikingly awful, that is.

Morrison had hired costume design icon Tony Duquette to create the club's interior. Armed with around a hundred grand ($1.5 million today), Duquette set out to fashion something unique and modern. This eventually translated into a Latin American–inspired main room, walls adorned with paintings by Jane Berlandina, and a large aviary containing twenty-one parakeets, four macaws, and a cockatoo.

The aviary actually delayed Mocambo's opening, originally slated for New Year's Eve 1941. Animal-rights advocates wanted assurance that the birds wouldn't be harmed by exposure to the excessive noise. Sadly, those advocates (clearly not candidates for the Audubon society) stood down after Morrison observed that the birds were actually "enjoying themselves." Also, the owner promised to close the drapes during the day so they could get more sleep.

Featuring big band music, Mocambo quickly became the town's premiere place to dance until you dropped. Ella Fitzgerald, Perry Como, Edith Piaf, Liberace—virtually every headliner around graced its stage. Lana Turner one night dropped $40,000 on a birthday party, while Myrna Loy and Arthur Hornblow went there to celebrate their divorce. When Charlie Morrison died in 1957, leaving his wife with no money, his friend Frank Sinatra had his solo debut there and sang for the next two weeks in an effort to pay for the funeral. Lucille Ball and Desi Arnaz thought so highly of the place they modeled the Tropicana club in *I Love Lucy* after it.

Nothing quite like the Desilu stamp of approval. ★

JACKIE GLEASON

1916–1987

ACTOR AND COMEDIAN

"I'm no alcoholic; I'm a drunkard. There's a difference. A drunkard doesn't go to meetings."

Best known for an Oscar-nominated performance in *The Hustler* (1961), and ribald turns as Ralph Kramden in the TV series *The Honeymooners*, and Buford T. Justice in the 1970s camp classic *Smokey and the Bandit*. Jackie Gleason was raised by his mother in Brooklyn after his father walked out. He fell in with gangs and hung out in pool halls as a teenager, but eventually started performing at amateur nights. He was discovered by Jack Warner in 1940 while working at New York's Club 18. He landed a job as host of the CBS variety show *The Cavalcade of Stars* (1950), which was renamed *The Jackie Gleason Show* two years later. One of Gleason's recurring characters, bus driver Ralph Kramden, was spun off into *The Honeymooners*. Though only thirty-nine episodes were initially completed (not counting later revivals and specials), *The Honeymooners* became one of the most beloved shows in the history of television and remained a syndication fixture for decades. Gleason played mostly bit parts in film, but his career revived with the original *Smokey and the Bandit* (1977) and its two sequels.

---- ★ ----

WHAT BETTER WAY for two friends to spend the afternoon? In one corner was Jackie Gleason, biggest television star in the world. In the other, Toots Shor, most beloved bar owner in Manhattan. The two were squaring off in a heavyweight-title bout of boozing. Gleason, as was his custom, was armed with a fifth of scotch; Shor, with a bottle of fifteen-year-old brandy. Nothing on the line but bragging rights.

During the 1940s and '50s, Toots Shor's was the biggest sports bar and restaurant in Manhattan. Some called it a gymnasium with room service, though the health benefits were questionable. Toots, the owner, had worked his way up from bar back to bouncer to bartender, befriending the city's elite along the way. His was an affectionately insulting brand of charm—"crum-bum" was his go-to nickname—and his clientele ate it up. DiMaggio, Mantle, Sinatra, Bogart, Chaplin, Berle, Cronkite were all regulars. But few loved the place, or its proprietor, as much as Gleason. When Gleason was down on his luck, the stretch between his failure in Hollywood and his job with CBS, Shor had taken care of him: At one point Shor estimated Gleason had owed him $10,000 in loans and unpaid bar tabs. Gleason never forgot it.

Most famously, Gleason bet Shor double or nothing on his bar tab that he could beat him in a race around the block. The only stipulation was they had to run in opposite directions.

In later years, Gleason would call Shor the best friend he ever had. That didn't mean, however, that he wasn't willing to take the piss out of him from time to time. In fact, Gleason and Shor were constantly one-upping each other, always engaging in some stupid wager or another. Most famously, Gleason bet Shor double or nothing on his bar tab that he could beat him in a race around the block. The only stipulation was they had to run in opposite directions. Shor accepted. As soon as Gleason saw Shor round the corner, he hailed a cab, drove around the block, and was patiently waiting at the bar when Shor returned, huffing and puffing.

This latest drinking contest had started at noon. And by the time most of Manhattan was knocking off work for the day, both men were well into their second fifths. Gleason was talking trash about his opponent to everyone in earshot. At one point Shor had enough. "You've got the face of a pig," Shor told him. Gleason shot right back: "Well, you've got the body!" Around 6 p.m., Gleason excused himself from the table. Said he needed to the use the bathroom. He stumbled across the bar, then did a face-plant at the entrance to the dining room—right in the path of everyone who wanted to step inside. The maître d' and a waiter naturally rushed to pick him up.

"Leave him," Shor instructed. "I want 'em all to see what happens when you mess with the champ." ★

CARY GRANT

1904–1986
ACTOR

"A shot of brandy can save your life, but a bottle of brandy can kill you."

Known for his debonair, sophisticated manner, transatlantic accent, and formidable comedic talents, Cary Grant was born in England as Archibald Leach, and ran away from home as a teenager to join a troupe of acrobats. His first big break came when Mae West chose him as her leading man in *She Done Him Wrong* and *I'm No Angel* (both 1933). Grant's career skyrocketed after signing with Columbia in 1936 and starring in such films as *The Awful Truth* (1937), *Bringing Up Baby* (1938), *Only Angels Have Wings* (1939), and *His Girl Friday* (1940). Later he was known for his seminal work with Alfred Hitchcock (*Suspicion*, 1941; *Notorious*, 1946; *To Catch a Thief*, 1955; and *North by Northwest*, 1959). A savvy businessman, he was the first major star to break away from the studio system and hire himself out as an independent contractor. Grant founded his own production company in the mid-fifties, through which he made a number of his later hits, including *Operation Petticoat* (1959). Although he received two Academy Award nominations during the first half of his career—*Penny Serenade* (1941) and *None but the Lonely Heart* (1944)—he didn't take home an Oscar until 1970, when he was presented with a lifetime achievement award. Grant was married five times but hounded by rumors of homosexuality throughout his life, largely due to his close relationship with actor Randolph Scott. He was also an outspoken proponent of LSD.

———————— ★ ————————

FOR FIVE DECADES, CARY GRANT played Hollywood's consummate gentleman. His dashing looks, combined with his grace and humility, became the standard by which debonair leading men have since been judged. Add to that the slightly continental accent, the final coat to Grant's patina of real-life aristocracy.

But as we know, there's most always a gap between the person and the persona. And for Grant that gap was a yawning chasm—the pedigree behind that upper-crust accent being far less than blue blood. Grant was born Archibald Leach and raised in Bristol, where his clinically depressed mother was committed to an institution when he was ten. At the time, Grant was simply told she had gone on a long holiday. Already his father had abandoned the family for a new wife and a new baby. So adrift was young Grant that for the next twenty years he believed his mother was dead, until he found her living in an institution in the late 1930s. By then, Archibald Leach had changed his name from the one his parents had given him to his stage name, Cary Grant, and his transformation—from the goofy, insecure orphan into the avatar of worldly confidence—was nearly complete.

As he once confessed, "I pretended to be somebody I wanted to be until finally I became that person. Or he became me."

But what few would ever know, perhaps even Grant himself, was exactly who the real Cary Grant was. As he once confessed, "I pretended to be somebody I wanted to be until finally I became that person. Or he became me." Still, it's remarkable that Grant managed to overcome such childhood trauma, to stitch himself up and live the rest of his life as a movie star. Though he didn't do it alone. Rather, the threading Grant used was an unusual blend of psychotherapy, psychedelics, and good old-fashioned booze.

Having arrived in the United States at only sixteen, Grant took to drink early. In New York City, while juggling and performing acrobatics in vaudeville, he bartended at a speakeasy with his roommate, the future costume designer Orry-Kelly. Some say they owned and operated the speakeasy out of their little apartment—and that they were lovers, too (there was similar speculation regarding Grant's later "roommate" actor Randolph Scott). But Grant's sexuality is just another part of the mystery, even in those early days, when he would walk on stilts in the morning and get legless at night, drinking bootleg beer across not much more than an ironing board. He would later claim, "a man would be a fool to take something that didn't make him happy." And perhaps for him, it was a happy time.

Jump-cut thirty years later to Grant as the elegant advertising executive Roger O. Thornill in *North by Northwest*. Sitting across the table from Eva Marie Saint in that famously impeccable gray glen check Savile Row suit, sipping a Gibson martini. He was still a mystery—one of the few consistencies being his thirst. Though now, even in the throes of celebrity, he would say, "You know what whiskey does when you drink it all by yourself—it makes you very, very sad." Had Grant become a fool? On set, he would hide his liquor in his coffee cups. On the streets, he had already been extricated from two drunken-driving incidents. Soon he would wake up in the hospital with alcohol poisoning, having been discovered unconscious in the bedroom of his home. Acknowledging that he had "spent the greater part of my life fluctuating between Archie Leach and Cary Grant, unsure of each, suspecting each," he started seeing a psychiatrist in search of answers.

Unexpectedly, it would be through therapy that Grant was first exposed to LSD. This as far back as 1957—LSD something not then or since to be found in a gentleman's handbook. Grant was striving to better understand himself and, through the Psychiatric Institute of Beverly Hills, was let into early experimental trials. Some of the other patients supposedly included Aldous Huxley, Jack Nicholson, Rita Moreno, and musician André Previn. He would go on more than a hundred acid trips, lauding the drug for its therapeutic benefits. "I was an utter fake . . . until one day, after weeks of treatment, I did see the light."

But what did that light reveal to our consummate gentleman star? In an interview nearing the end of his life, Cary Grant would point out, "Everybody wants to be Cary Grant." To which he added, "So do I." And so the question still remains—just who was he? ★

CARY GRANT'S TASTE for alcohol reflected both his lower-class upbringing and his upper-class screen persona. Among his favorite drinks were such British classics as a Shandy Gaff, a mixture of beer and ginger ale (basically, a poor man's Half and Half) and a Black Velvet, a mixture of beer and champagne (basically, a rich man's Half and Half). Like Archibald Leach and Cary Grant, both cocktails have something to offer.

SHANDY GAFF

6 OZ. LAGER BEER OR AMBER ALE

6 OZ. GINGER ALE SODA

Pour beer into a chilled beer mug or pint glass, add ginger ale. Stir.

BLACK VELVET

6 OZ. CHILLED STOUT

6 OZ. CHAMPAGNE

Pour stout into a chilled Collins glass, add champagne. Stir.

Note that both these cocktails can also be served layered. To create that effect, you pour the lighter beverage (ginger ale or champagne) first. Then pour the beer in slowly, over the back of a spoon. Do not stir.

STERLING HAYDEN

1916–1986

ACTOR

"Let's face it—alcohol has a million good functions."

Best-known roles: Jack D. Ripper in *Dr. Strangelove* (1964) and the corrupt police chief in *The Godfather* (1972). Sterling Hayden dropped out of high school in Maine to work as a mate on a schooner and spent the next several years sailing. He cashed in on his good looks and towering stature (he stood six-five) with modeling jobs. This led to a contract with Paramount in 1941. Hayden made just two pictures—with the studio promoting him as "the most beautiful man in the movies"—before the onset of World War II. He enlisted as a Marine and served as an OSS agent in Yugoslavia and Croatia, then returned to Hollywood after the war. He received accolades for starring roles in John Huston's *The Asphalt Jungle* (1950), Nicholas Ray's *Johnny Guitar* (1954), and Stanley Kubrick's *The Killing* (1956), but had more success as a character actor. Hayden had briefly been a member of the Communist party, and he did name names before the House Un-American Activities Committee, an action that haunted him the rest of his life. In the 1970s, he enjoyed something of a resurgence playing smaller parts for auteur directors: Coppola cast him in *The Godfather*; Altman in *The Long Goodbye* (1973); Bertolucci in *1900* (1976). Hayden divided his time between an apartment in Sausalito, a home in Connecticut, and a barge in Paris. In later years, he grew a long gray Ahab beard and frequently wore a biblical robe.

★

STERLING HAYDEN HAD A SAYING: "If you're doing anything for money, you're going down. If you're doing anything only for money, you're going down perpendicularly." But now Hayden was in London on a five-week deal making a B-movie called *Venom* for a producer he thought was a "senior-grade asshole" and an angle hadn't yet been invented for how he was going down.

Venom was about an insidious criminal plot to kidnap a wealthy couple's child. The plan goes tragically awry when everyone involved is trapped in the couple's home with a supremely pissed-off black mamba snake. Clearly, this was to be real Oscar bait. Co-starring was Oliver Reed, a burly English actor with two primary ambitions in life, "to drink every pub dry and to sleep with every woman on earth." Basically, Hayden was getting paid fifty grand a week to hang out with a drunken Reed, whose main amusement on set (apart from the booze) was calling their other costar Klaus Kinski "fucking Nazi bastard" at every opportunity. Which might have been fun, had Hayden not just gone on the wagon—yet again.

He also had two books to his name: an autobiography, *Wanderer*, and a novel, *Voyage*. But both of those were written in what he called the "alcoholic style of life," which he'd had to give up for health reasons, and which he now thoroughly missed.

Hayden had been off the studio radar for some time, though really he'd only ever had one foot in it to begin with. An incurable drifter, he'd only gotten into pictures in the first place as a way of financing a boat he wanted to purchase. He never really bought into the system, and the system, in turn, never really bought into him. But by the 1970s, a new generation of directors—including Francis Ford Coppola, Robert Altman, Bernardo Bertolucci—who knew Hayden from such films as Stanley Kubrick's *Dr. Strangelove* and Nicholas Ray's *Johnny Guitar*, and who revered him for his eccentric, bohemian lifestyle (he once lived on a barge on the Seine called the *Who Knows?*), were eager to hire him.

So it's not as if Hayden *needed* this *Venom* thing. He also had two books to his name: an autobiography, *Wanderer*, and a novel, *Voyage*. But both of those were written in what he called the "alcoholic style of life," which he'd had to give up for health reasons, and which he now thoroughly missed. To Hayden, who in WWII had received a Silver Star, a commendation from Marshal Tito, as well as a Bronze Arrowhead for parachuting behind enemy lines, quitting booze "made combat look like going down an elevator."

But what the hell—just because he'd written two books under the influence of alcohol didn't mean he needed it. Besides, what else was he going to do in his London hotel room? So one night, around 3 a.m., he sat down and started writing a new autobiography. He hadn't had a drink in three or four months, but to his surprise, the writing felt *great*. So great, in fact, he figured he might as well—nah, he shouldn't. Well, on second thought, why not—two double shots would be a great way to celebrate his sober literary prowess.

Three days later, Hayden informed *Venom*'s director that he was too drunk to continue on the picture. And just like that, he was gone. *Venom* would be his last film. ★

WILLIAM HOLDEN

1918–1981
ACTOR

"I don't really know why, but danger has always been an important thing in my life."

A clean-cut and traditionally handsome (on screen, anyway) leading man, William Holden established himself as a serious talent with the Oscar-nominated starring role in Billy Wilder's *Sunset Boulevard* (1950). Holden won the Academy Award three years later, for his performance as a prisoner of war in *Stalag 17*. He headlined numerous war pictures through the 1950s—*The Bridges at Toko-Ri* (1954), *The Bridge on the River Kwai* (1957)—while also proving himself as a romantic lead. His career hit a lull in the 1960s but was resurrected with his appearance in Sam Peckinpah's *The Wild Bunch* (1969). Holden received his third and final Oscar nomination (for Best Supporting Actor) as a television news executive in *Network* (1976). He divided his time between Hollywood, a home in Switzerland, and a wildlife preservation in Kenya, of which he was a partner. A dedicated boozer, he was convicted of vehicular manslaughter for a 1966 drunk-driving accident in Italy. And in 1981 he bled to death in his Santa Monica home after cracking his head on a table in a drunken fall.

———————— ★ ————————

FOR ALL SHE KNEW, this was typical. Kim Novak was still new to Hollywood. In the last year (her first in the business) she'd made three pictures, and this one, *Picnic*, looked like it might be the biggest yet. After all, she was starring opposite William Holden—the same William Holden she and a gathering crowd in Hutchinson, Kansas, could now see some fourteen stories up at the Baker Hotel, dangling from a windowsill.

Holden had always been something of a

daredevil. As a boy growing up in Pasadena, he'd once crossed the famed Colorado Street "suicide bridge" (where many local residents jumped to their deaths during the Depression) walking on its outer railings . . . *on his hands.* The only thing that ever truly frightened Holden was acting, and for that he had alcohol. Billy Wilder once told a *Time* reporter that Holden was an "inhibited boy" and that he drank to "pull himself together." He routinely took two shots of whiskey before a scene. And his office at Columbia was fully stocked at all times with top-shelf liquor, making it one of the most popular hangouts on the lot. Dean Martin, unsurprisingly, was a frequent guest, but there was no shortage of heavy drinkers to chum around with. Sterling Hayden was a dear friend, as was Dana Andrews. Ronald Reagan was a good pal, too, though far more temperate.

In fact, Dana Andrews tells a story about a night when Holden, Reagan, and he went to dinner following a Screen Actors Guild meeting. All three friends ordered drinks and chatted away. When the waiter returned, Holden and Andrews ordered a second round. Reagan was perplexed, "Why do you want another drink? You just had one." As Andrews would later point out, "See what happened—Bill and I became alcoholics, and Ronnie became President of the United States."

Of course hindsight is 20-20. Novak wouldn't find out until many years later what Holden was doing dangling up there on the fourteenth-floor windowsill of the Baker Hotel. As a newcomer, she didn't feel it was her place to question the leading man. But what she would eventually learn was that, on that day, Holden's natural courage had been amped with a healthy dose of liquid courage—in the form of martinis, to be specific. It seems he and the director of *Picnic,* Josh Logan, were discussing the film's final scene, in which Holden's character, Hal, says good-bye to Novak's character and jumps aboard a moving train. Holden was trying to convince Logan they could do it all in one unbroken shot—and that he could personally perform the stunt. Logan refused to consider it; it was too dangerous. So to prove his point, Holden jumped out the window of Logan's suite and hooked his elbow over the sill. Actress Rosalind Russell, who was there, too, begged him to come back inside, but this only caused Holden to hang by his hands. Logan turned away, refusing to look. There were pleas to reenter, as Holden started to lift his fingers one at a time, until he clung by just two. Logan, too, now begged Holden to come back inside. Holden told him he'd only do so if Logan looked. Finally, Logan did. ★

CIRO'S

8433 SUNSET BLVD.

A FEW YEARS AFTER entering the night-club business with the ultra-exclusive Café Trocadero, *Hollywood Reporter* founder Billy Wilkerson cemented his status as impresario of the Sunset Strip with this swank playground for the industry elite. Taking over the space that once housed Club Seville—a garish and ill-fated monstrosity where patrons were wowed (or not) by the prospect of dancing the night away on a glass floor laid atop a pool filled with live carp—Ciro's opened in January 1940 to the same steady thump of self-generated publicity Wilkerson had employed at the Troc'.

"Everybody that's anybody will be at Ciro's," his full-page ads in the *Reporter* said, and from the start the ads were on the money. One could spy Sinatra or Bogart, Marilyn Monroe or Judy Garland, Cary Grant or Spencer Tracy, scattered among the banks of silk sofas lining the club's perimeter. Xavier Cugat was a regular headliner on the bandstand, as were Dean Martin and Jerry Lewis in the years

before they became the biggest act in show business. In 1951 a group known as the Will Mastin Trio played Ciro's as part of an Academy Awards afterparty, launching the career of its youngest member, Sammy Davis, Jr.

Given Wilkerson's background in news, it's no wonder the antics at Ciro's, real or imagined, often made it into the scandal sheets. One of the most notorious rumors, and likely just that, involved the exquisite Paulette Goddard, film star and one-time wife of both Charlie Chaplin and Burgess Meredith. Supposedly, in 1940 not long after Ciro's had opened, during dinner with European director Anatole Litvak (*The Snake Pit*), Goddard's shoulder strap popped. Some accounts described Litvak as trying to shield Goddard's exposed chest. Others would say diamonds fell to the floor. Whatever the inciting incident, it caused Litvak to drop under the table where supposedly, in full view of the other patrons, he made love to Goddard in what was described at the time as the "French fashion." This despite Litvak being Hungarian. The story caught fire and, while nobody was found to have actually witnessed the event, it would plague Goddard for the rest of her life.

Scandalous indeed—but the nightclub's crowning moment wouldn't come until years later, on April 8, 1947. No rumor, this was the night Frank Sinatra punched Hearst columnist Lee Mortimer outside the club. Mortimer had written a series of widely read columns alleging that Sinatra was a communist and a supporter of fascist dictators. This insanity had been brewing since 1945, when Sinatra began speaking out against segregation, racism, and religious bigotry. And not just speaking out in some canned magazine story; he sang about it in the Oscar-winning short film *The House I*

Live In (1945), he wrote high-profile letters to newspapers, and he performed at a high school in Indiana white students were boycotting due to a recent order of integration. In *House*, he said anyone who couldn't see these fundamental truths was either an idiot or a Nazi.

Eventually, someone decided it was time to shut him up. And Mortimer, a red-baiting Hearst stooge, almost succeeded in destroying Sinatra's career: The name "Sinatra" was uttered during at least a dozen HUAC hearings. MGM Pictures, Columbia Records, Sinatra's radio station, and his agent all dropped him within months.

Then he clobbered Mortimer at Ciro's. When Mortimer filed a lawsuit, Sinatra claimed that Mortimer called him a dago. But it was Sinatra's reputation that took a beating, and a jury trial looked sure to make things worse. Even though he settled the case, everyone in Hollywood, with the exception of his friends, thought Frank's career was over. And for the next four years, it was. ★

JOHN HUSTON

1906–1987

DIRECTOR, SCREENWRITER,
ACTOR

• • • • • • • • • • • • • • • • • • • •

*"I prefer to think of God
as not dead, just drunk."*

A director of rare breadth and impeccable taste, John Huston helmed an impossible number of Hollywood classics: *The Maltese Falcon* (1941), *The African Queen* (1951), *The Misfits* (1961), and at least a dozen more. His father, Walter Huston, was an actor, and Huston initially followed in his footsteps but turned to writing in his twenties, selling two short stories to H. L. Mencken for publication in the *American Mercury*. He landed a writing contract with Warner Bros. and earned two Oscar nominations for *Dr. Erlich's Magic Bullet* (1940) and *Sergeant York* (1941). His next script, *High Sierra* (1941)—which launched Humphrey Bogart's career—convinced Warner Bros. to allow him to direct his first feature, an adaptation of Dashiell Hammett's *The Maltese Falcon* (1941), with Bogart as the lead. It proved to be a huge hit, garnering Huston Academy Award nominations for Best Picture and Best Screenplay. Huston went on to direct the majority of his screenplays from that point forward. Against Hollywood tradition, he rarely gave his films happy endings; the journeys his heroes undertook usually ended in failure. He turned to acting in the 1960s, with notable appearances in Otto Preminger's *The Cardinal* (1963), for which he received a Best Supporting Actor nomination, and Roman Polanski's *Chinatown* (1974). In 1985, at age seventy-nine, Huston became the oldest person to receive a best director nomination, for *Prizzi's Honor*—his fifteenth nomination overall.

———————————— ★ ————————————

IT WAS A HANGOVER only a bullet could cure. That's how John Huston described it. He'd spent the night at Bogart's house because, during a party that climaxed with a game of indoor football, he'd gotten as drunk as he'd ever been in his life. Now it was morning, late morning, and he was waking up to the sound of Bogart in the other room on the phone. "Yes, Sam, he's here."

Sam? *Shit.* Sam Spiegel. The MGM meeting.

Huston, fresh off *Key Largo* and the expiration of his contract with Warner Bros., had recently agreed to partner up with German émigré Sam Spiegel to form a production company called Horizon Pictures. Spiegel, an independent producer whose biggest credit in the U.S. thus far was Orson Welles's *The Stranger,* had set up a meeting with Louis B. Mayer and other MGM bigwigs to pitch Horizon's first project: *We Were Strangers*, a feature-length adaptation of a story by *New York Mirror* reporter Robert Sylvester. Huston was slated as the writer-director, but in his drunken stupor, had forgotten all about the meeting. Spiegel had spent the entire morning on the phone looking for him before finally striking gold with Bogart.

To save time, Bogart's driver dropped Huston off at Spiegel's place, where he quickly showered, shaved, and dressed—in a suit borrowed from the much shorter Spiegel. The sleeves of the jacket rode up to Huston's elbows. "Sam, I can't do it!" Huston implored, his head pounding. "I don't even remember what the hell the story's about!" But Spiegel convinced him they at least had to show up. It wasn't wise to stand up Louis Mayer.

Huston was useless during the meeting. Apart from a "How do you do?" at the beginning and a "Good-bye" at the end, he kept his mouth shut, watching Spiegel wing the entire presentation on his own. It was, Huston said, "one of the finest demonstrations of pure animal courage I've ever witnessed." Mayer, however, didn't see it that way. He found Spiegel too "streetwise" for his taste. Huston, on the other hand—so wrecked he could barely speak—struck him as the sort of calm, cool, and collected gentleman with whom he could do business.

MGM did eventually make an offer on *We Were Strangers*, but not before Columbia made a better one. Mayer still landed Huston, signing him to a two-picture deal that resulted in *The Asphalt Jungle* and *The Red Badge of Courage.* As for Spiegel? As the producer of *The African Queen, On the Waterfront, The Bridge on the River Kwai*, and *Lawrence of Arabia,* he and his upstart company did just fine. ★

BEAT THE DEVIL (1953)

John Huston's *Beat the Devil* was a total disaster almost from the start. Maybe total disaster is a little strong, since by some miracle nobody actually ended up dead. The film, directed by Huston and featuring Humphrey Bogart, Jennifer Jones, Peter Lorre, and Gina Lollobrigida was to be shot largely on location in Ravello, Italy, a picturesque mountain village high up on the Amalfi coast.

There were some early warning signs: First, the sexy Italian actress, Lollobrigida, had never been in an English-speaking film before. This, most likely, was because she could barely speak English. Second, traveling into Ravello, the Italian chauffer driving Huston and Bogart got into a car accident. Huston was fine, but Bogart was pitched forward, cracking some teeth and badly gouging his tongue. So even before shooting commenced, the female lead couldn't speak English and the male lead couldn't speak at all. And third, to complicate things even further, neither Lollobrigida nor Bogart—nor the rest of the cast—had yet to see any of their lines. Reason being, Huston had thrown a party the weekend before the start of principal photography during which he tore up the entire script. It was a tearing-up-the-script party. Apparently, the original draft, written by Anthony Veiller and Peter Viertal, had run into trouble with the Motion Picture Production Code and besides, nobody liked it much anyway.

At the recommendation of renowned producer David O. Selznick, Huston had flown novelist Truman Capote over to Italy to write the new script on a day-to-day basis, as they shot. It should be noted that Selznick was not officially involved with the film. However, since his wife Jennifer Jones was one of the stars, he was unofficially involved—in a Selznick kind of way. Selznick happened to be one of Hollywood's most prolific memo writers. After receiving a number of such memos, Huston sent him a three-page reply. Huston numbered the pages one, two, and four. This so that Selzick would spend the rest of production looking for page three. And so the filming of *Beat the Devil* began.

Capote would work through the night and pages would be handed out to the cast in the morning. Lollobrigida would learn her lines phonetically. Bogart, until his mouth healed, would mime his lines, which would later be dubbed. Conceivably, it could have worked, had only the cast and crew not decided to embark on a bender of legendary proportions. Capote (or "Caposy," as Bogart had begun to fondly call him) soon began to feel that Bogart and Huston were trying to kill him with their dissipation. He described everyone as "half-drunk all day and dead-drunk all night," noting that "once, believe it or not, I came around at six in the morning to find King Farouk doing the hula-hula in the middle of Bogart's bedroom." It seemed Huston had not created a very productive work environment.

In Yiddish folktales, the Russian city of Chelm is depicted as a city of fools. Jennifer Jones's character in *Beat the Devil* was named Mrs. Gwendolen Chelm—an insider's wink, some believe, at what the production had become. Certainly, Huston seemed self-aware. In an interview years later he would say, "It was a bit of a travesty—we were making fun of ourselves." Some critics would see the picture as one of the first examples of camp, arguing that Huston and Bogart were hell-bent on parodying the noir classics (*The Maltese Falcon, Key Largo*) they themselves had crafted. But that didn't mean the mayhem wasn't real.

Both Huston and Capote tell a story about Bogart arm wrestling all comers in the lobby of the Hotel Palumbo. He even challenged little "Caposy," wagering five dollars. Astonishingly, Capote upped it to fifty dollars and then actually beat Bogart rather effortlessly, pushing his arm flat. Everyone was wide-eyed. "I'd like to see you do that just one more time," Bogart said. Double or nothing, but again Capote pushed his arm down. Then once more, Bogart losing a total $150. Not having it, Bogart started to wrestle around with the writer, whom Huston now considered "a little bulldog of a man." And here again, Capote somehow managed to trip Bogart, flipping the hard-boiled screen legend onto his ass and in the process hurting Bogart's elbow so badly they had stop production for three days. "Huston, we have a problem," to borrow a phrase from the production's cinematographer, Oswald Morris.

In fact, Morris himself tells another story of being sent to fetch Huston early one morning, only to get a strong whiff of smoke as he approached Huston's room. It seemed the bottom half of the bedroom door, from the doorknob to the floor, was red-hot ash. The door was cracked open enough for Morris to slip inside, where he found the director crashed out on the bed, empty bottles of Jack Daniel's, a couple of sooty ashtrays and script pages littering the floor. Apparently, an electric room heater had been pushed too close to the door and was about to set the room ablaze. Morris reached out and shook Huston's shoulder. "John, it's Ossie."

A muffled, "How's the boy?"

"John, your bedroom door is alight." Silence. Again, "John, your bedroom door is alight!"

And then, only, "Oh, how I love the smell of burning wood." As Huston rolled over and went back to sleep.

But in the end the film was finished, and nobody had died. Bogart would go on to *The Caine Mutiny* and Huston would spend another thirty years directing films. *Beat the Devil*, however, would be both a commercial and a critical flop. But then over time that, too, would change, and it is now considered something of a cult classic. As for those lines of Bogart's, the ones to later be dubbed, this was done during post-production at England's Shepperton Studios. A young British actor was hired to provide Bogart's voice, a remarkable mimic—his name was Peter Sellers. At last, a professional comedian had come on board.

ROBERT MITCHUM

1917–1997

ACTOR

"The only way to get rid of people is to out-drink them."

K nown for playing sleepy-eyed antiheroes that made him the defining star of film noir. It was once said Robert Mitchum had "an immoral face," and indeed he grew up a troublemaker. He rode boxcars across the country as a teen, and as young man served time on a Georgia chain gang for vagrancy. Moving to Long Beach, California, in 1936 Mitchum landed bit parts in Westerns and B-movies, and finally gained notice with a supporting role in *30 Seconds Over Tokyo* (1944). Mitchum earned an Oscar nomination for Best Supporting Actor—the only nomination of his career—for *The Story of G.I. Joe* (1945) but was drafted into the army shortly after the film's completion. He returned to acting after an eight-month enlistment, kicking off his film noir period that included, among others: *Undercurrent* (1946), *Pursued* (1947), *Crossfire* (1947), and *Out of the Past* (1947)—the last considered one of the genre's best. Mitchum spent six weeks on a prison farm after an arrest for marijuana possession in 1948, but the ensuing publicity— *Life* published a pictorial with him in a prison uniform—had no negative impact on his popularity. His chilling performances as a duplicitous preacher in *The Night of the Hunter* (1955) and vengeful ex-con in *Cape Fear* (1962) are among the most memorable of his career. Final roles included narrating 1990 Western *Tombstone* and minor parts in Martin Scorsese's *Cape Fear* remake (1991) and Jim Jarmusch's *Dead Man* (1995).

———————— ★ ————————

IT IS REALLY A SIMPLE RULE, you drink a lot, you piss a lot. Robert Mitchum, Mitch to pals, drank a lot. He also fought a lot and screwed a lot. He also pissed a lot.

The title of Lee Server's wonderful biography, *Baby, I Don't Care* (taken from a line in Mitchum's noir masterpiece *Out of the Past*) is a perfect encapsulation of the star's utter and complete indifference to his own career. When asked about his celebrity status, Mitch would point out that Rin Tin Tin, one of the biggest stars in the world, was really just a four-legged bitch. Before McQueen, Marvin, or Eastwood, Mitchum was the original bad-boy outsider and one of the coolest cats Hollywood has ever known.

Mitchum was two when his father was crushed to death while working in a trainyard. By fourteen, he had already left home and was riding the rails himself. It was the Great Depression and the young teenager was jumping freight cars and sleeping in hobo jungles. Before reaching Hollywood, Mitchum's resume would include stints as a dishwasher in the Midwest, a fruit picker down South, and a coalminer in Pennsylvania. Patches of marijuana grew wild along the train tracks—"poor man's whiskey," Mitchum would call it—and he developed a fondness for it that lasted a lifetime. These were tough times. Mitchum recalls riding a refrigerator car near Idaho Falls. It was winter, ice cold outside, and all the teenager had eaten in the last twenty-four hours were frozen peaches. Having stuffed newspaper up his pant legs to keep him warm, he was sleeping when a hobo's campfire sparked to his cuffs, setting his legs ablaze and burning his only pair of trousers. As Server points out, "When you are standing with no pants under a streetlamp in Idaho in the middle of winter, trying to find some frozen clothes to steal off a clothesline," there is nowhere to go but up.

None of this, by the way, is an excuse for all the pissing that Server describes later. It's just a little context, before jump-cutting from the boy to the man—1948, Mitchum at thirty-one years old and very much a star. He and his wife Dorothy were visiting New York City when he received a call from David O. Selznick, the producer of *Gone with the Wind* and, along with RKO, the co-owner of Mitchum's contract. Selznick was adapting Ibsen's *A Doll's House* and had a role to discuss. Mitchum was to come to the Hampshire House at 3 p.m. And so, in typical Mitchum fashion, he found the nearest bar and had a couple of drinks. Then heading off down the street, he bumped into screenwriter Herman Mankiewicz and the two popped into another bar for a few more drinks. Finally making it to the Hampshire House, he ran into a friend in the lobby and together they had a few more still. By the time Mitchum rolled into Selznick's suite, he was very loaded. Selznick hustled out past receptionists, publicists, and writers to meet one of his stable's finest thoroughbreds. He offered the actor yet another drink and Mitch, perhaps unwisely, opted for a double scotch and water. It was then, locked in a chair in a hotel room, listening to the great producer play the great producer—Selznick pitching on and on—that Mitchum realized he had to relieve himself. But there was no stopping Selznick's endless enthusiasm for the brilliant Norwegian playwright Henrik Ibsen, even more so when paired with an A-list director and an A-list star—blah, blah, blah. While Mitchum, feeling his bladder extend and extend some more, at last and to Selznick's astonishment—unzipped his fly, leaned to one side, and much like a thoroughbred, hit the Hampshire House carpet with a strong cord of urine. Then Mitchum stood up, thanked the producer, and wobbled off. Suffice to say, he didn't get the part.

Another story, another producer—this more than five years after the Hampshire House incident. Mitchum was filming Charles Laughton's dark directorial triumph, *The Night of the Hunter*. By the end of production, the picture was way over budget and relationships were strained. In part, this was due to Mitchum's drinking and drugging. There had been times when Laughton had been unable to shoot the star's scenes. To the producer Paul Gregory, despite Mitchum's charm, the star had begun to resemble the frightening preacher he was playing—*LOVE* tattooed across one set of knuckles, *HATE* the other. During one of the finals days of shooting, Mitchum showed up bombed, his face swollen, his eyes red, yet still insisting he could act. Laughton phoned Gregory, who raced over to the location in his Cadillac convertible to try to handle the situation. Already at the end of his rope and not interested in sugarcoating, Gregory let loose on Mitchum. The producer argued that the star was in no shape to perform. It was then, as Gregory would tell Server, that Mitchum unzipped his fly and pulled out his penis. The door of the Cadillac was open and Gregory stepped back as Mitchum moved behind it. Gregory assumed this was out of modesty. But suddenly, that strong cord of urine began to rain down on the driver's seat, where the producer had just been sitting, creating a puddle. Mitchum zipped back up. As with Selznick, he wobbled off.

Before McQueen, Marvin, or Eastwood—Mitchum was the original bad-boy outsider, the first sleepy-eyed hipster, and one of the coolest cats Hollywood has ever known.

There were other incidents, of course. In France, the press asked Mitchum if he knew any French. "Cognac," Mitchum responded. Then later, he took a leak in the street, apparently right under a sign which read, in French, DO NOT PISS IN THE DOORWAY. In Ireland, trapped for months in Dingle for *Ryan's Daughter,* Mitchum had little to do but drink with costar Trevor Howard (by all accounts a first-rate inebriate) and horse around with leading lady Sarah Miles. Miles, curiously, was a practitioner of urine therapy, and accordingly drank her own urine. But that had little to do with Mitchum's behavior. One day, he was stranded in mud for over an hour waiting for the legendary—and legendarily tyrannical—British director David Lean to finish another scene. Mitchum held off until the next time he was sure cameras were rolling, then once again, he unzipped and let loose.

It is a simple rule—you drink a lot, you piss a lot—and clearly, one of the few that Mitchum followed. ★

ROBERT MITCHUM WAS by and large a vodka man. He would hide it around the set—in tall glasses, neat, so that it looked like water. He liked smoking joints, too, some said up to eight a day. But in the morning it was bourbon. Mitchum's hangover cure, discovered in his personal guest file at the Beverly Hills Hotel, was bourbon and orange juice blended with honey and egg. It hovers somewhere between a hangover cure and an eye-opener, embracing the stay-drunk philosophy. It actually tastes better than it sounds, but then, it sounds awful.

MITCHUM'S EYE-OPENER

2 OZ. BOURBON

3 OZ. FRESHLY SQUEEZED ORANGE JUICE

1 OZ. HONEY

1 RAW EGG

Put all ingredients into a blender, add a scoop of ice. Blend on high for several seconds until universally combined. Pour into a double Old-Fashioned or a Collins glass.

NOT AS A STRANGER (1955)

When producer Stanley Kramer decided the time had come for him to take a seat in the director's chair, he went big. With such hits as *High Noon* and *The Wild One* to his credit, he acquired the rights to Morton Thompson's *Not as a Stranger*, a medical melodrama nearly a thousand pages in length that was one of the best-selling novels of 1954. For his cast, he assembled a collection of heavy-hitters few could match: Robert Mitchum, Olivia de Havilland, Frank Sinatra, Gloria Grahame, Broderick Crawford, Charles Bickford, and Lon Chaney, Jr.

Once filming finally got underway, it was clear Kramer had little idea what he'd gotten himself into: An experience he would later describe as "ten weeks of hell." Mitchum, Sinatra, Crawford, and Chaney were four of the most fearless drunks in the business—and they quickly proved uncontrollable. Sets and trailers were demolished. Stars tearing phones from walls. "It wasn't a cast," Mitchum said, "so much as a brewery." Myron McCormick, who played Dr. Snider, would pass out during takes, wake up screaming, then tumble off the set.

And then there was the fighting. One night, after shooting had wrapped for the day, Kramer begged his cast to go home and get a decent night's sleep, as they had an important scene scheduled for the next morning. Later, on his drive home, he passed a bar near the studio where three or four of his actors were gathered outside—two of them pummeling each other. Then there was the day Crawford, teased one too many times by Sinatra (who used to call him Lenny, after the mentally handicapped character in *Of Mice and Men* he'd played on Broadway), held the singer down, tore off his toupee, and proceeded to *eat* the damn thing. When Mitchum tried to intervene, Crawford wound up belting him and then *they* went at it until Crawford, his throat lousy with artificial hair, started choking and one of the medical advisors had to rush over to help him puke it up. Shooting had to be temporarily delayed while Sinatra acquired a new rug.

But yet again, *Not as a Stranger* was every bit the success Kramer had hoped for. It was the fifth-highest-grossing picture of the year and highest of Mitchum's career.

· ·

DAVID NIVEN

1910–1983
ACTOR AND WRITER

· ·

"Champagne offers a minimum of alcohol and a maximum of companionship."

Best known for light, wry roles—*The Pink Panther* (1963), *Murder By Death* (1976)—and a courtly, sophisticated persona. Born into a family of British soldiers, David Niven served with the Highland Light Infantry in Malta and Dover before resigning out of boredom. He came to Hollywood in the early 1930s, spent the decade playing bit parts, and subsequently returned to the British army in 1939 and served for the duration of World War II. For a short period, he and pal Errol Flynn shared a house in Malibu dubbed Cirrhosis-by-the-Sea. His American career took off with the lead in *Around the World in 80 Days* (1956), which he followed in 1958 with an Oscar-winning performance in *Separate Tables*. Niven would also go on to host the Academy Awards on three occasions. He appeared in more than thirty films over the next twenty-five years, in addition to completing two bestselling memoirs and two novels.

———————————— ★ ————————————

EVER THE SOLDIER, DAVID NIVEN was simply following orders. In 1938, when John Ford took him aside on his twenty-eighth birthday and told him he should celebrate by getting drunk, Niven felt he had no choice. After all, Ford was a director known to be intimidating, if not at times downright mean.

They were in the middle of shooting *Four Men and a Prayer*, a mystery in which Niven had a small part playing the son of a colonel in the British Indian Army, and he wasn't scheduled for much the next day. Nothing a hangover would interfere with, at least. So Niven went out with Errol Flynn, his former housemate, on a pub crawl of epic proportions.

But when morning rolled around, as mornings tend to do, there seemed to be a problem—a big one. Ford didn't have any memory of the conversation whatsoever. And how *dare* this limey—that's the term Ford used—show up for work still drunk from the night before! In fact, so furious was Ford that he sent for producer Darryl Zanuck—let the boss deal with this. It seemed clear to Niven that if he didn't sober up quick, he might be out of a job.

In truth, a similar situation had occurred on an earlier Ford production, *The Informer*. Its star, Victor McLaglen, had been particularly anxious about a climactic scene in which he had to defend himself to his best friend's IRA pals. The night before the scene was scheduled, Ford had taken McLaglen aside and told him it was postponed. Why not go out that night and relax? It would do him some good. In fact, there was a party some of Ford's friends were planning to attend and McLaglen should tag along.

Much like Niven, McLaglen had taken Ford at his word. The next morning—early—McLaglen received a call at his hotel telling him that the scene was back on the schedule and he needed to report to set immediately. McLaglen was in no shape for it, but he somehow fought his way through. He won an Academy Award for the performance the following year. In that case, Ford—who knew all along the scene was still scheduled—was trying to bring out the best in an actor overwhelmed with anxiety.

In Niven's case, however, Ford was just bored. He was under contract to Twentieth Century–Fox and not especially enthusiastic about *Four Men and a Prayer*. It was one of those experiences he referred to as a "job of work." He had to get his kicks when he could. There wasn't any anxiety he wanted to help Niven work through—he just felt like a cheap laugh at the kid's expense.

The scene Niven had to film that morning was simple: all he had to do was bandage the arm of costar George Sanders, whose character had just been shot. But when Zanuck arrived and demanded to see a take, well, that made it a challenge. What's more, Ford was upping the ante: he suddenly wanted Niven in a white coat, with a first-aid kit added as a prop. On cue, Niven was now supposed to reach into his coat pocket for a stethoscope while also opening the first-aid kit. He was either to do this—or else.

At "action," Niven grabbed the stethoscope by its tubing and pulled it out of his pocket. Only it wasn't tubing he grabbed—it was the body of a snake. Niven immediately dropped it, trying his best to remain focused. But then he opened the first-aid kit, which was filled with tiny green turtles. It was too much. Niven shrieked, flinging the kit into the air. Behind the camera, Ford yelled, "Print it!" The Niven gag reel was a staple of Ford parties for years to come. ★

HOTEL BEL-AIR
701 STONE CANYON RD.
OPEN!

EVEN IN A CITY with no shortage of celebrity-friendly hotels (Beverly Hills Hotel, Chateau Marmont), the ultra-exclusive Hotel Bel-Air exists in a category all its own. A secluded hideaway in the hills just north of UCLA, this twelve-acre, 103-room resort has been the choice lodging of the world's most famous figures for more than sixty years. Not just movie stars: cultural icons as well. Howard Hughes stayed there; so has Oprah Winfrey. Grace Kelly stayed the night she won the Oscar for *Country Girl* and was such a regular, they named a suite after her. So discreet is the staff, that at one point, the three surviving Beatles (McCartney, Harrison, and Starr) all stayed at the hotel unaware that their

former bandmates were there, too. Cary Grant, Lauren Bacall, Jimmy Stewart, and Marilyn Monroe have all been among the hotel's honored guests.

Founded by Texas entrepreneur Joseph Drown in 1946, the Bel-Air was built on the far end of the personal estate of oil magnate Alphonzo Bell, who in 1921 purchased more than 1,700 acres of land in west Los Angeles, 600 of which he intended to develop as a new neighborhood catering to the film-industry elite. (Not that he'd sell to just anyone: When William Randolph Hearst went house-shopping for his mistress, Marion Davies, Bell—a devoutly religious man and also a business rival of Hearst—refused to accommodate the man.)

Construction began with the conversion of what had been Bell's sales office. A stable the family owned, once used to store horses that appeared in cowboy movies, became one of the more popular guest suites. What had been a riding ring was turned into a pool. When Bell's son Alphonzo, Jr., met Marlene Dietrich at a Palm Springs party years later, he had to fight back the urge to let her know her favorite room had once been a manure depository. (That's Hollywood for you—turning horseshit into gold.)

One particular story, involving Elizabeth Taylor and Michael Jackson, pretty effectively sums up the Hotel Bel-Air experience. It seems one night in 1990, Taylor and Jackson were scheduled to meet for dinner at the hotel's restaurant. Taylor arrived on time, but Jackson kept her waiting for an hour. She waited patiently for a while, eating caviar and drinking champagne, but by the time Jackson finally arrived, she was livid. Her anger only intensified when she found out the reason for his tardiness: He'd been sitting in the parking lot the whole time, on the phone in his Rolls Royce, talking to Jackie Onassis. "I will not play second fiddle to any woman," she barked, "not even *that* woman."

Jackson, as a peace offering, reached into his coat and took out a pair of turquoise earrings—they were loose in his pocket—embedded with diamonds. Taylor snagged the earrings, gathered her belongings, and stormed out without saying another word.

Presently owned by Hassanal Bolkiah, the Sultan of Brunei, after a two-year renovation (at an unconfirmed cost of $100 million), the hotel reopened in 2011 to much acclaim. Actor Robert Wagner perhaps put it best, "They just take care of people—the very best way they can be taken care of." ★

JACK PALANCE

1919–2006

ACTOR

"Alcohol, after all, is good for nothing except when you need a bullet removed from your behind."

B est known for tough-guy roles in Westerns and noirs (*Shane, Sudden Fear*) and for his one-handed push-ups after winning the 1991 Best Supporting Actor Oscar. Jack Palance worked in the Pennsylvania coal mines and briefly as a boxer before entering the Army Air Forces in World War II. After studying drama at Stanford postwar, his big break came as Marlon Brando's understudy in the Broadway production of *A Streetcar Named Desire* (1947). His first movie role was *Panic in the Streets* (1950). Palance was nominated for an Oscar as Best Supporting Actor for his third movie, *Sudden Fear* (1952), as well as his fourth, *Shane* (1953). He became a fixture of action movies and Westerns over the next several years, also playing a Hollywood producer in Jean-Luc Godard's *Le Mépris* (1963, released in America as *Contempt*). Having achieved early success in television, winning a Best Actor Emmy in 1957 for a *Playhouse 90* production of *Requiem for a Heavyweight,* he returned to the medium as his film career slowed. Palance's tenure as host of *Ripley's Believe It or Not* (1982–1986) put him back in demand as an actor, a resurgence that culminated with his third Oscar nomination and first win for a supporting role, in *City Slickers* (1991).

———————————— ★ ————————————

THEY SHOULD PROBABLY HAVE called it a night hours ago. The evening had begun, after all, with a brawl at a charity dinner set up by RKO's publicists. (The dinner, that is, not the brawl.) Jack Palance and Robert Mitchum, currently in Mexico City filming *Second Chance,* were supposed to present the local chapter of Boys Town with a $5,000 donation on the studio's behalf. That part of the event had gone just fine. But then some American college students showed up, and one of them, eager to see just how tough a guy Mitchum really was, challenged him on the way to the men's room. Mitchum, of course, laid him out. When the kid's friends decided to make a bigger issue of it, Palance and Mitchum were ushered out the back door—and taken (for some inexplicable reason) straight to a nightclub on the Reforma.

So began round two.

There'd been drinks at the dinner, of course, and more at the club. Mitchum's wife, Dorothy, had tagged along, as had Emilio "El Indio" Fernández, a famous actor and director of Mexican cinema. The trouble began when a drunken general approached the group's table. Palance and Mitchum would offer differing versions of exactly what happened next. Mitchum said the general hit Fernández in the head with the butt of a .45. Palance told Mitchum biographer Lee Server that the general tried to hug him (Palance)—and that he'd pushed him—and the general, being drunk, had fallen. However it actually happened, as Palance would note, "suddenly there was this big drama going on."

And by "drama," he meant "machine guns."

> However it actually happened, as Palance would note, "suddenly there was this big drama going on." And by "drama," he meant "machine guns."

Two machine guns, courtesy of the general's entourage. By the time bullets started to fly, Mitchum and Dorothy were already in the limousine. Palance was still inside—though not for long. He picked up a table, hurled it at one of the general's men, then hurried through the kitchen, while Fernández, who apparently also had quite a temper and carried a pistol at all times, provided cover. Once Palance was out, Fernández followed. Mitchum said Fernández made it to the limousine and promptly collapsed—"a delayed knockout from the general's strike."

It was now time for Palance to disappear. The general, not surprisingly, had a nasty reputation (false arrests, torture), so Palance switched hotels, registered under an assumed name, and kept as low a profile as possible until RKO spread enough money around to make the problem go away.

"Of course, when I got back to the States," Palance later said, "I found old Mitchum had taken all the credit for my rescue." ★

ANTHONY QUINN

1915–2001

ACTOR

"*Life is what you do, till the moment you die.*"

Known for exotic starring roles, Anthony Quinn was born in Chihuahua during the Mexican Revolution (his father rode with Pancho Villa). He moved with his family to El Paso, then to Los Angeles, where his father found work as a cameraman. Initially, he went into acting as a way of overcoming a speech impediment. By his early twenties, he had befriended both John Barrymore and W. C. Fields, becoming the youngest member of the Bundy Drive Boys and making his big-screen debut in *Parole!* (1936). He appeared in more than fifty films over the next decade—primarily in "ethnic" roles—before Elia Kazan cast him as Stanley Kowalski in a lengthy touring stage production of *A Streetcar Named Desire* (1948). Quinn returned to movies in the early 1950s and won his first Oscar for Best Supporting Actor opposite Marlon Brando in Kazan's *Viva Zapata!* (1952). He won a second such Oscar with his brief performance in the Van Gogh biopic *Lust for Life* (1956) and was nominated as Best Actor the following year for *Wild Is the Wind*. Quinn reached the pinnacle of his career in 1964 with what became his trademark role, *Zorba the Greek*, for which he received yet another Oscar nomination as Best Actor. He continued to work until his death, with parts in *Jungle Fever* (1991) and *Last Action Hero* (1993). Quinn was also an accomplished painter, with numerous international exhibitions, and the author of two memoirs.

★

ANTHONY QUINN WAS DOING HIS BEST to keep it together, but it wasn't easy. Quinn, Errol Flynn, and Gene Tierney were doing a live radio broadcast promoting war bonds and blood drives in St. Louis.

Quinn hated this kind of crap, hated selling himself to the public, especially when it involved travel. So the night before, he and Flynn (a fellow Bundy Drive Boy) had gone out and gotten all tore up, finally climbing into bed just before dawn. At around seven in the morning, Flynn—chipper as a jaybird, somehow—wandered into Quinn's room and told him the radio spot, originally scheduled for 11 a.m., had been moved up, and they had to get to the studio immediately.

So now here Quinn was in the broadcast booth, head pounding, trying to get through this whole business as quickly as possible. "You go to a place, you give a pint of blood, it's very simple," he said into the microphone. "They give you a very nice big glass of milk afterward—"

"Is there brandy in it?" Flynn suddenly chimed in.

"I beg your pardon?" Quinn replied. What the hell was Flynn doing?

"Is brandy in the milk? They call that a Velvet Cow in Australia."

Quinn tried to steer the conversation back to the blood drive, but Flynn was just getting started. "As a matter of fact," Flynn went on, "you know this program" (meaning the radio show they were appearing on), "you know damn well it's a lot of crap." He was on a roll now. He referred to Quinn as "this fucking Indian" and "the son-in-law of that son-of-a-bitch Cecil B. DeMille." (Quinn was married to DeMille's daughter Katherine.) Of Tierney, Flynn said into the mic, she was a "real fucking sweetheart" and that he had no intention of sleeping with her, "but if she would like to try to change my plans, I would be open to suggestions." Quinn couldn't believe what he was hearing. Neither could the studio director, who stormed into the control room, demanding they be taken off the air. Flynn responded by wrestling the man to the ground.

By the time Quinn returned to his hotel, word of the radio fiasco had apparently already reached Hollywood. Louella Parsons and Hedda Hopper had both left messages. DeMille—to whom Quinn rarely spoke to apart from work and family functions—called to tell him how badly this reflected on the family, and how he worried Quinn wasn't serious enough to have a real career. Then his wife Katherine called, then Quinn's agent. And then, lastly, Flynn called—apparently, he had one thing he needed to say.

"Gotcha, Tony."

The whole thing—the early start time, the lack of script, the profanity, the fight, the phone calls—had been one big ruse orchestrated by Flynn. They were never on the air.

Quinn was relieved. Because not only was his career not in peril, but if all these important people were willing to go to this much trouble to prank him, his career must be going pretty damn well. ★

VILLA CAPRI
1735 N. MCADDEN PL.
6735 YUCCA ST.

IT'S NOT HARD TO GUESS how the modest Italian joint Villa Capri became one of Hollywood's favorite haunts when it launched in 1950: the owner, Patsy D'Amore, was generally thought to cook the best pizza west of the Hudson after he opened his Farmers Market booth in 1949. Frank Sinatra liked it so much he became a partner in the restaurant. With him came the usual suspects, the Bogarts and Bacalls, the Garlands and the Lufts, the Joey Bishops and the Bobby Darins. But it was a relatively unknown actor who became the restaurant's most famous patron.

During the short time between his arrival in Los Angeles (1954) and his death (1955), James Dean became such a fixture at Villa Capri that he had a booth

permanently reserved for him. Once he got famous, he entered through the back door, and if he didn't find any of the Rat Pack at the restaurant, he'd sit alone, smoking and drinking scotch and water. At the time of his death, Dean was even living in a house he'd rented from the restaurant's maître d'. Dean's passing drew legions of fans to the place.

Villa Capri moved to Yucca Street in 1957, and Sinatra hosted his radio show there for a couple of years. The restaurant closed in 1982, but D'Amore's daughter Filomena still serves her father's recipe at the Farmer's Market, using the same red-brick oven they've had since 1949. ★

NICHOLAS RAY

1911–1979
DIRECTOR

"I haven't had a drink for fifteen months. If I had, I would be dead now, and that would make me furious."

D arling of auteur theorists, Nicholas Ray created stylish paeans to the alienated and disaffected that were a huge influence on Jean-Luc Godard, Wim Wenders, and Jim Jarmusch (Ray's assistant at the time of his death). A Wisconsin native, he studied architecture with Frank Lloyd Wright as a Taliesin Fellow before transitioning into theater. He moved to New York in 1932, where he came under the tutelage of Elia Kazan and John Houseman. Ray directed his first Broadway production in 1946, and his first feature, the Houseman-produced *They Live by Night*—considered a forerunner of *Bonnie and Clyde* and *Badlands*—the following year. (*Night* would be remade by Robert Altman as *Thieves Like Us* in 1974.) He directed Bogart in one of his most underrated performances, *In a Lonely Place*, in 1950, and in the mid-fifties directed his two signature pictures: *Johnny Guitar* (1954) and *Rebel Without a Cause* (1955). But Ray's proclivity for alcohol and drugs resulted in his marginalization within the industry. He was dismissed as director of *55 Days at Peking* (1963) after collapsing on set and never completed another feature. He turned to academia in the 1970s, teaching at Binghamton University, the Lee Strasberg Institute, and NYU.

———————————— ★ ————————————

THOUGH THE ICONIC 1955 film *Rebel Without a Cause* now plays like a quaint relic, the story of the man who directed it grows more unlikely (and insane) with each passing year. Such was the life of Raymond Nicholas Kienzle, known to cinema buffs as Nicholas Ray. Ray's filmography is a study in intelligent and ambitious eccentricity, from the talky Bogart noir *In a Lonely Place* (one of the best films of the era; see it immediately) to the feminist Western *Johnny Guitar*, to the endless (and endlessly wacko) Jesus biopic *King of Kings*. Even his worst films were intensely personal—if nothing else, because it was no great leap to believe they'd been made by a crazy Midwesterner who'd stalk his sets always drunk, turning every obstacle into an argument. Director Jim Jarmusch, one-time student of Ray's, described him as "my idol—a legend, the outcast Hollywood rebel, white hair, black eye-patch, and a head full of subversion and controlled substances."

Predictably, the thing that makes Ray's work so great—his absolute and steadfast refusal to do anything at less than full-bore crash-and-burn intensity—made his personal life an epic mess. An example: In 1948, Ray married the actress Gloria Grahame. She gave birth to their only child six months later, which might have led people to conclude they'd gotten married because she was pregnant—except Ray had already been telling this to anyone who'd listen since the wedding was announced. It was his way of declaring his unreserved contempt for her. And instead of doing something simple—like maybe not marrying her—Ray made a further and very public display of his feelings when he gambled and lost his entire life savings playing roulette the night before their wedding because (he claimed) he "didn't want this dame to have anything of mine." That plan didn't quite work out: three years later (and still somehow married to Grahame), Ray came home to find her in bed with a teenage boy: his thirteen-year-old son, from a previous marriage. Ray moved out the next day. While Grahame would in fact marry the son, nine years later.

So yes, you'd be correct in assuming that Ray's relationship to booze wasn't confined to the occasional Mint Julep over Derby weekend. After divorcing Grahame, Ray would shack up with a woman named Hanna Axmann. A German dabbler in film acting and screenwriting, with some success, she recounted her time with Ray thusly, "The hundreds of nights I spent, with Nick drinking . . . at four or five in the morning he'd start talking nonsense; by seven he'd be more or less fresh, contemplating his feet a bit to get back to earth. Then he would go off every morning to his psychoanalyst, Dr. Vanderhyde, come back and start drinking."

> Predictably, the thing that makes Ray's work so great—his absolute and steadfast refusal to do anything at less than full-bore crash-and-burn intensity—made his personal life an epic mess.

Admittedly, Ray may have been in a dark place at the time, given the wife/son thing. Yet, consider this final example, in the fall of 1973, more than twenty years after the Grahame episode. Tom Luddy of Pacific Film Archives invited Ray to Berkeley, California, for a retrospective of the director's work. By this point, Ray was half-blind from an embolism, still near always drunk, and fond of toting a briefcase filled with needles, pills, speed, and hash. Before he arrived in Berkeley, while teaching at Harpur College at Binghamton University in New York, he and his students had shot an experimental feature called *We Can't Go Home Again*. For some reason, Ray had the notion to finish it in Berkeley. Francis Ford Coppola, who was cutting *The Conversation* at the time, offered use of his editing suite to Ray during the off-hours, from midnight to 8 a.m.

Not surprisingly, Ray immediately became a squatter at Zoetrope: sleeping in screening rooms during the day, then getting up to work in the middle of the night. It was supposed to just be a short stay, but three weeks after Ray arrived, it became apparent to Luddy that Ray had no intention of folding up his tent. Some days, they'd find Ray passed out with a bottle of Almaden Mountain Rhine wine beside him. On the rare occasion that he'd actually leave the building to go drinking, Ray would set off Zoetrope's complex security system, costing the company money with each false alarm. Adding to this, Ray started making expensive phone calls on Zoetrope's dime. Finally, after Ray somehow broke the editing machine, Coppola pulled the plug on the arrangement.

By the time Ray left Berkeley, the only thing he'd accomplished was alienating everyone who'd tried to help him. He once asked Luddy if he knew where he could get $36,000. When Luddy said no, Ray replied, "How about six dollars? If I had six dollars, I could buy a hamburger and a bottle of Almaden." ★

LAWRENCE TIERNEY

1919–2002
ACTOR

"Heck, I threw away about seven careers through drink."

Best known to modern audiences as Joe, the gangster mastermind in *Reservoir Dogs* (1992), Lawrence Tierney had a string of tough-guy roles dating as far back as 1945. A star athlete at his Brooklyn high school, he received a scholarship to Manhattan College but dropped out to work as a laborer on the New York Aqueduct. After a few theater productions, he signed a contract with RKO in 1943. The titular role in *Dillinger* (1945) became the template for his on-screen persona, as he was continually cast as a traditional tough guy (*Badman's Territory* and *San Quentin*, 1946) to outright sociopath (*Born to Kill* and *The Devil Thumbs a Ride*, 1947). Numerous run-ins with the law for drunken behavior and fighting destroyed his career before it really even started. Landing parts here and there—John Cassavetes cast him twice, in *A Child Is Waiting* (1963) and *Gloria* (1980)—Tierney rarely worked again as an actor until the 1980s, when he was cast in a series of guest-starring roles on TV shows like *Hill Street Blues*, *Fame*, *Star Trek: The Next Generation*, and *The Simpsons*. His final film was the low-budget feature *Evicted* (2000), written and directed by his nephew.

★

THEY WEREN'T SUPPOSED TO let him drink. They had been warned. But something needed to be done. The entire cast and crew of *Reservoir Dogs* had, in one short week, come to despise Lawrence Tierney, the irascible seventy-something actor.

During the most recent day of shooting, director Quentin Tarantino and Tierney had to be physically separated from one another. When Tierney stormed off, the crew broke into applause. Tim Roth had declared he didn't even want to be in the same room with the guy. Only Michael Madsen wanted to make an effort. *Tierney had earned it, hadn't he?*

Known as one of film noir's consummate tough guys in the 1940s, Tierney claimed to loathe the parts he was given. "I thought of myself as a nice guy who wouldn't do rotten things," he once told an interviewer. But as real-life gangster Mickey Cohen once hypothesized about Tierney, reflecting on the actor's behavior after his turn as John Dillinger, "I guess when actors are given a certain part to portray, and they portray it year in and year out, they begin to play it somewhat for real."

By 1955 Lawrence Tierney had been arrested sixteen times. He spent three months in jail in 1948 for breaking a man's jaw in a gin mill. Later that year he was arrested for kicking a cop. (For good measure, he was arrested for punching one eight years later.) In 1952 he fought with a welterweight boxer outside a bar in New York City—a feat he topped in 1975 when he took on an accomplished knife fighter and wound up getting stabbed in the gut. Such was his reputation among Los Angeles police that when Robert Mitchum was awaiting trial for marijuana possession in 1948, two cops taunted the actor by saying, "Hey Bob, we're keeping Lawrence Tierney's cell warm for ya."

Tierney gave up drinking—mostly—in 1982, after he suffered a stroke. It was around that time that he finally started getting work again, primarily in television. By then, old age and sobriety had rendered him largely harmless, but he still had the ability to put the fear of God in people. His opportunity to become a recurring character on *Seinfeld* (as Elaine's dad) was probably squandered when he "jokingly" threatened Jerry Seinfeld with a butcher's knife he'd attempted to steal from the set.

And so, on the set of *Reservoir Dogs*, Michael Madsen decided to see if he could help settle Tierney down. He took the old man to Musso and Frank's for vodka tonics. Everything was going fine until Tierney excused himself to go to the bathroom—and didn't come back. Just as Madsen started to wonder what happened to him, he heard commotion outside the restaurant. Honking—lots of honking. Madsen got up to investigate. When he looked outside, there was Tierney, in the middle of Hollywood Boulevard, pants down, wagging his finger at every car that swerved past him—a miracle it was just his finger. ★

BOARDNER'S

1652 NORTH CHEROKEE AVE.

OPEN!

ON A SIDE STREET within spitting distance from Musso and Frank's, this neighborhood bar ("a local hang for the Who's Who and Who Cares") has been a hometown favorite since 1942—not quite as long as its more famous neighbors, but an unheard-of length of time by L.A. standards. The space was leased by singer Gene Austin in the early 1930s (he named it My Blue Heaven, after his biggest hit) and had already undergone three different incarnations, including those of a restaurant and a gay bar, when Steve Boardner, a longtime bartender who'd most recently manned the bar at the landmark Crossroads of the World on Sunset, took over the lease in January 1944.

A former athlete with social ties to both the sports and film worlds, Boardner brought with him a built-in crowd of celebrities, including Errol Flynn, W. C. Fields, Wallace Beery, and boxing promoters George Parnassus and Suey Welch. Members of Xavier Cugat's band would drop by, as did singers Jack Leonard and Phil Harris. (Harris, legend has it, would eat dinner with his wife at Musso and Frank's, then meet his mistress at Boardner's later that night.) A postwar mob hangout with insider protection provided by notorious L.A.P.D. lieutenant Harry Fremont, who used to play craps in the drained fountain on Boardner's patio, it was seedy enough to attract Charles Bukowski and rowdy enough to humble Lawrence Tierney, who reportedly called the cops when a wrestler pal of Boardner's had the guts to stand up to him. Such was the bar's reputation, it was even rumored to be the last known sighting of Elizabeth Short the night she died in the infamous Black Dahlia murder case.

In 1980, with failing health and accumulating debt, Boardner sold the bar to Dave Hadley and Kurt Richter, two regulars who'd made their money in porn (they were among the first to sell X-rated movies on videotape). The new owners had planned on turning it into a regular destination for employees of the adult-film industry. That plan never quite materialized, but Hadley kept the place going for more than twenty years, even after his partner died behind the bar on Christmas night in 1997. These days, Boardner's has expanded to include an additional nightclub and a full kitchen; it caters to a younger crowd with such tired standbys as Goth Night and 80s Night. But the bar still opens every day at five, the better to soak in whatever remains of its heyday. ★

JOHN WAYNE

1907–1979

ACTOR

"Tequila makes your head hurt. Not from your hangover. From falling over and hitting your head."

Strong and silent onscreen, hawkish and ultraconservative off, John Wayne transcended cinema so thoroughly he became the ultimate symbol (for better or worse) of American ideals and values. Born Marion Morrison, he adopted the nickname "Duke" as a kid. He played football for the USC Trojans until an injury ended his athletic career. After floundering in B-movies, Westerns, and serials, John Ford made him a star with his breakthrough role in *Stagecoach* (1939). Wayne and Ford went on to work together more than twenty times over the years, in such enduring classics as *She Wore a Yellow Ribbon* (1949), *The Searchers* (1956), and *The Man Who Shot Liberty Valance* (1962). Wayne won his only Oscar as Best Actor—after a prior nomination for *Sands of Iwo Jima* (1949)—for his portrayal of the flawed Rooster Cogburn in *True Grit* (1969). (Jeff Bridges would be nominated for an Oscar in the same role more than thirty years later.) Wayne is credited for directing two films over the course of his career: *The Alamo* (1960), which was nominated for Best Picture, and *The Green Berets* (1968), which came out unabashedly in favor of the Vietnam War. His humility and honesty earned him the begrudging respect of even his enemies, and he remains the most towering single image of an American ever produced by Hollywood.

★

1. MEET JOHN WAYNE. 2. Go to Disneyland. Those were the two items on Nikita Khrushchev's wish list during his 1959 visit to Los Angeles. The *only* two. So it came to pass that John Wayne

allegedly stood at a private bar, tossing back tequila and vodka with Soviet premier Nikita Khrushchev. It was, to put it mildly, an unlikely scenario: one of America's most famous anti-Communists chumming around with one of Communism's most prominent leaders. When President Eisenhower first proposed the meeting, Wayne initially said yes solely out of respect for the president. But then, on a personal level, he did have a motive all his own — a certain question that had been gnawing away at him. And there at the bar, with the aid of an interpreter and who knows how many shots, he popped it: "So, Nikita" — that's not actually how he brought it up, but let's pretend — "exactly why are your people *trying to kill me*?"

You see, Wayne believed that the Communists had been trying to murder him for over a decade. In 1951 two Russian hit men had supposedly tried to gun him down outside his office at Warner Bros. (Federal agents, acting on a tip, foiled the plan.) Another time, in 1955, a group of American Communists in Burbank had their plot to kill Duke broken up by a group of stuntmen who'd caught wind of the operation. And if Wayne was to be believed, these instances were the direct result of orders issued by Khrushchev's predecessor, Josef Stalin.

> As for the two attempts on Wayne's life, [Khrushchev] didn't know anything about those. Perhaps they were Stalin loyalists beyond his or anyone's control. Perhaps they were followers of Mao Tse-tung, who had also been involved in Stalin's plans. Regardless, Wayne shouldn't let his guard down.

In 1983 Orson Welles (by no means a kindred spirit of Wayne politically, though he liked the man) corroborated the Stalin story. The tale Welles told is long and convoluted (and again, the product of hearsay), but the essence is this: In 1949, Stalin had sent a movie director, Sergei Gerasimov, to an international conference in New York with explicit instructions to denounce Hollywood's lack of morals and to promote Stalinism. While there, Gerasimov learned about Wayne — at that time the president of the Motion Picture Alliance for the Preservation of American Ideals. When Gerasimov returned to the Soviet Union with news of this man's aims and his power, Stalin responded as though America had "invented some new secret weapon," a weapon he intended to neutralize.

Khrushchev didn't deny Stalin's intent. He said it was a product of Stalin's "last five mad years," and that the order had long been rescinded. As for the two attempts on Wayne's life, he didn't know anything about those. Perhaps they were Stalin loyalists beyond his or anyone's control. Perhaps they were followers of Mao Tse-tung, who had also been involved in Stalin's plans. Regardless, Wayne shouldn't let his guard down.

Three months after their drinking session, a large wooden crate marked CCCP arrived at Wayne's offices. Inside, packed in straw, were several cases of premium Russian vodka, along with a note that said, "Duke. Merry Christmas. Nikita." Wayne quickly returned Khrushchev's gesture, sending the Soviet leader a few cases of Sauza Conmemorativo with a note of his own: "Nikita. Thanks. Duke."

And so the story ends, with one small caveat: Nobody knows how much of it is true. But then, as the line goes, from the Wayne classic *The Man Who Shot Liberty Valance,* "When the legend becomes fact, print the legend." And if there is a larger truth to be had, maybe it is this—John Wayne liked drinking more than he hated Communists. ★

DOESN'T JOHN WAYNE seem like an eat the worm kind of guy? After all, his favorite booze was tequila—Sauza Conmemorativo, to be exact—though there is no worm in that bottle. Still, as he would tell *Playboy* magazine in 1971, Sauza is "as fine a liquor as there is in the world. Christ, I tell you it's better than any whiskey; it's better than any schnapps; it's better than any drink I ever had in my life."

That's quite an endorsement, and this from a man who truly knew. Wayne was, if you can believe it, one of the very first drinkers to try a margarita. The time was 1948, and the place, Acapulco. The Duke had a vacation house down there, near the Flamingo Hotel, and would pal about with the likes of Lana Turner, Fred MacMurray and others—pal around being a euphemism for drinking yourself stupid. Conrad "Nicky" Hilton of the Hilton Hotel chain was there, too, as was Joseph Drown, who owned the Bel-Air. The group would gather at the home of Dallas socialites Bill and Margaret "Margarita" Sames. (Maybe you can see where this story is going . . .)

Legend has it, the gang began to tire of the standard fare (Bloody Marys, Screwdrivers, beer). Wayne and his cohorts wanted something new under the sun, and they challenged their hostess, Margarita, to come up with it.

MARGARITA

LIME WEDGE
COARSE SALT
2 OZ. SILVER TEQUILA
1 OZ. COINTREAU
¾ OZ. FRESH LIME JUICE

Rub the rim of the cocktail glass with a lime wedge and press into a plate of salt. Pour all ingredients into a cocktail shaker filled with ice cubes. Shake well. Strain into the cocktail glass. Garnish with the lime wedge.

The Margarita is also frequently served on the rocks in an Old-Fashioned glass.

Part Four

1960'S & NEW HOLLYWOOD

1960–1979

"It was one long party. Everything old was bad, everything new was good. Nothing was sacred; everything was up for grabs. It was, in fact, a cultural revolution, American style."

—PETER BISKIND, film historian

RICHARD BURTON

1925–1984

ACTOR

"My liver is to be buried separately from the rest of me, with full honors."

A star of the stage in London and on Broadway, Richard Burton carved out a niche onscreen headlining historical epics. But however well he wore a crown, it was his series of tumultuous marriages to Elizabeth Taylor in the 1960s that cemented him as one of the biggest stars in the world. Welsh, he came to Hollywood after a much-lauded portrayal of Prince Hal in *Henry IV, Part I* (1951). His debut in *My Cousin Rachel* (1952) earned him the first of seven Oscar nominations (though he never won). Burton's portrayal of Jimmy Porter, an angry young man, in *Look Back in Anger* (1959) helped spawn the next generation of British actors. In 1963, he fell in love with Taylor on the set of *Cleopatra*, at the time the most expensive movie ever made. They tied the knot the following year and made numerous pictures together, most notably *Who's Afraid of Virginia Woolf?* (1966). The film would garner thirteen Academy Award nominations. (Taylor would win, for Best Actress, while Burton, nominated for Best Actor, would not.) The stress of playing the dysfunctional couple at the heart of the movie was said to take a toll on their real-life marriage. The couple divorced in 1974, remarried in 1975, then divorced for good in 1976. Burton received a final Oscar nomination for *Equus* (1977). His last movie was a well-regarded adaptation of Orwell's *1984* (1984).

★

HE THOUGHT IT WAS IN THE BAG. After much persuasion, Mike Mindlin had finally convinced Richard Burton to go through with the Ed Sullivan taping. Mindlin was handling publicity for *Becket,* currently in production at Shepperton Studios outside London, with Burton and Peter O'Toole in starring roles.

Ed Sullivan had just flown to England with the express purpose of interviewing them on location. Burton, however, had decided at the last minute that he'd cancel the appearance if he didn't receive his normal television fee. Fortunately, now that he'd had a few drinks, he wasn't feeling quite so obstinate. On the contrary: he was holding court in the lobby of the Dorchester Hotel, tourists everywhere, his new love, Elizabeth Taylor, by his side. One minute he was quoting Dylan Thomas and the next—well, the next, he was throwing up. Everywhere. It was an instance in which Burton, legendary for his capacity to consume alcohol, had gone beyond even his limit.

> This was a man who at his peak (or valley) was known to drain three bottles of vodka in a day—a man who once proclaimed, "If you can't do *Hamlet* straight through with a hangover, you ought to get right off the damn stage."

This was a man who at his peak (or valley) was known to drain three bottles of vodka in a day—a man who once proclaimed, "If you can't do *Hamlet* straight through with a hangover, you ought to get right off the damn stage." According to Robert Sellers's terrific biography *Hellraisers,* during the theatrical run of *Camelot,* starring opposite Julie Andrews, Burton wagered that he could start with a bottle of vodka while performing the matinee and then work through a bottle of cognac during the evening performance—without showing the effects. After the last curtain fell, Andrews, not even realizing he was drunk, commented that his performance was "a little better than usual." Performing in John Gielgud's production of *Hamlet,* Burton downed a whole quart of brandy in one evening's performance. The only noticeable difference, a critic would note, "was that he played the last two acts as a homosexual."

And now, here in London, it seemed he and O'Toole were in the midst of a friendly but intense competition. *Becket* was the first time the two men had worked together, and from a collaborative standpoint, they'd been excited from the start. O'Toole himself was a phenomenal lush and something of an eccentric, with a habit of getting drunk enough to pick fights with policemen and a proclivity for climbing walls. One night, after having been booed on the London stage, O'Toole got pissed on homemade mead and was locked up for disturbing a building. In court the next morning, he confessed to bursting into song in an attempt to seduce an insurance office.

But once they arrived on set, what the two stars were especially curious to discover was who could perform better under the influence. So they made a pact: both would remain on the wagon until they felt fully comfortable in their roles. After that, all bets were off. Sobriety had lasted all of ten days, when Burton suggested they deserved a little snifter—after which, the pair drank straight through the next two days. For the rest of the five-month shoot, they were perpetually wasted. Burton later described O'Toole's performance, a scene where King Henry puts a ring on Becket's finger, as a man threading "a needle wearing boxing gloves."

Mindlin knew all of this. It was impossible to visit the set and *not* know. So as embarrassing as Burton's public puking might have been—and even Burton himself felt humiliated—it didn't come as a total shock. Mindlin just walked Burton and Taylor to the elevator, wished them a good night, and told them he'd see them for the Sullivan interview tomorrow.

The next morning, Peter Glenville, the director of *Becket*, phoned Mindlin and urged him to schedule the Sullivan taping before lunch. Burton and O'Toole sometimes went to a local pub, the King's Head, on their break, and if that happened, there was no telling what shape they'd return in. Mindlin arranged for everyone to meet at the studio at noon. Ed Sullivan was there on time. So was O'Toole. No Burton. For hours. Around 5 p.m., Burton and Taylor finally arrived, epically sloshed. Burton, attempting to put on his Becket costume, kept trying to pull his tights over his trousers. Taylor laughed as though she'd never seen anything so funny. Sullivan began the interview by asking Burton if this was the first time he and O'Toole had worked together; Burton slurred that it was, and would "prolly fucking be the lashed." Tape rolled for another fifteen minutes before everyone involved gave up. Suffice to say, the segment never aired. ★

NIGHT OF THE IGUANA (1964)

When filming began on Tennessee Williams's *Night of the Iguana*, director John Huston gave each member of his principal cast the gift of a gold-plated Derringer. One each for Ava Gardner, Deborah Kerr, Sue Lyon, Richard Burton, and finally, Elizabeth Taylor (who wasn't in the movie, but was hanging out because she was in love with Burton). Inside the box for each gun were four bullets engraved with the names of the other costars. By the time all was said and done, he figured the bullets might come in handy.

The location for *Night of the Iguana* was Mismaloya, a remote village in Mexico, a few miles off the coast of Puerto Vallarta. Huston's plan was to house the cast and crew in the village, and to that end he ordered the construction of a small American suburb: a restaurant, bar, and living quarters; roads, power plants, and water storage facilities; plus an editing room and the film's one set, an old hotel. It was a beautiful setting, but there wasn't a lot to do besides work. And drink. This would seem to be a theme of many of Huston's productions.

Despite an entire cast of all-star tipplers, the lion's share of the drinking fell to Burton and Taylor, at that time the most gossiped-about couple in the world. (That Taylor was still technically married to singer Eddie Fisher only added grist.) The day the couple arrived in Mexico, the mob that swarmed them was so overwhelming that they were forced to run from the plane to their car, with Taylor being groped and Burton punching anyone who got in their way. Later, Burton issued a statement to the press: "This is my first visit to Mexico. I trust it shall be my last."

But to their surprise, Burton and Taylor fell in love with the place. Specifically Casa Kimberley, a house they'd rented in Puerto Vallarta (they had refused to stay in the primitive Mismaloya digs), which they promptly announced their intention to buy. The only drawback to staying in Puerto Vallarta was the trip across the water to the set each morning. This journey involved wading out to a canoe, then paddling over to a motorboat that, after crossing a short patch of Pacific, would land at the foot of what was more or less a rope ladder. The ladder led to a wooden staircase that was then climbed to a rough footpath. When Taylor heard Gardner whining about how unpleasant the boat ride was, she suggested Gardner water-ski across instead. Which is exactly what Gardner started doing: one hand holding the towline, the other a cocktail. Given the heat, the discomfort, and the boredom, cocktails only seemed to help.

Drinking started early and never stopped: Burton insisted that the set of stairs he had to climb at the Mismaloya boat-landing be equipped with two bars: one at the bottom, one at the top. Taylor, since she wasn't working, began her days at 10 a.m. at the Oceana Hotel bar, starting with vodka, then moving on to tequila. Burton would start his day with beer, this at 7 a.m., so that by the time shooting was over he would have polished off a case. Joining Taylor at the bar, he would shift to hard liquor. There was a joke around the set—to make a Burton cocktail you first take twenty-one shots of tequila. Quite literal, the joke stemmed from the time Burton took twenty-one shots of tequila. His one big booze discovery in Mexico—a cactus brandy called *raicilla*, which he swore you could feel move through your intestines, though somehow that doesn't seem so pleasant.

Equally unpleasant was the smell of Burton. Apparently, he consumed so much alcohol throughout the day and well into the night that his 80-proof sweat threw off an incredibly foul odor. Working under a hot Mexican sun, this posed a unique challenge to his costars. Still, Taylor put it up with it, as she did his rudeness. Though deep in the throes of courtship and soon to marry, the couple found time to fight, publically and awfully. When Taylor paraded around set in ever-more revealing bikinis, Burton would comment that she looked like a tart. During a conversation at a dinner party in which Taylor insinuated Burton might be an opportunist for getting involved with her, Burton brought her to tears with his response: "You scurrilous low creature, you." So irritated did Burton get with Taylor's constant fussing over him that once, after she insisted on fixing the job his hairdresser had just finished, he poured an entire beer over his head and asked, "How do I look now, by God?"

Luckily, it seems the golden bullets were forgotten somewhere along the way.

RICHARD BURTON'S DRINKING ability was nothing less than miraculous, described by biographer Robert Sellers as "one of the wonders of the twentieth century." Alan Jay Lerner, the creator of *Camelot* and one of Burton's drinking mates, when looking for an explanation for his friend's gift, went so far as to consult a doctor, who said, "Welsh livers and kidneys seem to be made of some metallic alloy, quite unlike the rest of the human race." But really there is no explanation. Add to this that until the age of forty-five, Burton claims to have never had a single hangover.

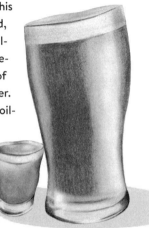

One of his favorite drinks in those early years was a Boilermaker—a sudsy speedball of booze that combines a glass of beer and a shot of whiskey. There are several methods for tossing this mixture back, but Burton's method, appropriately dramatic, was to line up pints of beer threaded in shots of whiskey, then go chugging down the row. He once took on a rugby team of

RICHARD BURTON'S BOILERMAKER

. . . .

1 OZ. WHISKEY

1 PINT LAGER BEER

Pour whiskey into a shot glass and beer into a pint glass or mug. Throw back the shot and chase it with the beer.

COACH BUTTERMAKER'S BOILERMAKER

. . . .

12 OZ. CAN OF BUDWEISER

2 OZ. JIM BEAM

Open can of Budweiser and take a good sip. Refill with Jim Beam. Drink down.

Welsh miners, managing to kill off nineteen such Boilermakers. Details remain fuzzy as to exactly who won.

Changing genres, there is also a comedic Boilermaker to be had. In *The Nutty Professor*, Jerry Lewis, as Buddy Love, orders one, saying, "I've decided that I shall not continue the flight on the gas I've got, so give me a Boilermaker, and heavy on the boil." Unfortunately, we never get to see the results. But in the opening credits of *The Bad News Bears*—the wonderful comedy created by Bill Lancaster and based upon his father, Burt—Walter Matthau couldn't be more obliging. As the booze-soaked Coach Buttermaker, he makes his own uniquely hilarious Boilermaker, this in the front seat of his car.

And finally, one last genre: horror (or maybe more accurately, tragedy). When Bela Lugosi, B-movie star of Count Dracula fame, among other monsters, wasn't on screen sucking on necks, he was off screen sucking down Boilermakers. Lugosi was also a well-known morphine addict and, in later years, nearly destitute. Ed Wood, B-movie director and himself a fiend with the bottle—whether wearing a skirt and pumps or not—recounts one particularly frightening tale.

It was three in the morning, and Wood had been asked to bring the Prince of Darkness some scotch, only to find him in his living room standing behind the curtain. This was where Lugosi would go when he wanted to fix. Having shot up, the Count stepped out, his body shaking and his face streaked with tears. In his hand there was a gun and it was pointed at his friend. "Eddie, I'm going to die tonight. I want to take you with me." Fortunately Wood, who had taken several bullets in WWII, kept cool enough to see a way out—Boilermakers.

That night Lugosi would forsake glassware. The canned beer was to be room temperature—the Count was European after all—the scotch he just drank from the bottle. Soon enough, Lugosi put the gun away in a drawer and continued to drink his Boilermakers. At least the two old friends, the unemployed monster and the angora fetishist, had each other. After a while, Lugosi started to mix paraldehyde in with the beer, which he drank with the scotch. A sedative used to treat alcoholics for delirium tremens, paraldehyde smelled a bit like ether and helped induce sleep. The sun, after all, was just breaking and the Prince of Darkness would soon be heading off to bed.

JOHN CASSAVETES

1929–1989

DIRECTOR AND ACTOR

"I don't really have to direct anyone or write down that somebody's getting drunk; all I have to do is say that there's a bottle there and put a bottle there and then they're going to get drunk."

J ohn Cassavetes forged one of the most unique careers in the history of cinema, capitalizing on his success as a character actor in traditional Hollywood pictures to direct a series of revolutionary, personal films that set the course for modern American independent filmmaking. A fixture of television in the 1950s, he made his feature debut with Sidney Poitier in *Edge of the City* (1957), a drama about interracial relationships. Cassavetes returned to that same subject matter with his first directorial effort, *Shadows* (1959), a largely improvised, low-budget affair shot with handheld cameras on the streets of New York. He was hired to direct two Hollywood features, *Too Late Blues* (1961) and *A Child Is Waiting* (1963), but frustrations with studio interference inspired him to swear off the traditional system for all future endeavors. As a means of financing his own work, Cassavetes took roles in such movies as *The Killers* (1964) and *The Dirty Dozen* (1967), for which he received an Oscar nomination as Best Supporting Actor. His next film as a director, *Faces* (1968), was nominated for three Oscars: Best Screenplay, Best Supporting Actor (Seymour Cassel), and Best Supporting Actress (Lynn Carlin). Gena Rowlands and Cassel, along with Peter Falk and Ben Gazzara, made up the core stable of actors Cassavetes would utilize throughout his singular and influential career. At the time of his death, he had written more than forty unproduced screenplays.

★

HE REALLY WANTED HER TO WIN. He knew how much it would mean to her. It was morning at the

Beverly Hills Hotel, and later that night, the 1974 Golden Globes ceremony were taking place not far away, at the Beverly Hilton.

Cassavetes and his wife, Gena Rowlands, had both been nominated for *A Woman Under the Influence:* her for acting, him for writing and directing. The night before, at the Polo Lounge, Cassavetes had thrown a few back with Richard Harris, who was in town as a scheduled presenter. What they had talked about, Cassavetes couldn't precisely recall, but here this morning was Harris again, in a slightly more sober state, to refresh his memory. Unfortunately.

It seems that when Cassavetes found out Harris was presenting the award for Best Actress, he'd drunkenly let slip just how badly he wanted his wife to win. The conversation had gone something like this:

Harris: "You want her to win it?"

Cassavetes: "Of course"

Harris: "Okay then, she's won it. I'll just pull the envelope out of my pocket, open it, and say she's won. You want me to do it?"

Cassavetes: "Yes . . . definitely."

Presumably they then celebrated with another round.

But now, in the harsh light of day, Cassavetes wanted to take it back as quickly as possible. He begged Harris not to go through with it. "Don't worry, it's no big deal," Harris said. "They won't find out until it's over, and then I can just say I made a mistake, or I couldn't read, or I'm dyslexic, or something."

Hours later, during the ceremony, Cassavetes and Rowlands were seated at a table right in front of the stage when Harris came out to present the Best Actress award. Cassavetes immediately started shaking his head, "No no no." Harris opened the envelope, smiled and announced the winner: "Gena Rowlands."

Afterward, Cassavetes asked who really won the award.

"Faye Dunaway," Harris replied, "for *Chinatown*." The director spent the next few hours in a spiral of guilt and shame. Imagining his friend's state, Harris decided to help. In the wee hours of the morning, a huge floral arrangement and a bottle of champagne were delivered to Cassavetes and Rowlands at their hotel room. They were from Harris. And there among the flowers was the card he'd read from during the ceremony. The name on the card: Gena Rowlands. ★

SAMMY DAVIS, JR.

1925–1990
SINGER AND ACTOR

"Sober up, and you see and hear everything that you'd been able to avoid hearing before."

Born to a vaudeville family, Sammy Davis, Jr., spent his childhood as part of the Will Mastin Trio, named after his uncle and also featuring his father. He struck out on his own in the 1950s, with solo records and a starring role on Broadway in *Mr. Wonderful* (1956). Later he would become a top attraction in Las Vegas as part of the Rat Pack, along with Frank Sinatra and Dean Martin. Davis had a successful (if not terribly distinguished) film career, most notably appearing in the Rat Pack vehicle *Oceans 11* (1960) and the *Cannonball Run* series. He scored a surprise number-one radio hit with "The Candy Man" in 1972 and became a regular fixture on television through the 1970s and 80s, guest-starring on sitcoms (*All in the Family, The Jeffersons, The Cosby Show*), game shows (*Family Feud*), even soap operas (*General Hospital, One Life to Live*). Davis shared one of the first interracial onscreen kisses, with Nancy Sinatra during a 1967 television special, but his romantic relationships with white women—including a marriage to Swedish actress May Britt—were a constant source of controversy. So, too, was his conversion to Judaism and his public support of Richard Nixon. Despite it all, Sammy remained to the end one of the country's most beloved performers.

★

IT WAS SUPPOSED TO BE the happiest day of his life. Almost midnight at the Copa, January 10, 1958, and Sammy Davis, Jr., had just gotten married. The lucky woman was Loray White, a singer at a Vegas nightclub called the Silver Slipper. They'd met three years earlier in L.A., dated for eight months, then gone their separate ways—until a week ago when Davis came looking for her and proposed.

She showed up for the wedding an hour late. Both were so nervous, they accidentally called her "Leroy" on the marriage-license application. The ceremony lasted two minutes. And now, at the Copa, he'd just finished his regular evening performances and everyone around him was celebrating his marriage, his shows, his success. But all Davis could do was cry. Cry and drink himself stupid.

What made the occasion particularly strange is that just ten days prior, on New Year's Day, a *Chicago Sun-Times* columnist named Irv Kupcinet had leaked the news that Davis was intending to marry actress Kim Novak, whose family hailed from Chicago. Novak had denied the story, but Kupcinet claimed he'd found an application for marriage with both their names. The story made headlines the world over. But now Davis was marrying another woman?

Rumors of a Novak-Davis affair had been floating in gossip columns long before Kupcinet reported it. The two met sometime in 1957 at a party thrown by Tony Curtis and Janet Leigh, and spent the evening chatting away. The next morning, word was in the papers. Davis realized the harm this could do to both their careers, so he called Novak to assure her he hadn't planted the information. She invited him over for spaghetti. And thus a clandestine relationship blossomed. Being driven to see her, Davis would lie on the floorboard of the car, a blanket draped over him.

But no level of discretion was going to keep the Novak-Davis pairing a secret for long. When word got back to Columbia Pictures head Harry Cohn—who'd been grooming Novak as the studio's new "it" girl (a replacement for the uncontrollable Rita Hayworth)—he had not one, but *two* heart attacks. Literal put-you-in-the-hospital heart attacks. Fearing the harm the story might do to Novak's career (read: his investment), Cohn hired some tough guys to drive Davis out to the desert and explain things. But Davis was tipped off to the plan and fled to the Sands in Las Vegas, under the protection of mob boss Sam Giancana.

Eventually, all parties decided the best way to put this whole business behind everyone was for Davis to pay another woman to marry him as quickly as possible, a black woman. (This would also have the added advantage of quieting the black press, which was livid over Novak.) Davis sat down and started flipping through his address book, looking for a wife. And then he came upon White.

The happy couple would divorce a few months later. For her trouble, White received $25,000. Cohn, despite securing his investment, would die of a heart attack the next month. As for Sammy—his heart would only be broken. ★

THE MAGIC CASTLE
7001 FRANKLIN AVE.
OPEN!

PRIVATE CLUBS IN LOS ANGELES have found varying levels of success over the years (the Clover Club worked where the Embassy Club didn't), but the mysterious and legendary Magic Castle, located in the Hollywood Hills, has been going strong for over fifty years.

The name's no joke: Originally built in 1909 as the private estate of banker/developer Rollin B. Lane, the chateau—a replica of the landmark Kimberly Crest house in Redlands, California—was leased by television writer Milt Larsen (of *Truth and Consequences* fame) in 1961, with the express of purpose of converting it into an exclusive hangout for magicians. (Larsen's father had been one).

Today, the Academy of Magical Arts—as the Castle's fraternity is known—boasts five thousand members, including at one time or another such famous types as Orson Welles, Johnny Carson, Muhammad Ali, Cary Grant, Steve Martin, and Tony Curtis.

With multiple dining rooms, bars, and nightly performances in several theaters (the Palace of Mystery, the Parlor of Prestidigitation), it's one of Hollywood's most unique nightlife experiences, but only open to Academy members and their guests—and only if their guests follow the dress code. (It's called a tie, people.) This means anyone hoping to marvel at Irma, the phantom pianist, or participate in one of the Castle's regular Houdini Séances ought to get working on their sleight of hand, or start hanging out at toddlers' birthday parties. ★

RICHARD HARRIS

1930–2002
ACTOR, SINGER, AND WRITER

"I often sit back and think,
I wish I'd done that,
and find out later that
I already have."

Born and raised in Ireland, the young Richard Harris was a talented rugby player, but his career was cut short by tuberculosis. After a decade of obscurity in London theater, he landed his first movie, *Alive and Kicking*, in 1959. His supporting roles in *The Guns of Navarone* (1961) and *Mutiny on the Bounty* (1962) led to his first lead performance in *This Sporting Life* (1963), for which he received the best actor award at the Cannes Film Festival and a Best Actor nomination at the Academy Awards. It was a performance that would propel him into the ranks of British Cinema's "angry young men." In 1967, Harris played King Arthur in the film adaptation of the musical *Camelot* and embarked on a music career, releasing the smash hit single "MacArthur Park" and the first of several full-length albums, *A Tramp Shining* (1968). He also published an acclaimed book of poetry, *I, in the Membership of My Days* (1973). Though Harris continued to act over the next two decades, it wasn't until *The Field* (1990) that he played another part of consequence; for his performance, he received his second Oscar nomination as Best Actor. Harris went on to have something of a renaissance, appearing in *Patriot Games* (1992), *Unforgiven* (1992), *Gladiator* (2000), and the early Harry Potter films.

★

THEY WERE CUTTING IT TOO CLOSE. The stagehand was in a panic. It was the middle of a performance of the play *The Pier* at the Bristol Old Vic, and as usual, Richard Harris and Peter O'Toole had ducked out for an unscheduled intermission. Enthusiastic and dedicated drinking buddies, they were blessed each night with one glorious twenty-minute stretch during which neither was required onstage. It was long enough to dash across the street (in full costume) to the local watering hole. Ordinarily they would toss a few back, while keeping a close eye on the clock, and return to the theater just before they were due back on. But not this night.

"Harris!" the stagehand screamed, throwing open the door of the bar. "For god's sake, you're on!"

In his professional life, Harris wasn't known to allow drink to interfere with his work. In his personal life, however, he was known for his disappearances. Once, while living in London, he told his wife, Elizabeth, that he was going out for a newspaper. What he didn't tell her was he was going to get it in Dublin. Five weeks of a massive bender passed before word got to him that Elizabeth was planning to divorce him. When he finally returned home, and an expressionless but clearly angry Elizabeth met him at the door, he asked—as sincerely as he could—"Why didn't you pay the ransom?"

Of course, that was Dublin—a city that holds you hostage. It held the same allure for O'Toole as it did for Harris, "With Dublin the only thing you can do is turn up the collar of your coat, pull your hat down over your eyes and walk straight through it: otherwise you're there forever."

> It was the middle of a performance of the play *The Pier* at the Bristol Old Vic, and as usual, Richard Harris and Peter O'Toole had ducked out for an unscheduled intermission.

Biographer Robert Sellers tells another story involving a Harris disappearance. Extremely loaded one night, Harris first closed down a pub in London, then—ever thirsty for more—hopped a train with the hope that the train's bar car would still be open. It was, and so Harris never bothered to ask where they were heading. He arrived in Leeds at well after midnight, pissed out of his mind. Spying a light on in a nearby house, he tossed a stone at a windowpane and drew out the owner. Naturally, the owner was quite angry at first, but then recognized the movie star and invited him in. Harris would stay there for the next four days, bombed the entire time.

But when it came to acting, both Harris and O'Toole knew their priorities. And so the two Irishmen slammed back their beers and took off for the theater. Just as Harris hit the stage door, he heard his cue and frantically scrambled toward the stage. His entrance, however, did not go as planned. Right as he was about to appear on the set, he tripped over a wire, sliding all the way down to the footlights, where his head landed practically in the lap of a woman in the front row. Catching the scent of alcohol on his breath, the woman shouted, "Good god! Harris is drunk!"

"Madam," Harris replied without missing a beat, "if you think I'm drunk, wait until you see O'Toole." ★

RICHARD HARRIS COULD DRINK two bottles of vodka a day (to Burton's three, though that is hardly indicative of greater restraint) and usually finish by 7 p.m. At which time, he would "break open a bottle of brandy and a bottle of port and mix the two." Given the degree of inebriation, there was likely little nuance involved, but for those who would like to try it . . .

PORT AND BRANDY

. . . .

1¼ OZ. PORT

1 OZ. BRANDY

Pour ingredients into a snifter or, if one isn't handy, a wine glass. Then maybe light a cigar.

• •

DENNIS HOPPER

1936–2010
ACTOR AND DIRECTOR

• •

"People used to ask how much drugs I did. I only did drugs so I could drink more."

P rimarily a character actor, as writer-director of *Easy Rider* (1969), Dennis Hopper epitomized the rebelliousness of Hollywood in the immediate poststudio era. He was heavily influenced by James Dean, the star of Hopper's first two major gigs—*Rebel Without a Cause* (1955) and *Giant* (1956). A method actor, who studied under Lee Strasberg, Hopper developed a reputation as being unmanageable early in his career. As a director, he bombed with his *Easy Rider* follow-up, *The Last Movie* (1971), but found work as a reliable wild-card type in a series of low-budget and European productions over the next several years. He earned accolades for his supporting role in Francis Ford Coppola's *Apocalypse Now* (1979) and a starring role in *Out of the Blue* (1980). But it was his terrifying performance as Frank Booth in David Lynch's *Blue Velvet* (1986) that gave his career new life, followed by an Oscar nomination for Best Supporting Actor in *Hoosiers* (1986) and critical acclaim for his fourth directorial effort, *Colors* (1988). An accomplished artist, his paintings, photographs, and sculptures were the subject of an exhibition at the Museum of Contemporary Art in Los Angeles.

———————————— ★ ————————————

RIGHT BETWEEN THE EYES—that is where the blade was. Just moments before, Rip Torn, Terry Southern, and Peter Fonda were in Fonda's New York townhouse, ostensibly working on the script for *Easy Rider,* but mostly just drinking. Suddenly, the film's director, Dennis Hopper, had blown in, at first looking wild-eyed and irrational, and then just royally pissed off.

The problem: While Hopper was down South, risking life and limb to scout locations, they hadn't written a thing. "I couldn't even stop in Texas," Hopper said. "They're cutting dudes' hair with rusty razors!" Rip Torn, a Texan, rose to his feet. "Take it easy," he said, "not everyone from Texas is an a-hole."

Hopper picked up a steak knife from a nearby table. No account of the evening chronicles what Hopper had consumed before he arrived at Fonda's townhouse, but his track record speaks for itself. While on location in Cuernavaca in the early 1980s, shooting a West German sexploitation picture called *Jungle Warriors*, he locked himself in his hotel room with a bottle of tequila (plus who knows what else) and before long was hearing voices of people being tortured and murdered around him. When he started to see bugs and snakes crawling beneath his skin, he stripped off his clothes and ran into the forest, where he "saw" two armies engaged in battle. Oh, and a flying saucer. "I thought the Third World War had started," he later said of the incident. "I masturbated in front of a tree and thought I'd become a galaxy—that was a good mood!" At that point in his life, Hopper was downing a half-gallon of rum, twenty-eight beers, and three grams of coke—*a day.*

Substance abuse was such an inextricable part of his life, filmmakers actually accounted for it in their production plans. One director, knowing Hopper might do one drug in the morning, and another in the afternoon—resulting in two different performances that couldn't possibly be cut together—went through the script with Hopper beforehand and, scene by scene, determined what drugs he'd be taking when. Seriously: *his drug schedule was included on his call sheets.*

But back to the knife fight. Hopper didn't have the upper hand for long. Rip Torn, a former military policeman (an amusing thought) quickly disarmed him. It was at this point Hopper threatened to pull out a second knife, a buck knife. Torn told him he'd wait for him in the street: "Bring your guns. Bring your knives. Bring your pals, and we'll find out in about three seconds who the punk is." With that, Torn went outside and waited. He knew Hopper had a buck knife; he didn't know what he was going to do if he had a gun. Fortunately, Torn never had to find out. Hopper stayed inside.

But within weeks, Hanson, the role Torn was supposed to play, was given to Jack Nicholson.

In fairness to Hopper, it should be noted that a year later while filming the movie *Maidstone,* Torn struck his director Norman Mailer in the head with a hammer—a hammer! Not afraid to mix it up himself, Mailer responded by pining Torn down on the grass and biting off a chunk of his ear. Cameras were rolling and the scene would end up in the movie.

Years after such mayhem, during a 1994 appearance on *The Tonight Show,* Hopper told the knife story to Jay Leno—only in his version, Torn was the first one to pull a blade. Torn, who was experiencing a career resurgence thanks to a starring role on HBO's *The Larry Sanders Show,* sued him for defamation—and won. The reason? The judge claimed Hopper wasn't a credible witness. ★

APOCALYPSE NOW (1979)

Harebrained is not a bad word for it. If there is any indication of just how harebrained, consider the original thinking. Back in 1971, it was suggested that *Apocalypse Now* be shot on location in Vietnam—yes, the war was still on. It would be a lean, vérité-style production; you just shoot it in 16 mm for a few million dollars. *Hmmm?*

Mercifully, that didn't happen (not hard to imagine why), but in 1976 when *Apocalypse* was finally launched, the plan was no less ill-conceived. Francis Ford Coppola, both producing and directing, was fixed on the Philippines. Never mind that the dictator Ferdinand Marcos had placed the entire country under martial law four years earlier, or that the production's helicopters might be called away to fight the active rebel insurgency—or that the script written by John Milius in 1969 was being rewritten by the director on the fly. Oh yeah, and the rainy season was fast approaching.

When Coppola asked legendary director Roger Corman for advice (Corman had experience filming in the Philippines), he replied, "My advice, Francis, is—Don't go." It is sort of reminiscent of Charles de Gaulle telling President Kennedy that in Vietnam he would "sink bit by bit into a bottomless military and political swamp."

Should Coppola have listened? He might have at least given pause. Not unlike the United State's involvement in the real war, they could have been better prepared. After all, there must've been at least the scent of impending disaster—the lead role of Capt. Willard was turned down by no less than McQueen, Nicholson, Redford, and Pacino.

One look at the cast and you knew. Martin Sheen, coming straight from a film in Italy, noted, "I had some personal concerns about my own physical condition." This in part because he was smoking two packs a day and fighting a decade-long battle with booze. Captaining a Navy patrol boat, the thirty-five-year-old actor also couldn't swim. When on the first day Sheen asked for a life jacket, the crew—assuming it must be a joke—laughed.

Or Dennis Hopper, who by his own estimation arrived "not in the greatest of shape." By this he must have meant drunk and high, with photographer Caterine Milinaire, the daughter of the Duchess of Bedford, in tow. Oscillating between erratic and out-of-his-mind, depending on what he was on, Hopper got into his role by connecting to the Fool, as in the card from the Tarot deck. He rarely bathed and chose not to wash his costume for the most of the shoot. Brando refused to be in the same room with him, a stipulation that made filming their scenes together a bit more complicated.

Not that Brando reported to duty in ship-shape. Hired for three weeks at $1 million a week, he arrived weighing almost three hundred pounds. Coproducer Gray Frederickson remarked, "You couldn't see around him." Tennessee Williams observed that they must be paying him by the pound. Added to this, Brando hadn't even bothered to read *Heart of Darkness*—the book upon which *Apocalypse Now* was based.

Clearly, nobody in the cast had been to boot camp. Still, with a disciplined commanding officer, things might have been different. But Coppola at this time in his life was not that officer. For one thing, he had just begun smoking grass, an interesting hobby to take up at the onset of the most ambitious production of your career.

The pressure was unbelievable, a strain the director dealt with by ripping doors off hinges, throwing two-by-fours, and eventually falling into a full-blown epileptic seizure. According to actor Frederic Forrest, there were days when the shooting schedule simply read, "scenes unknown."

It was a production steeped in chaos and prone to excess, difficult in the best of circumstances but impossible given the jungle locale. Cast and crew were pushed eight to twelve hours a day, suffering from the heat, from tropical disease. Sam Bottoms, eighteen at the time, got hookworm. Forrest had blood oozing out of his ears. Almost from the start, the production was behind schedule and over budget as fourteen weeks turned into sixteen weeks, then twenty—*Apocalypse* hitting the one-hundred-day mark, then two hundred days.

In the second month of production Typhoon Olga slammed into the island: days of torrential rain that wiped out sets, shut down production and killed two hundred Filipinos. Is it any wonder the cast and crew partied like the world was going to end? There were hundreds of beer cans lined up around the pool at the Pagsanjan Falls Resort so you didn't need to get out of the water. Flaming mattresses were seen flying out of hotel windows (Hopper's), crew members dove off the hotel roof, and gunshots rang out in the night (again, Hopper). Bottoms, with refreshing candor, would point out that just below the production office there was a massage parlor where "you could go in there and get jerked off for five bucks." Who knows how this struck his fellow actor Laurence Fishburne—given that he was only fourteen at the time.

There's a story that, the day after drinking a great deal of tequila, Forrest simply passed out in the middle of filming, just dropped to the jungle floor. Hopper cracked, "Who do we have here? Humphrey Bogart?" But in reality, they were a long, long way from anything as quaint as Bogart and Hepburn squabbling over gin in *The African Queen*. Martin Sheen seems to have been one of the few who truly saw this. Reluctant to return to the production after the typhoon, he commented, "I was afraid I would not live through it."

One of the most famous scenes, both because of what happens on screen and what happened on set, involves Sheen. At the opening of the film, his character, Capt. Willard, is hunkered down in a hotel room, smoking and drinking himself numb, as he awaits his next assignment. The scene was shot on Sheen's thirty-sixth birthday and the actor had spent the day in the hotel room, smoking and drinking like Willard. By the time they were ready to shoot, he was so drunk he could barely stand up. In the outtakes you can hear Sheen mutter, "Give us a little booze here will ya . . ." In a sort of free-form improvisational tour de force, Sheen struck hand-to-hand poses in front of a mirror, accidently shattering the mirror glass and gouging his thumb. With blood leaking, Sheen naked and weeping, Coppola to his credit wanted to stop filming, but Sheen insisted they press on. What is captured on film is powerful and intimate, a troubled man going deeply inward.

Through the lens of several decades of sobriety, Sheen would come to understand that he was using alcohol as a tool, "an easy ticket to the emotional well," and that he had been for some time. But certainly, he wasn't the only member of the cast to do so. When Coppola asked Hopper what he needed to help get into character, Hopper replied, "an ounce of cocaine." He wasn't joking. For the documentary *Hearts of Darkness*, Bottoms acknowledged that "most of my character was done under the influence of pot." It was a time and place when alcohol and drugs seemed (to use Sheen's phrase) like a "legitimate professional aid," and a miracle that all the cast survived intact. Sheen in fact almost didn't—suffering a heart attack nearer the end of the production. Later, he would wonder if it wasn't a subconscious attempt to escape the insanity around him.

But escape finally did arrive. By then fourteen weeks had turned into more than fourteen months and the budget had gone from $13 million to over $30 million—and 250 hours of footage had been shot. Coppola, with the help of Brando's incredible improvisation, had finished the script and the shoot—"the horror, the horror" was over.

Premiering at the 1979 Cannes Film Festival, *Apocalypse Now* would win the Palme d'Or. At a press conference, Coppola declared, "My film is not about Vietnam, it is Vietnam"—an overstatement for sure, but not by much.

THE TROUBADOUR

9081 SANTA MONICA BLVD.

OPEN!

THE PREMIERE SHOWCASE for singer-songwriters of Southern California and beyond during the 1960s and 1970s, the Troubadour has occupied its current three-hundred-capacity theater just south of the Sunset Strip since 1961. Founded by Doug Weston, a towering longhair with Ben Franklin glasses who'd previously worked as a stage manager at the Apollo Theater, it began four years earlier as a humble sixty-five-seat coffeehouse on La Cienega, but with Weston's stewardship and keen eye for talent, it became a crucial performance space that helped make stars of Bonnie Raitt, the Byrds, Buffalo Springfield, Carole King, the Eagles, Jackson Browne, James Taylor, Joni Mitchell, Randy Newman, and Tom Waits (to name but a few).

Elton John, who made his U.S. debut with a six-night stand at the Troubadour (during which he was introduced by Neil Diamond), still considers that engagement the turning point of his career. Comedians, too, have played a pivotal role in the club's history. Lenny Bruce was first arrested for obscenity at the Troubadour. Richard Pryor recorded his first album there. It's where Steve Martin and Cheech & Chong were discovered, and where the Smothers Brothers launched their 1974 comeback. (That performance is best remembered for two famous hecklers in the crowd, Harry Nilsson and John Lennon, both of whom were thrown out by security.)

Yet despite the sentimental attachment performers had to the Troubadour, Weston's allegedly avaricious business practices caused no small degree of resentment. "The Troubadour is a gold mine that's been mined by everyone else," Weston once said. And as the club's international reputation grew—aided in part by the release of live albums by Diamond and Van Morrison—he wanted his cut. The most egregious of his demands was a "return engagement" contract that required acts to continue performing at the Troubadour no matter how popular they'd become—for the same fees they'd always been paid.

Capitalizing on the festering bad blood, a group that included producer Lou Adler and David Geffen opened the Roxy Theatre in 1973, a larger room that targeted the exact shows that had been the

Troubadour's bread and butter. Weston failed to meet the competition head on. By the early 1980s he'd abandoned his previous booking principles—that he would only present artists who had "something to say"—and started catering to the burgeoning heavy-metal scene on the Sunset Strip. (Metallica played their first headlining gig in L.A. at the Troubadour in 1982; four years later, a gig by Guns N' Roses convinced Geffen to sign the band.)

It was only after Weston partnered with businessman Ed Karayan, who reorganized operations, that the Troubadour started to reclaim some of its previous luster. These days, the club concentrates primarily on emerging artists and established independent acts, though the old guard continues to pop in from time to time. (James Taylor and Carole King, for instance, reenacted their Troubadour debut for a fiftieth-anniversary celebration in 2007.) And though Doug Weston passed away in 1999, a controversial figure to the end, his name still appears on the sign above the door. ★

ROCK HUDSON

1925–1985

ACTOR

"I love to drink and I hate to exercise. I built a gym in my house and I don't even like to walk through it."

Cast on the strength of his looks, Rock Hudson had just one line in his first picture, *Fighter Squadron* (1948), and needed thirty-eight takes to get it right. But years of extensive training in acting, dancing, singing, fencing, and horseback riding finally paid off with an Oscar nomination in 1956, for *Giant*. He became a bankable lead in romantic comedies, especially when cast opposite Doris Day: *Pillow Talk* (1959), *Lover Come Back* (1961), and *Send Me No Flowers* (1964). He would make nine films with Danish-German director—and something of a father figure—Douglas Sirk, melodramas that included *Magnificent Obsession* (1954), *All That Heaven Allows* (1955), and *The Tarnished Angels* (1958). Hudson transitioned into television in the 1970s, starring in the long-running NBC series *McMillan & Wife* with Susan Saint James. In 1985 Hudson publicly announced he had contracted AIDS—the first major celebrity to do so. Despite residual scandals, his disclosure made the disease a mainstream health issue and had a substantial positive effect on funding for research and treatment.

★

ROCK HUDSON WAS NERVOUS. Understandably so: the relationship had to be believable. Though he was one of Hollywood's most popular movie stars, he was also considered one of its worst actors, and this role, in George Stevens's *Giant,* was his chance to prove everyone wrong. Adding to the pressure, his onscreen rival, James Dean, was a product of the Actor's Studio in New York, the same school that had produced Marlon Brando and Montgomery Clift.

Fortunately, Hudson's onscreen wife, Elizabeth Taylor, was a close friend of Clift's and had some advice for her anxious costar: just add a little Method. If Hudson and Taylor were going to behave like a married couple in front of the camera, they should hang out as much as possible behind it. And in Marfa, Texas, the tiny cattle town in the desert where *Giant* was being shot, that meant one thing: they'd be drinking together—drinking a lot.

The bulk of the cast and crew were put up at Marfa's one large hotel, the Paisano (which even today is covered in *Giant* memorabilia). Apart from the hotel, the town consisted of mostly a half dozen cafés and bars, a grocery store, and a boarded-up movie theater the production was using to screen rushes. Still, Hudson and Taylor found their fun.

One night, when a crazy storm rolled through, they rushed outside with buckets, collecting the falling hail to use in Bloody Marys. Another night, on a whim, they decided to add chocolate liqueur and chocolate syrup to a vodka martini, thus creating—so the legend goes—what both considered the finest cocktail they'd ever tasted, the chocolate martini. Even after the production returned to Los Angeles, they were two peas in a pod. They capped off one drinking session by sampling nachos at a string of Mexican restaurants, then challenged one another to a belching and farting contest. (Taylor won.)

Naturally, all this carrying-on sparked rumors that Taylor and Hudson were an item, which were fueled even further by Taylor's on-set fights with her visiting husband, Michael Wilding. But Hudson was facing other romantic problems. Publicly, he was dating Phyllis Gates, the secretary of his agent, Henry Willson, and was being pressured on all sides to propose, not the least by Willson himself. Willson had received word that *Confidential* magazine was wise to Hudson's homosexuality, even offering $10,000 to two former lovers if they'd be willing to come forward, and knew it was only a matter of time before his top client was outed. To placate the tabloid, Willson had given up the goods on Tab Hunter, who'd recently fired him, but still, when this *Giant* business was over, he knew the next role Hudson had to sign up for: husband.

On October 3, 1955—days after Jimmy Dean's death near the end of production on *Giant*—*Life* ran a cover story on Hudson entitled "The Simple Life of a Busy Bachelor: Rock Hudson Gets Rich Alone." In the opening paragraph was this sentence: "Fans are urging twenty-nine-year-old Hudson to get married—or explain why not." That was it.

Willson told Hudson he had one month to marry Gates. They did so on November 9. *Giant* was released the following year. For his performance as husband (Taylor's that is), Hudson was nominated as Best Actor. ★

LEAVE TWO HARD-DRINKING international movie stars, in this case Rock Hudson and Elizabeth Taylor, stranded on location (*Giant*) in far west Texas for weeks on end and here is what you get: pure American kitsch, right down to the Hershey's chocolate syrup. Over the years, the original recipe (like so many others) has been unnecessarily spruced up, somewhat diluting its unique high desert meets high-society charm. But the truth is, when you mix chocolate in with anything, it's hard to miss.

CHOCOLATE MARTINI

1 OZ. VODKA
1 OZ. KAHLUA
½ OZ. HERSHEY'S CHOCOLATE SYRUP
½ OZ. HALF AND HALF
1 BAR OF DARK CHOCOLATE

Pour liquid ingredients into a cocktail shaker filled with ice. Shake, then strain into a cocktail glass. Garnish across the top with shavings from chocolate bar.

Spruced-up Godiva Version:

1½ OZ. VANILLA VODKA
½ OZ. GODIVA DARK CHOCOLATE LIQUEUR
½ OZ. GODIVA WHITE CHOCOLATE LIQUEUR
SPLASH OF HALF AND HALF
1 BAR OF DARK CHOCOLATE

Pour liquid ingredients into a cocktail shaker filled with ice. Shake, then strain into a cocktail glass. Garnish across the top with shavings from chocolate bar.

DEAN MARTIN
1917–1995
ACTOR, SINGER, AND COMEDIAN

"You're not too drunk if you can lie on the floor without holding on."

Best known as the straight man in the Martin and Lewis comedy team and a core member of Sinatra's Rat Pack. A former boxer, steel-mill worker, and croupier, Dean Martin came up as a nightclub singer on the East Coast before teaming with comedian Jerry Lewis in 1946. Their act, with Martin as a straight man whose performances are continually undermined by Lewis, became one of the biggest draws in the country, lasting ten years and earning both men millions. As a solo performer, he won acclaim for his roles in *The Young Lions* (1958), *Some Came Running* (1958), and *Rio Bravo* (1959), the last of which was a wonderful turn as the archetypal drunken cowboy. As a member of the Rat Pack, along with Frank Sinatra and Sammy Davis, Jr., he established himself as one of the giants of the Las Vegas casino circuit. He brought his wisecracking drunk persona into millions of homes on a weekly basis with two long-running NBC series, *The Dean Martin Show* (1965–1974) and *The Dean Martin Celebrity Roast* (1974–1984). To the end, Martin remained one of the most bankable and beloved stars in show business.

★

WITH DEAN MARTIN, YOU could never tell. His family and friends held firm that the actor's public persona—the jovial, unapologetic tippler—was exactly that, a persona. The truth was, they said, that while he liked a drink, it wasn't a way of life. *New Yorker* film critic Anthony Lane later observed the same thing: "Martin's trick was to appear drunk even when he was not, and to look even when he *was* drunk as if he were only pretending to be drunk and were fully in control of the situation—as, of course, he was, even though drunk." Sounds like maybe Lane was drunk. The most Martin would admit to was four or five cocktails in a given evening, plus wine. You be the judge.

Still, if the quantity of Martin's consumption was something of a mystery, the quality of his drinking buddies was not. They were the Rat Pack, probably the most storied collection of debauchers in the history of Hollywood, and Vegas, too—and that's no small feat. With Sinatra or Davis or Bishop or Lawford at his side, Martin suddenly became the town drunk.

One friend of the Rat Pack who seems to have made a hobby out of testing various pals' capacity for booze was the indomitable Jackie Gleason. In his autobiography, Jerry Lewis, who considered Gleason "the greatest party animal alive," describes a contest that took place in 1950 at Manhattan's legendary Toots Shor's restaurant. It seems that Gleason had been teasing Martin endlessly about his "wussy drinking," and on this night Martin had had enough. The two stars decided to go drink for drink, last man standing wins. Immediately, a crowd gathered around. Gleason quickly ordered two Boilermakers. After which, Martin ordered two Pink Ladies—it was meant as a joke, but they drank them. With round one over, the actors decided to raise the stakes to a thousand dollars, which in 1950 was roughly equivalent to ten thousand dollars. The crowd grew even bigger, with gamblers and drunks eager to watch this historic battle unfold. But within minutes, it was over. Who had won?

Nobody. They'd each downed exactly two drinks when retired Major League shortstop Leo Durocher walked into the restaurant with the most beautiful woman on earth. Lewis describes her as having "breasts far out enough to ring her own doorbell." Immediately, the contest was forgotten.

At night's end, however, it would be Lewis (not Martin or Gleason) who wound up taking the woman back to his hotel suite. At 4:15 a.m., there was a knock on his door, followed by this exchange:

Martin: "I want sharesies!"

Lewis: "We share sandwiches, makeup, towels, tux ties, but we never share ladies."

Martin (*burp*): "Did you ever hear of an amendment?"

Hmm, sounds pretty damn drunk. ★

NOT AN EASY COCKTAIL to approximate for the simple reason that it is totally absurd. But since the Alaskan Polar Bear Heater belongs to Dean Martin's one-time comedy partner Jerry Lewis, it's the best kind of absurdity. As Buddy Love in *The Nutty Professor,* Lewis's order is as follows, "Pay attention. Two shots of vodka, a little rum, some bitters, and a smidgen of vinegar . . . a shot of vermouth, a shot of gin, a little brandy, lemon peel, orange peel, cherry, some more scotch. Now mix it nice, and pour it into a tall glass."

If the vinegar doesn't give pause, how about being asked to add *more* scotch, when there's no scotch to begin with? What is easier to imagine is the hangover. As a matter of fact, *The Nutty Professor* goes on to depict one of the best hangover scenes ever portrayed on film. Buddy Love (back as his alter ego, Professor Kelp) arrives to teach a science class. With the sound heightened, his briefcase hits the floor like bricks, a book strikes a desk like a gong. All this, while the professor's tongue pushes sand around in his mouth. It is painful just watching.

ALASKAN POLAR BEAR HEATER

. . . .

2 MARASCHINO CHERRIES

2 OZ. VODKA

½ OZ. LIGHT RUM

3 DASHES ANGOSTURA BITTERS

¼ OZ. WHITE VINEGAR

1 OZ. VERMOUTH

1 OZ. GIN

¼ OZ. BRANDY

LEMON PEEL

ORANGE PEEL

Muddle cherries in the bottom of a mixing glass. Add other ingredients and stir. Pour into a Collins glass filled with ice cubes. Garnish with lemon peel and orange peel.

Though not for the Polar Bear purist, add 1 oz. of orange juice if desired.

LEE MARVIN

1924–1987

ACTOR

"Tequila. Straight. There's a real polite drink. You keep drinking until you finally take one more and it just won't go down. Then you know you've reached your limit."

Known for stone-cold badass characters in films such as *The Man Who Shot Liberty Valance* (1962) and *The Big Red One* (1980), Lee Marvin was named after the Confederate general Robert E. Lee, a first cousin (four times removed). He received a Purple Heart as a Scout Sniper in the Marines during World War II and turned to acting when he was no longer able to continue in the military. (And even then, largely by chance: while working as a plumber's apprentice near a summer-stock playhouse, he asked for an audition on a lark). Marvin would earn a spot in a Broadway production of *Billy Budd* in 1951 and make his movie debut later that year with *You're in the Navy Now.* He landed numerous supporting roles over the next several years, carving out a niche as cinema's definitive villain. Terrorizing everyone from kids to old ladies, one critic would comment that Marvin was "rapidly becoming the Number 1 sadist of the screen." It wasn't until NBC's *M Squad* (1957–1960) that he began to broaden his range. After a series of costarring roles with John Wayne (including *Liberty Valance*), he received top billing for the first time in the 1964 remake of *The Killers*, and won a Best Actor Oscar the following year for his dual role in *Cat Ballou* with Jane Fonda. After *The Dirty Dozen* (1967), he briefly became one of the highest paid actors in Hollywood, but his career started to fade in the 1970s as Westerns and World War II pictures proved less profitable.

★

JUST START DRIVING, he'll come down. At least, that was the logic. Director John Boorman and his wife, Christel, had just finished dinner with Lee Marvin at Jack's at the Beach in Santa Monica. Well, that's not entirely true. It had *started* as a dinner, but the hour was now 2 a.m.—and Marvin was ripped on martinis. They'd all arrived together in Marvin's car, which he now insisted on driving, even though Boorman was trying to take away his keys. "Fuck you," Marvin had said, rearing back, gesturing with an imaginary samurai sword. This was a man who had made twenty-one beach landings in the South Pacific during WWII. Still, the imaginary sword didn't prevent anyone from getting into the car. And so Marvin persisted. He felt he was completely capable of driving, and to demonstrate this, he climbed up onto the top of the vehicle like an orangutan and crouched on the luggage rack.

Pity John Boorman, the British filmmaker who was directing his first American feature, *Point Blank,* with Marvin as the lead. Boorman was as yet untested. He was also rewriting the script on the fly, since Marvin had thrown the original shooting draft, based on the pulp novel *The Hunter* by Richard Stark, out the window. Locations were being scouted, sets were being designed, and still no one knew exactly what they were filming. Boorman would regularly meet with Marvin at his Malibu beach house to apprise him of his progress. The meetings typically went well—unless Marvin had too much to drink. "Beyond a certain level of vodka," Boorman would write, "he sailed out on his own into deeper waters where no mortal could follow."

> Boorman would regularly meet with Marvin at his Malibu beach house to apprise him of his progress. The meetings typically went well—unless Marvin had too much to drink. "Beyond a certain level of vodka," Boorman said, "he sailed out on his own into deeper waters where no mortal could follow."

Indeed, when drunk, Marvin left everyone behind—often even himself. One morning, he arrived home from an all-nighter without his house keys. After ringing the bell, he was greeted at the door by an unfamiliar woman. When he asked what she was doing in his house, she replied, "You sold it to me three months ago." He had to buy a Star Map to figure out where he currently lived. Prior to *Point Blank,* Marvin had been in Vegas for production of *The Professionals.* One night, returning to his hotel after a long day's shooting in Death Valley, he'd put quarter after quarter into a slot machine he couldn't get to work—not realizing it was actually a parking meter.

Anyway—the luggage rack. Marvin's car was parked at the end of a pier jutting into the ocean. Boorman figured if he drove the length of the pier, he could demonstrate he was serious about this, and Marvin would relent. So he gave it a shot, to no avail. Before reaching the actual road, Boorman got out and asked Marvin if he was ready to come down. Marvin snarled. Boorman got back behind the wheel. It was late. The Pacific Coast Highway was practically deserted. And Marvin had left him no choice.

Boorman turned onto the highway and slowly headed toward Marvin's beach house. It wasn't long before rolling lights appeared in the rearview mirror. The police. Boorman pulled over. An officer approached the car, assessing the scene. Finally, he looked at Boorman and asked his first question: "Do you know you have Lee Marvin on your roof?" ★

DAN TANA'S
9071 SANTA MONICA BLVD.
OPEN!

BATHED IN BORDELLO RED and adorned with checkered tablecloths, Dan Tana's tiny dining room could pass for any number of East Coast family-run Italian pasta joints. But in keeping with Hollywood's taste for reinvention, the restaurant's namesake and owner not only isn't from New York or Italy—he's a former Yugoslavian soccer player who immigrated to Los Angeles in the 1950s.

Before opening his own humble establishment in 1964, Dan Tana worked in a variety of restaurants (and briefly as an actor). The place is famous for its steaks and martinis, but initially the restaurant's hours were its main appeal. In a city where even the most popular eateries shut down by 11 p.m., Dana Tana kept the kitchen open late. (Last seating is at 1 a.m., making it especially attractive to patrons leaving the Troubadour, located just down the block.)

Deliberately unfussy and stridently old-school, Dan Tana's has remained a favorite of L.A. celebrities young and old for nearly fifty years. MCA power broker Lew Wasserman was a regular up until his death in 2002. Fred Astaire and John Wayne loved the place. Drew Barrymore claims she's been going there so long, her diapers were changed in one of the booths. Dabney Coleman, James Woods, George Clooney, and Karl Malden all have items on the menu named after them, as does former L.A. Laker Vlade Divac. Phil Spector had drinks there the night he shot Lana Clarkson.

With the restaurant's "seen it all" cool, simply being famous is not enough to get you a table: seating is limited, and if you're not a regular, you may have a long wait ahead of you. Ask John Travolta:

at the height of his *Saturday Night Fever* fame, he showed up one night with a date but without a reservation. When told it would be two hours before he could be accommodated, Travolta dropped his name with a defiant "don't you know who I am?" tone.

"Well, for you, Mr. Travolta," the maître d' allegedly replied, "it will be three." ★

STEVE MCQUEEN

1930–1980

ACTOR

"When a horse learns to buy martinis, I'll learn to like horses."

K nown for his quiet cool and an affection for motorized vehicles, as showcased in *The Great Escape* (1963) and *The Getaway* (1972), Steve McQueen performed many of his own stunts. Abandoned by his father as a boy, he was remanded to reform school as a teenager and worked as a janitor in a brothel, a lumberjack, and an oil rigger before enlisting with the Marines at seventeen. After an honorable discharge in 1950, he went to New York to study acting. McQueen gained notoriety in B-movies (most notably *The Blob*, 1958) and television (*Wanted: Dead or Alive*) before *The Magnificent Seven* (1960) and *The Great Escape* established him as a major movie star. He had a string of successes throughout the decade and received his lone Oscar nomination for *The Sand Pebbles* (1966). By the time he made *The Getaway*, directed by Sam Peckinpah and costarring McQueen's future wife Ali MacGraw, he was the highest-paid movie star in the world. But he retreated from Hollywood shortly after release of *The Towering Inferno* (1974), appearing in only three movies over the next six years while battling cancer. His final picture was *The Hunter*, in 1980. McQueen's status as avatar of all things cool remains rock solid, as evidenced in the film *The Tao of Steve* (2000).

★

THE ROOM HADN'T SEEN many happy endings, but Steve McQueen intended to change that. After countless drinks and a couple tabs of acid, he and cheesecake actress Mamie Van Doren were alone in a bedroom at the home of hairdresser-to-the-stars Jay Sebring.

This had once, long ago, been the bedroom of MGM producer Paul Bern and his wife, Jean Harlow. As the story goes, Bern shot himself in the house because he was physically incapable of pleasing Harlow in the bedroom—*this* bedroom, the very one in which Mc-Queen and Van Doren, after a promising first encounter, were now tripping.

McQueen and Van Doren had met exactly two nights prior, at the Whisky a Go Go. McQueen was a regular, with his own permanently reserved booth. There'd been dancing and booze, and a drunken tryst back at Van Doren's house that hadn't gone quite as far as McQueen had hoped. But Van Doren promised there'd be other nights, and tonight was turning out to be one of them.

Just like before, they'd met at the Whisky. McQueen suggested they go to a party Jay Sebring was throwing at his house. The Bern-Harlow house. There, while drinking and hanging out by the pool, McQueen dug into his pocket and pulled out some LSD. Van Doren was hesitant. "No bad trips," McQueen assured her. "This stuff's pharmaceutical. It makes sex a totally new experience."

If there were two things McQueen lived for, they were sex and new experiences. Although a guy who drank Old Milwaukee by the case when he first arrived in Hollywood (and never stopped), by the late 1960s he was open to every substance that came his way: peyote, hash, cocaine, amyl nitrate. As for women, they were in no short supply. Friends would tell stories of casual evenings they'd had with McQueen while he sat across the room, going at it with two, three ladies at a time. "Look," McQueen would say, "a certain type of broad goes to a movie and there's this guy on the screen—it's like seeing a rock at Tiffany's. They go after what they want. . . . I'm being chased around by *them*." And he wasn't going to let his marriage get in the way.

> If there were two things McQueen lived for, they were sex and new experiences. A guy who drank Old Milwaukee by the case when he first arrived in Hollywood (and never stopped), he was open to every substance that came his way by the 1960s.

McQueen and Van Doren were in bed together by the time the acid kicked in. She would later describe the experience as flashes of light skyrocketing around the room. And that afterward, with McQueen asleep at her side, she hallucinated a nude Paul Bern in a full-length mirror across the room, a mask over his eyes, a gun in his hand. ★

WHAT'S THERE TO say? It is hardly novel. But then again, given all the craft/micro/artisanal beers out there—the pale ale, blonde ale, brown ale, oatmeal stout, dry stout, sweet stout, porter, wheat, etc.—maybe Old Swill has become novel. After all, Pabst Blue Ribbon has enjoyed a resurgence, made hip by Dennis Hopper in David Lynch's *Blue Velvet:* "Heineken? Fuck that shit! Pabst Blue Ribbon!"

Besides, Old Milwaukee was always good enough for McQueen.

OLD MILWAUKEE

. . . .

Drink in four swallows or less.
Crumpling can is optional.

WHISKY A GO GO
8901 SUNSET BLVD.

OPEN!

IT WAS DURING A TRIP across Europe in 1963 that former Chicago cop Elmer Valentine stumbled upon the germ of an idea that would transform the culture not only of Los Angeles but of the United States.

Traveling with money he'd made selling his interest in the restaurant P.J.'s in West Hollywood, Valentine stopped one night at a discotheque in Paris, where the sight of young people enthusiastically crowding the dance floor motivated him to return to the states and open his own club, one so closely modeled after its inspiration in Paris he even stole the name: Whisky a Go Go.

Though nominally a discotheque, Valentine's Whisky specialized in live music:

opening night, 1964, featured Johnny Rivers ("Secret Agent Man"), whom Valentine had signed to a one-year performance contract. Between sets, a DJ in a slit skirt shook and shimmied while spinning records in a cage suspended high above the crowd—a happy accident (the cage was planned; the skirt wasn't) that spawned the go-go dancing craze of the 1960s.

But the Whisky proved to be much more than a gimmick: historically, it's one of the most important rock venues of all time. When the Doors were still practically unknown, even in Los Angeles, Valentine hired them as the house band. (He later fired them, after hearing a drunk Jim Morrison sing the lyrics to "The End.") During a single two-week stretch in 1966, the band would open for Buffalo Springfield, Captain Beefheart and His Magic Band, Love, and Them (featuring Van Morrison). The Byrds could be seen at the club on a regular basis, as could Frank Zappa and the Mothers of Invention. Alice Cooper, Led Zeppelin, the Kinks, the Who, the Animals, Cream, Big Brother and the Holding Company, Jefferson Airplane, the Velvet Underground, War, the Zombies, King Crimson, Fleetwood Mac—name a band of the era, they played the Whisky.

The club was enough of a sensation to attract such Hollywood elite as Steve McQueen and Cary Grant, and even drew a reservation from President Lyndon Johnson (which he made only to appease his daughters; he never showed). The Whisky was eventually franchised across the country, with sister locations in Atlanta and San Francisco. When punk and new wave overtook metal and hard rock in the late 1970s, the original Whisky didn't miss a beat, booking the Ramones, Blondie, Talking Heads, Patti Smith, and locals such as the Germs (who recorded a live album there) even as they packed the place with future arena rockers like Mötley Crüe and Van Halen. As the novelty of punk started to wear off, however, the Whisky started to lose steam. Valentine, who by then had also opened the Roxy Theatre and the Rainbow Bar & Grill to tremendous success, eventually sold his share of the club. Though still active most nights of the week, today the club's glory is but a memory. ★

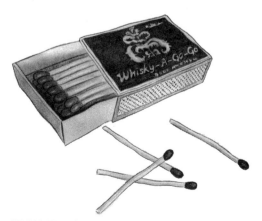

SAM PECKINPAH

1925–1984
DIRECTOR AND SCREENWRITER

"I can't direct when I'm sober."

Best known for *The Wild Bunch* (1969) and *Straw Dogs* (1971), Sam Peckpinpah was given the nickname "Bloody Sam" due to the violence in his films. A descendent of Western pioneers, his grandfather was a cattle rancher, superior court judge, and U.S. congressman. Peckinpah, who was frequently in trouble as a teenager, finished high school at a military academy, then obtained a master's degree at USC. He broke into television as a screenwriter in the late fifties, and on the recommendation of Brian Keith, star of *The Westerner,* landed his first feature directing job, *The Deadly Companions* (1961). His second film, *Ride the High Country* (1962), quickly became his calling card, but erratic behavior on the follow-up, *Major Dundee* (1965), which was plagued by budget overruns and delays, severely harmed his reputation. The runaway success of what would become Peckinpah's most famous film, *The Wild Bunch* (1969), earned him his lone Oscar nomination, for Best Screenplay. The early 1970s proved to be his most prolific and inspired period, as he completed four features— *The Ballad of Cable Hogue* (1970), *Straw Dogs, Junior Bonner* (1972), and *The Getaway* (1972)—in just three years. His next two pictures, *Pat Garrett and Billy the Kid* (1973) and *Bring Me the Head of Alfredo Garcia* (1974), proved to be the last worthy efforts of his career, as booze and drugs took their toll. He was known to carry a gun on set.

★

WHAT HAVE WE GOTTEN ourselves into? Bob Dylan didn't say it, but he didn't have to—the look on his face said it all. He was in a projection room in

Durango, Mexico, watching the first batch of dailies from *Pat Garrett and Billy the Kid*. Beside him were the film's star, Kris Kristofferson, and the film's director, Sam Peckinpah. Peckinpah was drunk and angry. After more than a week of shooting, Peckinpah declared every bit of footage unusable: "Can't I expect fucking focus?"

Dylan had been a last-minute addition to the cast. It was 1972, and Peckinpah was in that rare class of people who seemed never to have heard of him. But Rudy Wurlitzer, the film's screenwriter, and Gordon Carroll, its producer, were both fans, and they'd hoped to persuade Dylan to provide a few songs for the soundtrack. Through Kristofferson, a friend of Dylan's, they'd gotten Dylan a copy of the script, which he read and liked. After screening *The Wild Bunch* in New York, he signed on.

Peckinpah's first introduction to Dylan was over Thanksgiving weekend in Durango. After a ribald dinner, Dylan had played two songs he'd written for the movie, which sold Peckinpah on him immediately. Shortly thereafter, it was decided that including Dylan in the film itself could only help its commercial prospects, and so what had been a small part—Alias, a member of Billy the Kid's gang—was expanded and given to the singer. His scenes were among the first to be shot when cameras finally started rolling.

But the production of *Pat Garrett and Billy the Kid* was pure chaos from the get-go. Peckinpah, as had been the case for years, was drinking heavily and second-guessing plans he'd long since approved, from locations to costumes. Actor James Coburn, a loyal pal who had been cast in the role of Pat Garrett, put it well, "Peckinpah was a genius for four hours a day. The rest of time he was drunk." When Peckinpah's production manager suggested at one point that the director was "drinking this picture into the toilet," Peckinpah fired him. Then, at some point early on in the filming, the camera was apparently dropped, and unbeknownst to everyone, its mounting frame was bent.

Because the masters had to be sent to Los Angeles for developing, a week's worth of film was shot before anyone laid eyes on the footage. When it was finally screened (the episode described above), Peckinpah realized that half the frame was out of focus—in every scene! The entire week would have to be reshot.

Bob Dylan looked on as Peckinpah—disgusted and drunk—grabbed a folding chair and pulled it close to the screen. He climbed up, nearly falling as he did so, unzipped his pants, and proceeded to urinate his first initial all over the flickering images.

"From then on," second-unit director Gordon Dawson later said, "we watched dailies with this S-shaped piss stain on the screen." ★

THE GETAWAY (1972)

When Steve McQueen and publicist-turned-producer David Foster went in search of a director for *The Getaway*, a planned adaptation of the 1958 Jim Thompson novel, they had their sights on Peter Bogdanovich, fresh off his directorial breakthrough, *The Last Picture Show*. But Bogdanovich proved unavailable—officially, because he wanted to make *What's Up, Doc?*; unofficially, because he couldn't cast his lover, Cybill Shepherd, as the female lead. McQueen then suggested the hard-drinking Sam Peckinpah, with whom he'd recently worked on *Junior Bonner,* as a suitable replacement. Somehow, legendary Paramount producer Robert Evans agreed. And that little twist is what makes the production of *The Getaway* so interesting.

Let's back up a moment, because this is important. The bit where Bogdanovich wanted to cast Shepherd and couldn't? This was because Evans had *his* wife, Ali MacGraw, in mind. MacGraw, a relatively inexperienced actress but a bona fide star after the runaway success of *Love Story*, hadn't been in a movie in almost two years. At the time, she was waiting around on a Truman Capote–penned adaptation of *The Great Gatsby*, which Evans had planned to produce with MacGraw in the role of Daisy. But *Gatsby* was dragging on, and Evans was losing his mind fighting with Francis Ford Coppola over the editing of *The Godfather*, and ultimately, it seemed like the best possible thing for both of them was if she just went away to Texas for a couple months to make a picture. Unfortunately, with both a costar and a director who drank their way through every film they'd make—so would she. As you might guess, the film ended up destroying Evans and MacGraw's relationship.

The ensuing affair between MacGraw and McQueen is undoubtedly the best-known behind-the-scenes story of *The Getaway*. When Evans finally reunited with his wife after the picture wrapped, Evans found MacGraw "had as much interest in being with me as being with a leper. She was looking at me and thinking of Steve McQueen's cock." MacGraw eventually divorced Evans and, in 1973, married McQueen.

But the other story of *The Getaway*—as was typically the case on any film he directed—was Peckinpah's own insane boozing, by this point more out of control than anyone could have imagined. In the mornings, his hands would shake until he got a few eye-openers in him. Throughout the day, he called upon a prop-master—who had loaded up one of those trays beer-and-peanut vendors use at baseball games with a bucket of ice and assorted bottles of alcohol—to refill the tumbler of booze he kept in the drink-holder of his director's chair. The full extent of Peckinpah's drinking shocked his new bride, Joie Gould. "That he could stand up straight every day was extraordinary," she said.

According to biographer David Weddle, not only was Peckinpah able to stand up straight, he was remarkably productive. *The Getaway* was never meant to be high art. At the onset, Peckinpah himself had declared, "We're not doing *War and Peace* . . . get it on, get it over with, and get the fuck out." And even as the production traversed the Texas landscape, from Huntsville to San Antonio, from El Paso to the Mexico border, he kept things running smoothly, eventually wrapping the picture after two months of shooting, only four days behind schedule.

Because of the affair backstory, public anticipation for *The Getaway* was so high that it made more than twice its budget (pegged at just under $3 million) in exhibitor guarantees before a single theater screened it. By the end of its first year in release, it had grossed nearly $20 million, making it the biggest commercial success of Peckinpah's career, and the worst personal failure of Evans's.

BY MOST ACCOUNTS, Sam Peckinpah was a wildly indiscriminate drinker, downing his own lethal mixture of whatever was on hand: vodka, gin, whiskey, tequila, brandy. His gray hair wrapped in a bandana, his blue jeans grubby, sometimes carrying a pistol, sometimes throwing-knives. Peckpinpah would start drinking early—brandy and coffee, or maybe vodka and tonic, or maybe grenadine and water. By late morning, he might find some "alcoholic equilibrium," enjoying a few hours of focus and lucidity until at around 3 p.m. or so, when his cup runneth over. One type of liquor that seems to have played a starring role was Campari. A strong, bitter taste, you tend to either love it or hate it—like Bloody Sam's films, you're never ambivalent. On the set of *The Getaway,* Peckinpah would drink Campari with vodka and soda water. Pretty much as bitter as it gets. It's not a bad drink, if you like Campari, but maybe try a Negroni first. For that, just add sweet vermouth and while you can keep the vodka if you want, gin is more traditional.

CAMPARI & VODKA

. . . .

1½ OZ. CAMPARI

1½ OZ. VODKA

SODA WATER

ORANGE SLICE

Pour Campari and vodka into an Old-Fashioned or a Collins glass filled with ice cubes. Fill remainder of glass with soda water. Stir gently. Garnish with orange slice.

NEGRONI

. . . .

1 OZ. CAMPARI

1 OZ. GIN OR VODKA

1 OZ. SWEET VERMOUTH

ORANGE TWIST

Pour ingredients into an Old-Fashioned or a Collins glass filled with ice cubes. Stir gently. Garnish with orange twist.

OLIVER REED

1938–1999

CHARACTER ACTOR

"You meet a better class of person in pubs."

O liver Reed was known for playing burly Luddites, onscreen and off. Reed's first notable roles were in British horror movies produced by Hammer Films, including *The Two Faces of Dr. Jekyll* (1960) and *The Curse of the Werewolf* (1961), but his signature performance was as Bill Sikes in *Oliver!* (1968), directed by Carol Reed (his uncle). He frequently collaborated with Ken Russell; see roles in *The Devils* (1971), *Tommy* (1975), and his nude wrestling turn in *Women in Love* (1969). Beginning in the 1970s, Reed would star as Athos in three movies based on Alexandre Dumas's *Three Musketeers* novels and return to horror in 1979 with David Cronenberg's *The Brood.* He was largely relegated to straight-to-video releases by the 1980s, with the notable exception of *The Adventures of Baron Munchausen* (1988). Reed died at a bar in Malta while shooting Ridley Scott's *Gladiator* (2000).

★

OLIVER REED WAS WHAT you might call a "four-quadrant" drunk. Which is to say, whether you were male or female, under twenty-five or over, he would never fail to offend. A brawler, prankster, and unapologetic chauvinist (with a lifelong devotion to exposing his penis), Reed's besotted lunacy put him in a league of his own. Not surprisingly, it also helped sabotage any chance he ever had (and he had numerous) of becoming a Hollywood star. *Too drunk for Hollywood?* As a matter of fact, yes.

In the late 1960s, Reed was rumored to be the next James Bond, the replacement for Sean Connery. But for "unknown" reasons, the part went to

George Lazenby, an Australian whom Reed shortly thereafter attacked in a restaurant—slapping the MI6 agent in the face, then wrestling him to the ground amidst several servings of custard. In the early 1970s, Steve McQueen came to London with an interest in casting Reed in a major Hollywood production. Out on the town, Reed got so bombed he threw up on McQueen, splattering the superstar's jeans and shoes and forcing McQueen to spend the rest of the night reeking of puke. Once again, the role went to somebody else.

In the mid-1970s, in yet another display of his capacity for poor decision making, Reed reportedly passed up the role of Quint in Spielberg's *Jaws*. The part went to Robert Shaw instead, himself an impressive drinker, though somewhat less apocalyptic. It wasn't until the late 1990s, cast as Proximo the slave trader in that massive tentpole *Gladiator*, that Reed would again find himself within striking distance of international recognition. Sadly, in the final act of self-sabotage, he died during filming on the island of Malta, this while arm wrestling Royal Navy sailors in a pub, smashed on rum and his much-beloved whiskey. He was only sixty-one.

In the late 1960s, Reed was rumored to be the next James Bond, the replacement for Sean Connery. But for unknown reasons, the part went to George Lazenby, an Australian whom Reed shortly thereafter attacked in a pub—slapping the MI6 agent in the face, then wrestling him to the ground.

Still, as biographer Robert Sellers makes very clear, Reed's was a career worth noting, both on the silver screen and on the bar stool—a life filled with drunken antics that ranged from the violent to the humorous to the surreal. Focusing first on the violence, there were the typical fisticuffs: punch-ups with local toughs and sober citizens, the constables often called in. Sometimes things got a little out of hand, as on the night a West End heckler broke a glass on Reed's face that left him with thirty-six stitches and puckered scars for the next year. Naturally, there was the barroom arm wrestling, too, up until the day he died, as well as a game of head butting that was Reed's own invention. Simple enough, opponents were to continue to butt heads until one of them either backed down or buckled. But the roughneck stuff aside, what seems most curious was Reed's ever-increasing appetite for medieval weapons.

Even before he bought a fifty-two-bedroom country estate, Broome Hall, Reed had begun collecting broadswords, pikes, battle axes, and the like. Not a dangerous hobby in and of itself, but probably unwise for an angry young man so given over to drink. After enough booze, the monster inside would awaken. Like the time Reed lined up half a dozen drunken mates on his front lawn, armed them with antique weapons, and led an assault on the local police station. Or the night he forced a six-foot sword upon director (and enfant terrible) Ken Russell and insisted on dueling. Reed was not satisfied until Russell had cut open Reed's shirt, causing blood to pour down his chest. It was a passion that carried over into his film work. Cast as Athos in Richard Lester's *The Three Musketeers,* foregoing rehearsal, Reed would launch into sword fighting with such a frightening zeal that the terrified stunt team was reduced to drawing lots as to who would be matched up against him. There seemed to be no limit. While filming the Who's *Tommy* (Reed in the role of Uncle Frank), the actor quite naturally found a kindred spirit in legendary drummer Keith Moon, the two of them becoming running mates until Moon's untimely death a few year's later. Along with the orgies (the term seems almost too quaint), the television sets thrown out of windows, and the hotel wallpaper attacked with forks, there would be the odd duel at Broome Hall, this with double-edged swords. Moon even upped the ante with a new game: Reed was to run around the fields outside his estate, while Moon tried to run him down with his car.

It was dangerous, but comical, too, which more or less sums up Reed. Because along with the violence, there was humor—like passing out on the baggage carousel at Galway Airport or kidnapping famed producer David Puttnam. At a hotel in Madrid, Reed stole all the goldfish from the dining room pond and hid them in his bathtub. He replaced the school with fish-shaped carrots, then at breakfast made a singular display by diving into the water and eating what the other guests believed to be real fish. What can you say about a man like that?

On a bender in Los Angeles, Reed had a pair of eagle's claws tattooed on his penis. One can only imagine him waking up to find what he liked to call his "mighty mallet" swaddled in blood-soaked gauze. He went on to have an eagle's head tattooed on his shoulder. This, according to Sellers, so that when anyone asked why, Reed could tell them, *You should see where's it's perched.* ★

GUNK IS AN Oliver Reed original and a fitting accompaniment to his equally inventive head-butting game. Which is to say, both are easy to learn and cause a great deal of pain. To create Gunk, Reed would simply ask the bartender for an ice bucket and then ask him to pour every spirit behind the bar into it. Not unlike Ava Gardner's Mommy's Little Mixture, Gunk indicates a particular kind of wet-brained idiocy.

And here lies the classic chicken and egg debate. Only a man who has smashed his head into a great many things could come up with such a concoction. Or perhaps, only after drinking such a concoction could you swing your head about with true abandon.

THE VESPER MARTINI has little to do with Oliver Reed, and everything to do with James Bond. But then what if Reed had been Bond? It is hard to imagine. But some say that in 1969 he came quite close. He did after all best Bond (in the form of George Lazenby) that same year in a brawl in London. This all took place during the Sean Connery–Roger Moore transition. Foregoing Reed as Bond was a casting decision that the *Guardian* would describe as "one of the great missed opportunities of post-war British movie history."

As it stands, for most of James Bond's cinematic life, over which a great number of cocktails have been downed, he has almost always ordered a dry vodka martini, shaken, not stirred. A couple of not so small quibbles, like, why dry? The martini calls for vermouth and many feel strongly the wetter the better. And why shaken? It only dilutes it further. While we're at it—why vodka?

But then Bond is a creature of habit. After all, habit has kept him alive for a very long time. Pierce Brosnan, for one, looked like he actually enjoyed a martini and Roger Moore before him. Sean Connery seemed, well, more of a scotch man. But the truth of it is, while the Vesper martini was not introduced to movie audiences until the 2006 film adaptation of *Casino Royale,* that novel was Ian Fleming's first Bond book (1954) and the Vesper was actually the very first cocktail the character Bond ever ordered. It is about the Vesper that he first says "Shake it very well until it's ice cold."

On screen, Daniel Craig as Bond (the most Reed-like Bond yet) creates the drink and names it after his one true love, Vesper Lynd. It is her and perhaps sunset, the violet hour (not as much the evening prayers), that the name connotes. Worth mentioning is that in that same film Bond also finds himself tied to a chair naked and hit in the testicles with a heavy knotted rope. This seems very much a scene that Reed would have relished— and maybe even attempted in one configuration or another with Keith Moon. Likely, after drinking a bucket of Gunk (see above).

The cocktail, as written by Fleming: "Three measures of Gordon's, one of vodka, half a measure of Kina Lillet. Shake it very well until it's ice-cold, then add a large thin slice of lemon peel. Got it?" And here is the translation:

VESPER MARTINI

. . . .

3 OZ. GIN (PREFERABLY TANQUERAY OR BROKER'S SINCE GORDON'S HAS BEEN REFORMULATED).

1 OZ. VODKA

½ OZ. LILLET BLANC OR COCCHI AMERICANO (KINA LILLET IS NO LONGER AVAILABLE)

LEMON PEEL

Pour ingredients into a cocktail shaker filled with ice. Shake well, and then strain into cocktail glass. Garnish with lemon peel.

FRANK SINATRA

1915–1998
SINGER AND ACTOR

"I feel sorry for people who don't drink. When they wake up in the morning, that's as good as they are going to feel all day."

Frank Sinatra began as a singer, dubbed "the Voice" for his smooth inflections and distinctive phrasing. After fronting bands for Tommy Dorsey and Harry James, he embarked on a solo career in the early 1940s, quickly acquiring the sort of rabid teenage fan base that later coalesced around Elvis Presley and the Beatles. By the end of the decade, Sinatra had released a wildly successful solo record, *The Voice of Frank Sinatra* (1946), launched a weekly radio show, and teamed with Gene Kelly for three musicals: *Anchors Aweigh* (1945), *Take Me Out to the Ball Game* (1949), and *On the Town* (also 1949). Two years later, he struggled with hemorrhaging vocal chords and mentions in House Un-American Activities hearings. While attempting a singing comeback in Vegas, he accepted a paltry (by his standards) $8,000 fee to play Maggio in *From Here to Eternity* (1953), a part he desperately wanted. *Eternity* proved to be a major turning point, earning him an Oscar for Best Supporting Actor and laying the groundwork for such starring roles as *The Man with the Golden Arm* (1955). Despite inspired collaborations with Count Basie and Antonio Carlos Jobim, his record sales flattened as rock 'n' roll became the dominant sound of the sixties. Still, Sinatra would spend the rest of his life as an American icon. Becoming part owner of the Sands hotel and casino in Las Vegas, he earned $100,000 each week he performed. Sinatra announced his retirement in 1971 but continued to make sporadic appearances all the way up to his eightieth birthday, when he performed for the last time at the Shrine Auditorium in Los Angeles.

HOW DID SINATRA KNOW where to find her? No one bothered to ask. They were at the Villa Capri: Sinatra, Joe DiMaggio, Robert Mitchum, Lee Marvin, screenwriter Eddie Anhalt. Everyone but DiMaggio was out for yet another night of revelry during the production of the film *Not as a Stranger.* DiMaggio just had the misfortune of crossing their path—and he hadn't been feeling that well to begin with.

DiMaggio's marriage to Marilyn Monroe was basically over, everyone knew that. All he wanted to do was talk to her, he said. He'd spent days tracking her down, to no avail. It was tearing him apart. So Sinatra, DiMaggio's loyal friend, suggested that he and the rest of the guys help him find her. In fact, Sinatra happened to know where Monroe was right at that moment.

But first let's step back and acknowledge how astonishing it was that Stanley Kramer, director and producer of *Not as a Stranger,* had found it advisable to assemble this cast in the first place. In addition to Sinatra, Mitchum, and Marvin, he'd also hired character actors Broderick Crawford and Lon Chaney, Jr. It was the U.S. Olympic Dream Team of boozing—and much like their future basketball counterparts, they were unstoppable. The set was a free-for-all. Which is to say that a scheme like the one they were now hatching— the "Wrong Door Raid," the press would later call it—was definitely in their wheelhouse.

It took place the evening of November 5, 1954. Two years later it was aired out in court. DiMaggio never testified. Sinatra—who some believe perjured himself on the stand—insisted he stayed in his car, and that DiMaggio and two private investigators were the only ones directly involved. He didn't mention anyone else by name. Only Eddie Anhalt would speak publically about the incident, decades later, when all the other participants were dead. Anhalt said it went down like this:

After a few rounds at the Villa Capri, everyone present agreed to take DiMaggio to the apartment building where Sinatra said Monroe was hiding out. Apartment 3A. Sinatra said that's where they'd find her. What if she refused to answer the door, DiMaggio asked? Then they'd knock it down, Marvin replied. The only question now, *Whom could they get to knock it down?*

Sinatra, for one, was not a big man, at least in the conventional sense. When his one-time wife Ava Gardner was asked why she was with a one-hundred-nineteen-pound weakling, she remarked that "nineteen pounds is cock." However impressive that might be, it wasn't going to knock down a door. Soon all eyes turned to Mitchum. Not a small man, Mitch. But Mitch suggested Broderick Crawford—that Old Brod was big enough to do it.

> **Sinatra said that's where they'd find [Marilyn]. What if she refused to answer the door, DiMaggio asked? Then they'd knock it down, Marvin replied. The only question now, whom could they get to knock it down?**

By now the gang was drunk enough that the plan seemed foolproof. So they got in their cars, picked up Crawford at the Formosa (his regular hangout), and drove off to find Monroe.

Everyone staggered out of the car and up to the door of Apartment 3A. *Wham, wham*—Crawford kicked the door down just as he'd been asked to. And everyone piled in. Only Monroe wasn't there. In her place, they found a terrified fifty-year-old woman by the name of Florence Kotz—the apartment's actual tenant. Something along the lines of "oh shit" was collectively uttered, as Kotz grabbed her phone and called the police. By the time the law arrived, everyone was long gone.

Monroe, it turned out, was staying at the apartment house just next door.

"It was funny how Sinatra knew all this," Anhalt said. "Later I found out he was balling Marilyn himself, but we didn't think of that at the time." ★

THE MISFITS (1961)

In 1956, while living on a ranch outside Reno, Nevada (he was there establishing residency requirements to obtain a divorce), Pulitzer Prize–winning playwright Arthur Miller made the acquaintance of some old cowboys so desperate for money that they'd been reduced to capturing wild mustangs to sell to dog-food companies. A year later, divorced and in the full bloom of his relationship with Marilyn Monroe, Miller wrote about the cowboys for a short story eventually published in *Esquire*. And so began one of the most infamous productions in the history of American cinema—a film followed by the death of the two Hollywood icons who starred in it.

The principal cast was small but sensational: Monroe, Clark Gable, Montgomery Clift, Eli Wallach, and Thelma Ritter. The peerless John Huston would direct. Shooting on location in the Nevada desert was originally slated for March 3, 1960 (before the intense summer heat kicked in), but delays and prior commitments by Gable and Monroe pushed the start date to mid-July. By then, the desert was unbearable. Daytime temperatures could reach as high as 120° F. Dust was inescapable, requiring constant cleaning of camera lenses and generally making everyone uncomfortable. But that was nothing compared to the lack of comfort Monroe was creating.

Miller had written the script largely as a gift to Monroe, but by the time filming finally began, their marriage was in shambles. Monroe showed up having just completed *Let's Make Love*, during which she'd done just that with her costar, Yves Montand, and was now demanding that Montand be given a part in *The Misfits*. (She was eventually convinced that, yes, the request was outrageous.) For his part, Miller would meet Austrian photographer Inge Morath on the set and begin a relationship that would last the next forty years. Added to this, the problems between Monroe and Miller were not so subtly working themselves into the story, which Miller was rewriting on the fly, incorporating their private conversations as dialogue, almost taunting his wife.

Monroe showed up in Nevada with an entourage of her own personal hairdresser, body cosmetician, secretary, masseur, makeup artists, and an acting coach (Paula Strasberg). Gable initially referred to her as a "self-indulgent twat." Already heavily addicted to pills, she found a doctor willing to prescribe her three hundred milligrams of Nembutal—three times the maximum dosage. The night before her first scene with Gable, whom she'd idolized as a girl, she nervously popped the barbiturates like candy, nearly overdosing. She needed several hours to revive the next morning, and eventually her physical condition deteriorated to the point where she remained in her trailer for days at a time and finally had to be flown back to Los Angeles for a week to detox.

But Monroe wasn't the only one in poor health. Clift was losing his sight to cataracts and had his own on-set vices, carrying around a hip flask with a powerful combination of orange juice, vodka, and downers. To hear Monroe say it, "He's the only person I know who's in worse shape than I am." As for Gable—whose contract called for a salary of $750,000, ten percent of the gross, and weekly overtime payments of $48,000 if he was asked to work anything more than a nine-to-five day—he failed his preproduction physical and was told to give up smoking and drinking for good. (He followed this advice just long enough to pass a second exam.) Nearly sixty, Gable was also doing his own stunts; for one scene, he was dragged behind a truck traveling thirty-five miles an hour.

By the time production finally wrapped, The Misfits had gone forty days over schedule and a half-million dollars over budget. (There were rumors that the budget overrun was partly due to Huston's incessant gambling.) Two days after the final scene was shot between Gable and Monroe, Gable suffered a heart attack. Ten days later, he died. The Misfits was released on what would have been his sixtieth birthday, February 1, 1961.

Monroe, whose chaotic behavior caused Gable so much stress that she was blamed in some circles for his passing, attended the premiere a week before checking into a psychiatric ward. A year and a half later, she, too, died. The Misfits was her final completed picture. And Clift died five years later, having made only three more films. The night of his death, his secretary had asked him if he wanted to watch The Misfits on television. His response stands as his final words: "Absolutely not."

RAINBOW BAR & GRILL

9015 SUNSET BLVD.

OPEN!

FOUNDED IN 1972 BY Roxy Theatre owners Lou Adler and Elmer Valentine (the latter of whom also owned the Whisky a Go Go), the Rainbow occupies a lot that once belonged to Villa Nova, an Italian restaurant famous as the site where Vincente Minnelli asked Judy Garland to marry him, and where Marilyn Monroe and Joe DiMaggio had their first date. Its ties to the glamour of old Hollywood, however, end there.

The Strip had started to skew sleazy by the late 1960s, and while that didn't suit the image of Villa Nova (which reopened in Newport Beach), it fit the Rainbow like a glove. A grand opening party in honor of Elton John established the grill as a primary haunt of just about every major rock star of the time, including John Lennon and Led Zeppelin. (The Rainbow, it should be noted, is also one of two places rumored to have served John Belushi his last meal—Dan Tana's is the other.)

By the mid-eighties, the Strip had become ground zero for hair-metal: Members of Poison and Mötley Crüe were often seen at the bar; Guns N' Roses featured it in three separate videos. (And although it'd be sacrilege to lump him in with the lipstick-and-spandex crowd, it should be noted that Motörhead's lead singer and bassist, Lemmy Kilmister, was downing Jack and Coke there as long as any of them.)

Today, with hair-metal long dead, the Rainbow feels less like the hottest bar in town and more like a museum that serves steak. ★

ELIZABETH TAYLOR

1932–2011
ACTRESS

"The problem with people who have no vices is that generally you can be pretty sure they're going to have some pretty annoying virtues."

Born in London to American expatriates, Elizabeth Taylor's first screen appearance was Universal's *There's One Born Every Minute* (1942). But when she was cast the following year in MGM's *Lassie Come Home*, it kicked off a relationship with the studio that would last more than twenty years. She solidified her position as an up-and-coming star with *National Velvet* (1944) and transitioned seamlessly into more adult roles with *Conspirator* (1949). Her marriage to her first husband, hotel heir and socialite Conrad "Nicky" Hilton, lasted only months but generated great publicity for *Father of the Bride* (1950). The distinction between Taylor's personal and professional life would be forever blurred. She emerged as a fully-formed dramatic actress with *A Place in the Sun* (1951) and received Best Actress Academy Award nominations four years running: *Raintree County* (1957), *Cat on a Hot Tin Roof* (1958), *Suddenly, Last Summer* (1959), and finally, *Butterfield 8* (1960), which earned her her first Oscar. She ignited one of the biggest Hollywood scandals of the 1950s after the death of her third husband, Mike Todd, when she became romantically involved with singer Eddie Fisher. Taylor and Fisher married in 1959, but the relationship ended during filming of *Cleopatra* (1963), when she met and fell in love with her costar, Richard Burton—igniting an even bigger scandal. The couple's tumultuous relationship fueled the 1966 film version of *Who's Afraid of Virginia Woolf?*, resulting in a Best Actress Oscar for Taylor. While her box-office power diminished through the 1970s and 1980s, her celebrity and influence never did.

GIVEN EVERYTHING HE HAD heard about her, it's no wonder Richard Burton was wearing armor. By the filming of *Cleopatra,* Elizabeth Taylor had been married four times, divorced twice, widowed once, had three children with two different men and was in the process of adopting a fourth with her third. And she wasn't yet thirty.

It does suggest a certain take-no-prisoners attitude. But despite Burton's halter armor and leopard-pattern fur vest, his green silk tunic and matching leather wrist guards, he would end up falling on his sword—at least as Mark Anthony. This was the beginning of Liz & Dick, in hindsight a phenomenon whose scope and power was almost impossible to comprehend—a Grade 10 earthquake, a Category 5 hurricane that would rage throughout the remainder of the sixties and into the early seventies.

Their first scene together had no dialogue; they were just to look at each other. Burton showed up hungover—the attraction was instant and mutual. Still, at least in the beginning, the Welshman had intended it to be "once-over-lightly," a brief dalliance— he being a man who polished off women like pints. In the men's makeup trailer, Burton announced, "Gentlemen, I've just fucked Elizabeth Taylor in the back of my Cadillac!" A lout for sure, but even more so, a naïve lout: Elizabeth Taylor was no man's conquest.

At the moment, Taylor was married to Eddie Fisher. A feat that she accomplished by busting up his marriage to her good friend Debbie Reynolds. Fisher and Reynolds had been dubbed America's sweethearts, and the nation was not pleased. Three years later, in Italy, Fisher and Taylor's relationship was now winding down or, perhaps more accurately, exploding into a thousand pieces upon the world stage. Fisher initially objected to Burton constantly prodding his wife to drink, not that she needed prodding. The grape and the grain was something Taylor had embraced years earlier, during her brief first marriage to Conrad "Nicky" Hilton—heir to Hilton hotel fortune, and a young man with a gambling, boozing, wife-beating problem.

There had since been numerous stories of her drunken hijinks—different films, different leading men. Taylor drinking chocolate martinis with Rock Hudson while on location for *Giant.* Taylor jumping into a public fountain with Montgomery Clift while on location for *Raintree County.* It seemed standard movie star fare, but in matters of the liver, just as of the heart, Taylor rarely did anything half-assed. As her third husband, theater and film producer Mike Todd (born Avrom Hirsch Goldbogen), would note, "I have often seen her pour her own champagne for breakfast." And by this, he meant a bottle, sometimes two.

Cleopatra was to balloon into the most expensive movie ever made. And Liz & Dick's affair was to balloon into perhaps the biggest scandal ever. Taylor and Burton called it *le scandale,* an on-again, off-again juggernaut that whipped the paparazzi into an orgiastic frenzy never before seen. Even the Vatican piled on, publishing an open letter in the Vatican City weekly accusing the adulterers of "erotic vagrancy." Back in the States, Congresswoman Iris Blitch of Georgia attempted to have the couple barred from reentering "on the grounds of moral undesirability." Of the media spotlight, Burton remarked, "It's like fucking Khrushchev!" The man had a way with words. "I've had affairs before—how did I know the woman was so fucking famous!" But there was no stopping now.

Not the suicide attempts, not the drunken rows—often public and violent, Taylor giving as good as she got. It was a love affair set within the scorching hot crucible of movie magazine madness: flashbulbs popping, hands groping—constant pandemonium. When they arrived in Boston in 1964 from their honeymoon, hundreds of crazed fans flooded the tarmac and surrounded the plane. Mobbed at the hotel, Taylor was slammed into the wall, her hair pulled, Burton throwing punches. For the next ten years it was a nonstop circus as they crisscrossed the globe, emptying bottles together and making films together—*The V.I.P.s, The Sandpiper, The Taming of the Shrew, The Comedians, Boom!*—crap, really. The one exception being *Who's Afraid of Virginia Woolf?,* arguably the best performance of each of their careers. But how far from reality was it? A drunken Martha and George raging around the set during the day. A drunken Liz & Dick raging around the bedroom at night.

> **MARTHA**
>
> I'm loud, and I'm vulgar, and *I* wear the pants in the house because *somebody's* got to, but I am not a monster! I'm not!
>
> **GEORGE**
>
> You're a spoiled, self-indulgent, willful, dirty-minded, liquor-ridden . . .

> In matters of the liver, just as of the heart, Taylor rarely did anything half-assed. As her third husband, theater and film producer Mike Todd, would note, "I have often seen her pour her own champagne for breakfast." And by this, he meant a bottle, sometimes two.

No longer limiting herself to champagne, Taylor started her days with Bloody Marys, then turned things over to Jack Daniel's; Burton was plowing through three bottles of vodka a day or maybe taking it easy with five bottles of wine. It is a matter of debate as to who could drink more. But they were quite the pair, puking in hotel lobbies, falling down restaurant stairs, punching paparazzi, policemen, costars. Taylor would confess that her capacity was terrifying, saying—"I had a hollow leg. I could drink everyone under the table." She called Burton a burnout, talentless. He called her a "fat little tart."

Ugliness, made even more so by the backdrop of such incredible movie-star splendor. Biographer Robert Sellers describes celluloid gods with Rolls-Royces, mink coats (one for him, too), diamonds and more diamonds—Burton out-bidding Aristotle Onassis on a $1.1 million rock. In their massive dressing room suites, butlers and maids catered to a sprawling entourage of hairdressers, publicists, make-up artists, personal assistants, not to mention friends, family members, and hangers-on. Vacation homes and movie locations, traveling with a pack of incontinent dogs and ninety-three suitcases—how did they sustain it all? Physically, emotionally, let alone financially? And why did they want to?

Burton commented in private, "Elizabeth is more famous than the Queen. I wish none of it had ever happened." Taylor told the press, "I don't know how many plates I broke over his head." Finally in 1972, during the filming of *Divorce His-Divorce Hers* (a two-part TV movie), the well began to run dry. There is much irony here: they were back in Rome, telling the story of a marriage destroyed beyond repair. Burton was a mess physically, Taylor a mess emotionally, nothing new with that. There is a story of him inviting an attractive extra up to his room and Taylor leaping out from behind the couch. She breaks a liter of vodka and chases him around the room with the bottle neck—nothing new there, either. Just that maybe, after a decade, it finally felt old.

Back in Hollywood, the fighting would continue. One day Taylor showed up at the Beverly Hills Hotel. She walked into the bar, where she knew Burton would be, and punched him in the face. *Divorce His-Divorce Hers* had recently been broadcast on TV— and Taylor soon announced that she and Burton were officially separated. A year later they would get divorced.

Of course, a year after that, they would remarry. ★

SAID TO BE THE BIRTHPLACE of the Mai Tai, a rum concoction created by "Trader" Victor J. Bergeron, the in-house watering hole of Hilton's flagship Beverly Hills location was actually the fourth Trader Vic's in the U.S. when it opened in 1955. (The original was in Oakland; the second, in Seattle.) But with its high-profile clientele—boosted by the hotel's hosting of the Golden Globes every year since 1961—and international reputation, it elevated Polynesian-themed kitsch into something resembling (whoa) class, and later reappropriated as lounge cool.

Reflecting a nationwide trend toward island-themed bars (thatched palm ceilings, fishing nets, tiki masks), by the end of the 1960s, there were over twenty Trader Vic's outposts around the globe, many of them affiliated with Hilton hotels. The Beverly Hills location received benediction from such stars as Frank Sinatra, Dean Martin, Anthony Quinn, Mia Farrow, Nancy Sinatra, Jack Lemmon, Ronald Reagan, and Warren Beatty.

But despite the powerful allure of the Mai Tai or the equally tasty Scorpion Bowl, the widespread appeal of Trader Vic's diminished as the 1970s gave way to the 1980s and the tikiphiles grew older. Still, in Los Angeles, its appeal remained strong all the way into the twenty-first century. More than forty years after its founding, patrons included Kevin Spacey, Steven Spielberg, Tom Cruise, Matt Damon, Harrison Ford, Jodie Foster, and Russell Crowe.

Sadly, construction plans at the intersection of Santa Monica and Wilshire forced the closure of the original Beverly Hills Trader Vic's in 2007. Whereas before it was easily accessible to anyone via a street-level high-peaked Polynesian entrance marked by a giant totem pole, it's now a fully assimilated hotel amenity, with smaller, less colorful digs just off the Beverly Hilton pool. ★

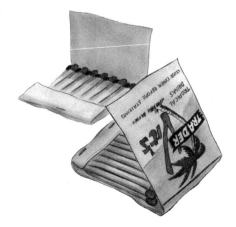

MAI TAI

. . . .

1 OZ. DARK JAMAICAN RUM

1 OZ. MARTINIQUE RUM

½ OZ. ORANGE CURACAO

¼ OZ. SIMPLE SYRUP

¼ OZ. ORGEAT SYRUP

¼ OZ. FRESH LIME JUICE

MINT SPRIG

FRUIT STICK (ORANGE SLICE
    AND CHERRY)

Pour all liquid ingredients into a cocktail shaker filled with ice. Shake, then strain into a double Old-Fashioned glass filled with crushed ice. Garnish with mint sprig and fruit stick. Serve with straw.

THE ROSETTA STONE of giant communal tiki drinks. The original 1946 version of the Scorpion Bowl serves about twelve people.

SCORPION BOWL

· ·

1½ BOTTLES PUERTO RICAN RUM
(RUM MERITO OR BRUGAL
SUGGESTED)*

½ BOTTLE WHITE WINE

2 OZ. GIN

2 OZ. BRANDY

16 OZ. FRESH LEMON JUICE

8 OZ. FRESH ORANGE JUICE

8 OZ. ORGEAT SYRUP

2 MINT SPRIGS

GARDENIAS

Mix all of the liquid ingredients in a punch bowl. Add cracked ice and let stand for 2 hours. Add more cracked ice. Garnish with mint and gardenias. Serve with straws.

*1½ bottles is about 36 ounces.

Another version, also delicious, was developed more that a decade later, in 1958, by restaurateur Steve Crane—one-time B-movie actor and owner of the Beverly Hills celebrity hotspot Luau. A successful restaurateur for twenty-five years who would leave his mark on Hollywood nightlife, Stephen Crane is also remembered as one of Lana Turner's ex-husbands (the second of seven).

Crane met Turner at Mocambo and married her three weeks later, somehow forgetting to mention he was not yet divorced from his first wife. The marriage was annulled, but after discovering Turner was pregnant (and once Crane was legally divorced), the couple remarried. They would divorce a second time one year later, and it was their daughter, Cheryl Crane, who at age fourteen famously stabbed gangster Johnny Stompanato to death in her mother's bedroom. Stephen Crane would be linked to numerous other starlets, including Ava Gardner and Rita Hayworth. It couldn't have been his B-picture good looks that seduced them—so maybe it was his bartending skills.

CRANE'S SCORPION BOWL

2 OZ. GOLD PUERTO RICAN RUM.

2 OZ. GIN

1 OZ. BRANDY

¾ OZ. SIMPLE SYRUP

1 OZ. ORGEAT SYRUP

1 OZ. FRESH LIME JUICE

2 OZ. FRESH ORANGE JUICE

8 OZ. CRUSHED ICE

Pour ingredients into blender and mix for several seconds until uniformly combined. Without straining, empty into what seems like the right-sized bowl. Drink by yourself—or share.

NATALIE WOOD

1938–1981

ACTRESS

*"My mother used to tell me,
'No matter what they
ask you . . . always say yes.
You can learn later.'"*

Best known as the beautiful lead in *Rebel Without a Cause* (1955) and *Splendor in the Grass* (1961). The daughter of impoverished Russian immigrants, Natalie Wood was pushed into show business by her famously ambitious mother, Maria "Mud" Gurdin, making her screen debut at age four in *Happy Land* (1943). She continued to work as a child actor, appearing in *Miracle on 34th Street* and *The Ghost and Mrs. Muir* (both 1947), before landing her first major role, opposite James Dean in *Rebel Without a Cause*, which earned her an Oscar nomination for Best Supporting Actress. Wood was again nominated for an Academy Award, this time for Best Actress, for *Splendor in the Grass*. This proved to be the most fertile period of her career, as she appeared in two musicals, *West Side Story* (1961) and *Gypsy* (1962), and the romantic comedy *Love with the Proper Stranger* (1963), for which she received another Oscar nod. After the birth of her first child in 1970, Wood would appear only sporadically on television and in the occasional feature. She drowned off the coast of Santa Catalina Island during a break in the picture *Brainstorm*.

★

IF THEY WERE GOING to do this, they needed to do it right. Dennis Hopper and Nick Adams, both cast in *Rebel Without a Cause,* had just returned from the liquor store with several cases of champagne. Little more than kids, obsessed with emulating their Hollywood idols, they'd decided what they really needed to do this night was have an orgy, because that's what John Garfield used to do. It would be the two of them and Natalie Wood. (Can you have an orgy with just three people? Isn't that called something else?) Wood had said she was up for it, under one condition: she'd need to bathe in champagne first—like Jean Harlow.

One of the perks of being a young star, as Natalie Wood had been, is that you get away with things other kids can't. The flipside, of course, is that you lose your childhood to Hollywood. At fifteen, Wood was sipping wine at Frank Sinatra's house, her mother, Mud, having thrust the teenager on the thirty-eight-year-old. Soon Wood began to smoke and to drink heavily. At sixteen she was ordering drinks at Villa Capri and Ciro's, passing out on Zombies at frat parties in the Hollywood Hills. By the time she hooked up with Hopper (he'd already been cast in *Rebel,* she had yet to be), she was more sophisticated than anyone she knew her age and in many ways more immature. Her friend Margaret O'Brien, similarly a former child star, described Wood's affectations, her mink stoles and cigarette holders, as nothing more than "a feint, a look, an attitude." A little girl playing dress-up.

> One of the perks of being a young star, as Natalie Wood had been, is that you get away with things other kids can't. The flipside, of course, is that you lose your childhood to Hollywood.

Hopper, just two years older, was a newcomer to the movie industry, but already was displaying the insolent, self-destructive behavior that would make him its enfant terrible by the 1970s. Eager to impress Wood—some said it was genuine affection, others opportunism—he'd taken her out drinking one night in Los Angeles before shooting began on *Rebel* and wound up flipping his car somewhere in Laurel Canyon. Wood, thrown into the street and knocked out cold, had to be rushed to the hospital. Drifting in and out of consciousness, she kept telling the police to call Nicholas Ray (the director of *Rebel* and her secret lover) instead of her mother, Mud. Wood's rebellious spirit, her desire to break away, impressed Ray greatly, who was at her bedside when she awoke. "They called me a goddamn juvenile delinquent," she told the director, "*Now* do I get the part?" As for Mud, she would eventually find out about both affairs, but according to Hopper, always looking to advance her daughter's career, complained to Warner Bros. only about him, not Ray. It would remain quite the circus, Wood sleeping with Ray and Hopper (and maybe Nick

Adams), and Ray sleeping with Wood and, given his bisexuality, maybe Sal Mineo. While James Dean was left odd man out.

Fast forward several months. *Rebel* was complete, and here were Wood and Hopper and Adams, living out their wildest movie-star fantasies at a cabin in the mountains northeast of Los Angeles. Eager to get the orgy underway, they poured bottle after bottle of champagne into the cabin's bathtub. Wood dipped her toe in: *this* was glamour. In went the rest of her—but not for long. Because as soon as her most sensitive areas came in contact with the alcohol, she shrieked in pain. Her vagina, she screamed, was on fire! And thus was the orgy extinguished. ★

The End

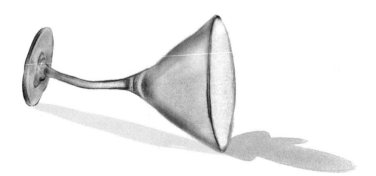

ACKNOWLEDGMENTS

We collaborated with a great many smart and talented people in getting this book to print.

First and foremost our extraordinary editor Andra Miller. We were lucky to have someone so intelligent, supportive, and funny, too. Incredibly patient, Andra worked long and hard to bring out the best in our words and art. She was a gift. And Keven McAlester, who is credited as a consulting writer. Much more than that, Keven became a partner, really, in shaping the text, and the book is so much richer for it. We would like to thank Algonquin's team. They seem to us the best team on the planet, and at every instance bent over backward to make decisions that worked for us. Anne Winslow was our remarkable creative director and Jean-Marc Troadec our truly gifted designer; it was their vision and style that wove the writing and illustrations together so beautifully. And a special thanks to Elisabeth Scharlatt, our publisher. Elisabeth never fails to put the book first, and told us early on that we could have as much time as we needed to get it right. Quite possibly she regrets having said that. Craig Popelars and Kelly Bowen in Algonquin's marketing and publicity, for all they have done and are planning to do. Drew Jacobson of Luminosity was our lead bartender, with the help of his business partner Paul Keo. Drew's terrific palate, deep knowledge, and cheerful perseverance (though really, who doesn't like testing drinks?) resulted in some delicious cocktail recipes. Our wonderful agent David Kuhn who seems to do everything and more—this book was David's idea. And our amazingly persistent researchers, all of them across the years: Tim Mackin and Emily Schlesinger, as well as Jordan Cohen, Joel Dando, Michelle Hovanetz, Aily Nash, and Georgia Stockwell. And of course, there are friends and family, too, who have so generously helped along the way—with ideas, advice, support: Madelyne Bailey, Paul Bailey, Edward Beason, Lyndie Benson, Minor Chavez, Chelsie Corbett, Gerlayn White Dreyfous, Karen Duffy, Eve Epstein, Joe Flanigan, Shannon and Drew Hayden, Taylor Johns, Sarah Johnson, Peter Kaplan, Andrew Karsch, Sheila and Chris Kennedy, Robert Kennedy Jr., Edward Klaris, John Lambros, Kim Lowe, Brendan

McBreen, Joe McDougall, Derek Newman, Jeanine Pepler, Robin Pogrebin, Edward Saxon, Stephen Sherrill, Franco Simplicio and his terrific Malibu restaurant the Sunset, Brian Strange, and Shamra Tankersley—thank you.

MARK BAILEY: I would specifically like to thank my wife, Rory. It is not always easy living with a writer, and living with a drinking writer is harder still. But a drinking writer who is writing a book on drinking—that takes a special kind of woman, which you are. This book is for you, with love.

And my children—Georgia, Bridget, and Zachary. Unfortunately, you are not allowed to read this until you are at least twenty-one.

EDWARD HEMINGWAY: Special thanks go to my family—Valerie, Vanessa, Sean, and Brendan Hemingway, for all having a terrific sense of humor, but more importantly, for always being there.

SOURCES

Below is a list of many wonderful books—biographies, autobiographies, memoirs, anthologies, urban histories, cultural histories, film histories, film analysis, celebrity interviews—as well as newspaper articles, magazine pieces, web posts, talk show appearances, and films.

We are greatly indebted to these very talented writers. We encourage interested readers to explore these sources. It is here that you will find the whole story.

Abrams, Brett L. *Hollywood Bohemians: Transgressive Sexuality and the Selling of the Movieland Dream*. Jefferson, NC: McFarland, 2008.

Alleman, Richard. *Hollywood: The Movie Lover's Guide*. New York: Broadway Books, 2005.

Austerlitz, Saul. *Another Fine Mess: A History of American Film Comedy*. Chicago: Chicago Review Press, 2010.

Bacall, Lauren. *By Myself and Then Some*. New York: HarperEntertainment, 2005.

Bach, Steven. *Marlene Dietrich: Life and Legend*. New York: William Morrow, 1992.

Barbas, Samantha. *The First Lady of Hollywood: A Biography of Louella Parsons*. Berkeley: University of California Press, 2005.

Barrymore, Diana and Gerold Frank. *Too Much, Too Soon*. New York: Henry Holt, 1957.

Barrymore, Elaine and Sanford Dody. *All My Sins Remembered*. New York: Appleton-Century, 1964.

Basinger, Jeanine. *Silent Stars*. New York: Alfred A. Knopf, 1999.

Bell, Alphonzo, with Marc L. Weber. *The Bel Air Kid*. Victoria, BC: Trafford, 2002.

Berg, A. Scott. *Goldwyn: A Biography*. New York: Riverhead Books, 1989.

Bessette, Roland. *Mario Lanza: Tenor in Exile*. Portland: Amadeus, 2003.

Birchard, Robert S. *Cecil B. DeMille's Hollywood*. Lexington: University Press of Kentucky, 2004.

Biskind, Peter. *Easy Riders, Raging Bulls*. New York: Simon & Schuster, 1998.

Bogle, Donald. *Bright Boulevards, Bold Dreams: The Story of Black Hollywood*. New York: One World Books, 2006.

Boller, Paul F., Jr., and Ronald L. Davis. *Hollywood Anecdotes*. New York: William Morrow, 1987.

Boorman, John. *Adventures of a Suburban Boy*. London: Faber & Faber, 2003.

Bosworth, Patricia. *Montgomery Clift: A Biography*. New York: Harcourt Brace Jovanovich, 1978.

Bragg, Melvyn. *Richard Burton: A Life*. Boston: Little, Brown, 1988.

Bret, David. *Clark Gable: Tormented Star*. New York: Carroll & Graf, 2007.

———. *Elizabeth Taylor: The Lady, The Lover, The Legend 1932–2011*. Vancouver, BC: Greystone Books, 2011.

———. *Tallulah Bankhead: A Scandalous Life*. London: Robson Books, 1996.

Brettell, Andrew. *Cut!: Hollywood Murders, Accidents, and Other Tragedies*. Barron's Educational Series. Hauppauge, NY: 2005.

Brian, Denis. *Tallulah, Darling: A Biography of Tallulah Bankhead*. New York: Macmillan, 1980.

Brooks, Louise. *Lulu in Hollywood*. Minneapolis: University of Minnesota Press, 1982.

Brownlow, Kevin. *Behind the Mask of Innocence*. New York: Alfred A. Knopf, 1990.

Calistro, Paddy, and Fred E. Basten. *The Hollywood Archive*. New York: Universe Publishing, 2000.

Callan, Michael Feeney. *Richard Harris: A Sporting Life*. London: Sidgwick & Jackson, 1990.

Capote, Truman, and Gerald Clarke. *Too Brief a Treat: The Letters of Truman Capote*. New York: Vintage, 2005.

Capua, Michelangelo. *Montgomery Clift: A Biography*. Jefferson, NC: McFarland, 2002.

Carey, Harry, Jr. *Company of Heroes: My Life as an Actor in the John Ford Stock Company*. Lanham, MD: Scarecrow Press, 1996.

Carter, Graydon, ed. *Vanity Fair's Tales of Hollywood*. New York: Penguin, 2008.

Chandler, Charlotte. *Marlene: Marlene Dietrich, a Personal Biography*. New York: Simon & Schuster, 2011.

———. *Not the Girl Next Door: Joan Crawford, a Personal Biography*. New York: Simon & Schuster, 2008.

Clarke, Gerald. *Get Happy: The Life of Judy Garland*. New York: Random House, 2000.

Cobb, Sally Wright, and Mark Willems. *The Brown Derby Restaurant: A Hollywood Legend*. New York: Rizzoli, 1996.

Cowie, Peter. *The "Apocalypse Now" Book*. Boston: Da Capo Press, 2000.

Cramer, Richard Ben. *Joe DiMaggio: The Hero's Life*. New York: Touchstone. 2000.

Crosby, Bing, and Peter Martin. *Call Me Lucky: Bing Crosby's Own Story*. Cambridge, MA: Da Capo Press, 1993.

Curtis, James. *W. C. Fields: A Biography*. New York: Alfred A. Knopf, 2003.

Curtis, Wayne. *And a Bottle of Rum: A History of the New World in Ten Cocktails*. New York: Crown, 2006.

Daniel, Douglass K. *Tough as Nails: The Life and Films of Richard Brooks*. Madison: University of Wisconsin Press, 2011.

Dardis, Tom. *Some Time in the Sun*. New York: Limelight Editions, 1976.

———. *The Thirsty Muse: Alcohol and the American Writer*. New York: Ticknor & Fields, 1989.

Davidson, Bill. *Spencer Tracy: Tragic Idol*. New York: E. P. Dutton, 1987.

Dick, Bernard F. *The Merchant Prince of Poverty Row: Harry Cohn on Columbia Pictures*. Lexington: University Press of Kentucky, 1993.

Drew, Bernard. "John Huston: At 74 No Formulas," in Robert Emmet Long, ed.

Eisenschitz, Bernard. *Nicholas Ray: An American Journey*. Trans. Tom Milne. London: Faber & Faber, 1993.

Eliot, Marc. *Cary Grant: A Biography*. New York: Three Rivers Press, 2004.

Ellenberger, Allan R. *Ramon Navarro: A Biography of the Silent Film Idol, 1899–1968*. Jefferson, NC: McFarland, 1999.

Evans, Peter and Ava Gardner. *Ava Gardner: The Secret Conversations*. New York: Simon & Schuster, 2013.

Evans, Robert. *The Kid Stays in the Picture: A Notorious Life*. New York: Hyperion, 1994.

Eyman, Scott. *Ernst Lubitsch: Laughter in Paradise*. New York: Simon and Schuster, 1993.

———. *Lion of Hollywood: The Life and Legend of Louis B. Mayer*. New York: Simon & Schuster, 2005.

Fagen, Herb. *Duke, We're Glad We Knew You: John Wayne's Friends and Colleagues Remember His Remarkable Life*. New York: Carol, 1996.

Fine, Richard. *West of Eden: Writers in Hollywood, 1928–1940*. Washington, DC: Smithsonian Institute Press, 1993.

Finstad, Suzanne. *Natasha: The Biography of Natalie Wood*. New York: Harmony Books, 2001.

Fishgall, Gary. *Against Type: The Biography of Burt Lancaster*. New York: Scribner, 1995.

———. *Gonna Do Great Things: The Life of Sammy Davis, Jr.* New York: Scribner, 2003.

Fleming, E. J. *The Fixers: Eddie Mannix, Howard Stickling and the MGM Publicity Machine*. Jefferson, NC: McFarland, 2004.

———. *Paul Bern: The Life and Famous Death of the MGM Director and Husband of Harlow*. Jefferson, NC: McFarland, 2009.

Flynn, Errol. *My Wicked, Wicked Ways*. New York: G. P. Putnam's Sons, 1959.

Folsom, Tom. *Hopper: A Savage American Journery*. New York: HarperCollins, 2013.

Ford, Dan. *Pappy: The Life of John Ford*. New York: Da Capo Press, 1998.

Fordin, Hugh: *MGM's Greatest Musicals: The Arthur Freed Unit*. Cambridge, MA: Da Capo Press, 1996.

Fricke, John. *Judy: A Legendary Film Career*. Philadelphia: Running Press, 2011.

Fussell, Betty Harper. *Mabel*. New Haven: Ticknor and Fields, 1982.

Gerhing, Wes D. *Laurel & Hardy: A Bio-Bibliography*. Westport, CT: Greenwood Press, 1990.

Giddins, Gary. *Bing Crosby: A Pocketful of Dreams—The Early Years, 1903–1940*. Boston: Little, Brown, 2001.

Godfrey, Lionel. *Cary Grant: The Light Touch*. New York: St. Martin's Press, 1981.

Good, Howard. *The Drunken Journalist: The Biography of a Film Stereotype*. Lanham, MD: Scarecrow Press, 2000.

Goodrich, David L. *The Real Nick and Nora: Frances Goodrich and Albert Hackett, Writers of Stage and Screen Classics*. Carbondale: South Illinois University Press, 2001.

Goodwin, Betty. *Chasen's: Where Hollywood Dined*. Santa Monica: Angel City Press, 1996.

Graham, Sheilah. *The Garden of Allah*. New York: Crown Books, 1970.

Grant, Barry Keith, ed. *Fritz Lang: Interviews*. Conversations with Filmmakers. Jackson: University Press of Mississippi, 2003.

Greenberg, Peter S. "Saints and Stinkers: The Rolling Stone Interview," in Robert Emmet Long, ed.

Grey, Rudolph. *Nightmare of Ecstasy: The Life and Art of Edward D. Wood, Jr.* Los Angeles: Feral House, 1992.

Guiles, Fred Lawrence. *Marion Davies*. New York: McGraw-Hill, 1972.

———. *Stan*. London: Michael Joseph, 1980.

Harris, Warren G. *Clark Gable: A Biography*. New York: Harmony Books, 2002.

Hecht, Ben. "Farewell, Soldier," in Christopher Silvester, ed.

Heimann, Jim. *Out with the Stars: Hollywood Nightlife in the Golden Era*. New York: Abbeville Press, 1985.

Hellman, Lillian. *Maybe: A Story*. Boston: Little, Brown, 1982.

Heymann, C. David. *Liz: An Intimate Biography of Elizabeth Taylor*. New York: Birch Lane Press, 1995.

Higham, Charles. *Orson Welles: The Rise and Fall of an American Genius*. New York: St. Martin's Press, 1985.

Higham, Charles, and Roy Moseley. *Cary Grant: The Lonely Heart*. San Diego: Harcourt Brace Javanovich, 1989.

Hiney, Tom. *Raymond Chandler: A Biography*. New York: Grove Press, 1997.

Hodges, Graham Russel Gao. *Anna May Wong: From Laundryman's Daughter to Hollywood Legend*. New York: Palgrave Macmillan, 2004.

Hofler, Robert. *The Man Who Invented Rock Hudson: The Pretty Boys and Dirty Deals of Henry Willson*. New York: Carroll & Graf, 2005.

Huston, John. *An Open Book*. New York: Alfred A. Knopf, 1980.

Inge, M. Thomas, ed. *Truman Capote: Conversations*. Jackson: University Press of Mississippi, 1987.

Jacobs, Diane. *Christmas in June: The Life and Art of Preston Sturges*. Berkeley: University of California Press, 1992.

Jensen, Richard. *The Amazing Tom Mix: The Most Famous Cowboy of the Movies*. Lincoln, NE: iUniverse, 2005.

Jordan, Stephen C. *Hollywood's Original Rat Pack: The Bards of Bundy Drive*. Lanham, MD: Scarecrow Press, 2008.

Kamp, David. "Cleopatra: When Dick Met Liz." In Graydon Carter, ed.

Kanfer, Stefan. *Tough Without a Gun: The Life and Extraordinary Afterlife of Humphrey Bogart*. New York: Vintage Books, 2011.

Kaplan, James. *Frank: The Voice*. New York: Doubleday, 2010.

Kashner, Sam. " 'Rebel Without a Cause': Dangerous Talents," in Graydon Carter, ed.

Kashner, Sam, and Jennifer MacNair. *The Bad and the Beautiful: Hollywood in the Fifties*. New York: W. W. Norton, 2002.

Keaton, Buster, and Charles Samuels. *My Wonderful World of Slapstick*. Garden City, NY: Doubleday, 1960.

Kelley, Kitty. *Elizabeth Taylor: The Last Star.* New York: Simon & Schuster, 1981.

——. *His Way: The Unauthorized Biography of Frank Sinatra.* New York: Bantam, 1986.

Kobler, John. *Damned in Paradise: The Life of John Barrymore.* New York: Atheneum, 1977.

Koszarski, Richard. *Von: The Life & Films of Erich Von Stroheim.* New York: Limelight Editions, 2001.

LaGuardia, Robert. *Monty: A Biography of Montgomery Clift.* New York: Arbor House, 1977.

Lane, Anthony. *Nobody's Perfect: Writings from "The New Yorker."* New York: Picador, 2002.

Langmead, Donald. *Icons of American Architecture: From the Alamo to the World Trade Center.* Wesport, CT: Greenwood Press, 2009.

Lazar, Irving, and Annette Tapert. *Swifty: My Life and Good Times.* New York: Simon & Schuster, 1995.

Leaming, Barbara. *If This Was Happiness: A Biography of Rita Hayworth.* New York: Viking Press, 1989.

——. *Marilyn Monroe.* New York: Crown Publishers, 1998.

——. *Orson Welles: A Biography.* New York: Viking Penguin, 1985.

Lenburg, Jeff. *Peekaboo: The Story of Veronica Lake.* New York: St. Martin's Press, 1983.

Leong, Karen J. *The China Mystique: Pearl S. Buck, Anna May Wong, Mayling Soong, and the Transformation of American Orientalism.* Berkeley: University of California Press, 2005.

Levant, Oscar. *The Unimportance of Being Oscar.* New York: G. P. Putnam's Sons, 1968.

Levy, Shawn. *Rat Pack Confidential: Frank, Dean, Sammy, Peter, Joey, and the Last Great Showbiz Party.* New York: Anchor Books, 1998.

Lewis, Jerry, and James Kaplan. *Dean and Me: A Love Story.* New York: Random House Large Print, 2005.

Lobenthal, Joel. *Tallulah!: The Life and Times of a Leading Lady.* New York: Regan Books, 2004.

Long, Robert Emmet, ed. *John Huston: Interviews.* Jackson: University Press of Mississippi, 2001.

Loos, Anita. *A Girl Like I.* New York: Viking Press, 1966.

——. *The Talmadge Girls: A Memoir.* New York: Viking Press, 1978.

Lord, Graham. *Niv: The Authorized Biography of David Niven.* New York: Thomas Dunne Books, 2003.

Louvish, Simon. *Mae West: It Ain't No Sin.* New York: Thomas Dunne Books, 2006.

——. *Man on the Flying Trapeze: The Life and Times of W. C. Fields.* New York: W. W. Norton, 1997.

Madsen, Axel. *John Huston: A Biography.* Garden City, NY: Doubleday, 1978.

Mank, Gregory. *Hollywood Cauldron: Thirteen Horror Films from the Genre's Golden Age.* Jefferson, NC: McFarland, 1994.

Mank, Gregory William, with Charles Heard and Bill Nelson. *Hollywood's Hellfire Club: The Misadventures of John Barrymore, W. C. Fields, Errol Flynn, and "The Bundy Drive Boys."* Los Angeles: Feral House, 2007.

Mann, William J. *How to Be a Movie Star: Elizabeth Taylor in Hollywood.* New York: Houghton Mifflin Harcourt, 2009.

Marx, Arthur. *The Nine Lives of Mickey Rooney.* New York: Stein and Day, 1986.

McBride, Joseph. *Searching for John Ford: A Life.* New York: St. Martin's Press, 2001.

McCabe, John. *Cagney.* New York: Alfred A. Knopf, 1997.

McCann, Graham. *Cary Grant: A Class Apart.* New York: Columbia University Press, 1996.

McGilligan, Patrick. *Fritz Lang: The Nature of the Beast.* New York: St. Martin's Press, 1997.

McNulty, Thomas. *Errol Flynn: The Life and Career.* Jefferson, NC: McFarland, 2011.

McPherson, Edward. *Buster Keaton: Tempest in a Flat Hat.* New York: Newmarket Press, 2005.

Meade, Marion. *Buster Keaton: Cut to the Chase.* New York: HarperCollins, 1995.

——. *Dorothy Parker: What Fresh Hell Is This?* New York: Penguin Books, 1989.

Meredith, Burgess. *So Far, So Good: A Memoir.* Boston: Little, Brown, 1994.

Meryman, Richard. *Mank: The Wit, World, and Life of Herman Mankiewicz.* New York: William Morrow, 1978.

Meyers, Jeffrey. *John Huston: Courage and Art.* New York: Crown Archetype, 2011.

Milland, Ray. *Wide-Eyed in Babylon: An Autobiography by Ray Milland.* London: The Bodley Head, 1974.

Miller, Gabriel, ed. *Fred Zinnemann: Interviews.* Conversations With Filmmakers. Jackson: University Press of Mississippi, 2005.

Milton, Joyce. *Tramp: The Life of Charlie Chaplin.* New York: HarperCollins, 1996.

Mitchell, Glenn. *The Laurel and Hardy Encyclopedia.* London: B. T. Batsford, 1995.

Morella, Joe, and Edward Z. Epstein. *Jane Wyman: A Biography.* New York: Delacorte Press, 1985.

Morris, Oswald, and Geoffrey Bull. *Huston, We Have a Problem: A Kaleidoscope of Filmmaking Memories.* Lanham, MD: Scarecrow Press, 2006.

Muller, Eddie. *Dark City: The Lost World of Film Noir.* New York: St. Martin's Griffin, 1998.

Munn, Michael. *John Wayne: The Man Behind the Myth.* New York: New American Library, 2004.

———. *Richard Burton: Prince of Players.* New York: Skyhorse, 2008.

Nelson, Nancy, and Cary Grant. *Evenings with Cary Grant: Recollections in His Own Words and by Those Who Knew Him Best.* New York: William Morrow, 1991.

Newquist, Roy. *Conversations with Joan Crawford.* Seacaucus, NJ: Citadel Press, 1980.

Niven, David. *The Moon's a Balloon.* London: Hamish Hamilton, 1971.

Norman, Marc. *What Happens Next: A History of American Screenwriting.* New York: Crown Archetype, 2007.

Norris, M. G. "Bud." *The Tom Mix Book.* Waynesville, NC: The World of Yesterday, 1989.

Paris, Barry. *Louise Brooks.* New York: Alfred A. Knopf, 1989.

Peters, Margot. *The House of Barrymore.* New York: Alfred A. Knopf, 1990.

Pizzitola, Louis. *Hearst over Hollywood: Power, Passion, and Propaganda in the Movies.* New York: Columbia University Press, 2002.

Porter, Amy. "Garden of Allah, I Love You," in Christopher Silvester, ed.

Powers, Stefanie. *One from the Hart.* New York: Gallery Books, 2010.

Prigozy, Ruth. *The Life of Dick Haymes: No More Little White Lies.* Jackson: University Press of Mississippi, 2006.

Quinn, Anthony, and Daniel Paisner. *One Man Tango.* New York: HarperCollins, 1995.

Quirk, Lawrence J., and William Schoell. *Joan Crawford: The Essential Biography.* Lexington: University Press of Kentucky, 2002.

Ray, Nicholas, and Susan Ray, ed. *I Was Interrupted: Nicholas Ray on Making Movies.* Berkeley: University of California Press, 1995.

Roberts, Jerry, ed. *Mitchum: In His Own Words.* New York: Proscenium, 2000.

Roberts, Randy, and James S. Olsen. *John Wayne: American.* New York: Free Press, 1995.

Rodriguez, Elena. *Dennis Hopper: A Madness to His Method.* New York: St. Martin's Press, 1998.

Ryan, Jim. *The Rodeo and Hollywood: Rodeo Cowboys on Screen and Western Actors in the Arena.* Jefferson, NC: McFarland, 2006.

Sahadi, Lou. *One Sunday in December.* Guilford, CT: Lyons Press, 2008.

Sandford, Christopher. *McQueen: The Biography.* New York: HarperCollins, 2001.

Sarlot, Raymond R., and Fred E. Basten. *Life at the Marmont.* Santa Monica: Roundtable Publishing, 1987.

Schickel, Richard. "Appreciation: The Genuine Article." In *Bogie: A Celebration of the Life and Films of Humphrey Bogart.* New York: Thomas Dunne, 2006.

———. *D. W. Griffith: An American Life.* New York: Simon & Schuster, 1984.

Schulberg, Budd. *The Four Seasons of Success.* Garden City, NY: Doubleday, 1972.

———. *Moving Pictures: Memories of a Hollywood Prince.* Chicago: Ivan R. Dee, 1981.

See, Lisa. *On Gold Mountain.* New York: Vintage Books, 1996.

Sellers, Robert. *Hellraisers: The Life and Inebriated Times of Richard Burton, Richard Harris, Peter O'Toole, and Oliver Reed.* New York: Thomas Dunne Books, 2008.

———. *Hollywood Hellraisers: The Wild Lives and*

Fast Times of Marlon Brando, Dennis Hopper, Warren Beatty, and Jack Nicholson. New York: Skyhorse Publishing, 2010.

Server, Lee. *Ava Gardner: "Love Is Nothing."* New York: St Martin's Press, 2006.

——. *Robert Mitchum:"Baby, I Don't Care."* New York: St. Martin's Press, 2001.

Sheen, Martin, and Emilio Estevez with Hope Edelman. *Along the Way: The Journey of a Father and Son.* New York: Free Press, 2012.

Shepherd, Donald, Robert Slatzer, and Dave Grayson. *Duke: The Life and Times of John Wayne.* New York: Citadel Press, 2002.

Sherman, Vincent. *Studio Affairs: My Life as a Film Director.* Lexington: University of Kentucky, 1996.

Shipman, David. *Judy Garland: The Secret Life of An American Legend.* New York: Hyperion, 1992.

Silvester, Christopher, ed. *The Grove Book of Hollywood.* New York: Viking Press, 1998.

Sinyard, Neil. *Fred Zinnemann: Films of Character and Conscience.* Jefferson, NC: McFarland, 2003.

Smith, Andrew Brodie. *Shooting Cowboys and Indians: Silent Western Films, American Culture, and the Birth of Hollywood.* Boulder: University Press of Colorado, 2003.

Smith, Don G. *Lon Chaney, Jr.: Horror Film Star, 1906–1973.* Jefferson, NC: McFarland, 1996.

Smith, Gus. *Richard Harris: Actor by Accident.* London: Robert Hale, 1990.

Soares, Andre. *Beyond Paradise: The Life of Ramon Novarro.* New York: St. Martin's Press, 2002.

Spicer, Christopher J. *Clark Gable: Biography, Filmography, Bibliography.* Jefferson, NC: McFarland, 2005.

Spiegel, Penina. *McQueen: The Untold Story of a Bad Boy in Hollywood.* New York: Doubleday, 1986.

Spoto, Donald. *A Passion for Life: The Biography of Elizabeth Taylor.* New York: HarperCollins, 1995.

Starr, Kevin. *Golden Dreams: California in an Age of Abundance 1950–1963.* New York: Oxford University Press, 2009.

Stenn, David. *Bombshell: The Life and Death of Jean Harlow.* New York: Doubleday, 1993.

Stewart, Donald Ogden. " 'Please—Don't Take a Sock at Me,' " in Christopher Silvester, ed.

Sturges, Preston. *Preston Sturges by Preston Sturges:*

His Life in His Words. New York: Touchstone, 1990.

Summers, Anthony, and Robbyn Swan. *Sinatra: The Life.* New York: Vintage Books, 2006.

Sweeney, Louise. "John Huston," in Robert Emmet Long, ed.

Taraborrelli, J. Randy. *Michael Jackson: The Magic and the Madness.* New York: Birch Lane Press, 1991.

——. *The Secret Life of Marilyn Monroe.* New York: Grand Central Publishing, 2009.

Taylor, Robert Lewis. "Mourning a Friend," in Christopher Silvester, ed.

Thomas, Bob. *Golden Boy: The Untold Story of William Holden.* New York: St. Martin's Press, 1983.

Tosches, Nick. *Dino: Living High in the Dirty Business of Dreams.* New York: Doubleday, 1992.

Vidor, King. *A Tree Is a Tree: An Autobiography.* Los Angeles: Samuel French, 1953.

Vieira, Mark A. *Irving Thalberg: Boy Wonder to Producer Prince.* Berkeley: University of California Press, 2009.

Viertel, Peter. *Dangerous Friends: At Large with Huston and Hemingway in the Fifties.* New York: Nan A. Talese, 1992.

Wallace, David. *Lost Hollywood.* New York: St. Martin's Griffin, 2002.

Walsh, John Evangelist. *Walking Shadows: Orson Welles, William Randolph Hearst, and "Citizen Kane."* Madison: University of Wisconsin Press, 2004.

Walsh, Raoul. *Each Man in His Time: The Life Story of a Director.* New York: Farrar, Straus & Giroux, 1974.

——. "Resurrecting Barrymore," in Christopher Silvester, ed.

Wapshott, Nicholas. *Peter O'Toole: A Biography.* New York: Beaufort Books, 1983.

Watts, Jill. *Mae West: An Icon in Black and White.* New York: Oxford University Press, 2001.

Wayne, Jane Ellen. *The Golden Girls of MGM.* New York: Carroll & Graf, 2002.

——. *Lana: The Life and Loves of Lana Turner.* New York: St. Martin's Press, 1995.

——. *The Leading Men of MGM.* New York: Carroll & Graf, 2005.

Weddle, David. *"If They Move . . . Kill 'Em!": The*

Life and Times of Sam Peckinpah. New York: Grove Press, 1994.

Wellman, William A. *A Short Time for Insanity: An Autobiography.* New York: Hawthorn Books, 1974.

Westbrook, Robert. *Intimate Lies: F. Scott Fitzgerald and Sheilah Graham—Her Son's Story.* New York: HarperCollins, 1995.

Whitefield, Eileen. *Pickford: The Woman Who Made Hollywood.* Lexington, KY: University Press of Kentucky, 1997.

Williams, Gregory Paul. *The Story of Hollywood: An Illustrated History.* Los Angeles: BL Press, 2005.

Yablonsky, Lewis. *George Raft.* New York: McGraw-Hill, 1974.

Young, Paul. *L.A. Exposed: Strange Myths and Curious Legends in the City of Angels.* New York: St. Martin's Griffin, 2002.

Zeitz, Joshua. *Flapper: A Madcap Story of Sex, Style, Celebrity, and the Women Who Made America Modern.* New York: Three Rivers Press, 2006.

Zollo, Paul. *Hollywood Remembered: An Oral History of Its Golden Age.* New York: Cooper Square Press, 2002.

MAGAZINES

Blum, David. "Slave of New York," *New York Magazine,* Sept. 5, 1988.

Callo, Jim. "Mavericks John Cassavetes and Gena Rowlands," *People,* Oct. 8, 1984. Vol. 22, No. 15.

Champlin, Charles. "A Laugh and a Tear for Toots," *Life,* July 6, 1959. Vol. 47, No 1.

Heaton, Michael. "It Hasn't Been an Easy Ride, but Hard-Living Dennis Hopper Is Out of Trouble—for Now," *People,* Oct. 24, 1983. Vol. 20, No. 17.

Houseman, John. "Lost Fortnight: 'The Blue Dahlia' and How It Grew Out of Raymond Chandler's Alcoholic Dash for a Deadline," *Harper's Magazine,* August 1965.

Hoyt, Caroline S. "Can the Gable-Lombard Romance Last?" *Modern Screen Magazine,* May 1939.

Kael, Pauline. "Raising Kane," *New Yorker,* February 20, 1971, and Feb. 27, 1971.

Kaftan, Jod. "Drink in Paradise," *Los Angeles Times Magazine,* Feb. 2010.

Liberty Then & Now, "Clara Bow: The Playgirl of Hollywood," Spring 1975.

Life, "Funnyman W. C. Fields Has Own Way of Keeping Himself Fit," May 12, 1941. Vol. 10, No. 19.

Life, "Lana Turner's Fourth and Positively Last Time," May 10, 1948. Vol. 24, No. 19.

Life, "Life Goes to a Big Marion Davies Party," Oct. 20, 1952. Vol. 22, No. 16.

Life, "The Simple Life of a Busy Bachelor," Oct. 3, 1955. Vol. 39, No. 14.

Los Angeles Confidential, "The Hollywood History of the Hotel Bel-Air," Oct. 28, 2011.

Oulahan, Richard. "A Well-planned Crawford," *Life,* February 21, 1964. Vol. 56, No. 8.

Playboy, "Playboy Interview: Lee Marvin," May 1971.

Rosenbaum, Jonathan. "Looking for Nick Ray," *American Film Magazine,* December 1981.

Time, "Trader Horn's Goddess," May 28, 1934. Vol. 23, No. 22.

Tynan, Kenneth. "The Girl in the Black Helmet," *New Yorker,* June 11, 1979.

Updike, John. "Smiling Bob," *New Yorker,* April 7, 1997.

Wiener, Jon. "Frank Sinatra: His Way," *Nation,* June 15, 2009.

NEWSPAPERS

Carter, D. Robert, "Edwina in Africa: Clouds on Bright Horizon," *Daily Herald,* Feb. 23, 2008.

——, "Edwina Endures Problems, Returns Home after Filming," *Daily Herald,* March 15, 2008.

Fernandez, Jay. "Raising a Glass to Great Imbibers," *Los Angeles Times,* Dec. 13, 2006.

Flatley, Guy. "Cary—From Mae to September," *New York Times,* July 22, 1973.

Guardian, "Devil of an Actor," May 7, 1999.

Harnisch, Larry. "Movie Comedian Stan Laurel Accused of Planning to Bury Wife in Backyard," *Los Angeles Times,* Jan. 2, 2009.

——. "Stormy Marriage Full of Off-Screen Drama for Stan Laurel," *Los Angeles Times,* June 21, 2009.

Harvey, Steve. "Don the Beachcomber Helped Launch Wave of Polynesian Restaurants," *Los Angeles Times,* May 1, 2011.

Hilburn, Robert. "A Man Who Had a Passion for Art of the Troubadour," *Los Angeles Times,* Feb. 16, 1999.

Lelyveld, Nina. "Landmark Stands in Changing Neighborhood," *Los Angeles Times,* Sept. 9, 2003.

Martin, Douglas. "Owner of Legendary Rock Venue Whisky a Go Go," *Chicago Tribune,* Dec. 11, 2008.

McLellan, Dennis. "Elmer Valentine, Co-founder of Whisky a Go Go, Dies at 85," *Los Angeles Times,* Dec. 7, 2008.

Nasaw, David. "Exit Laughing," *New York Times,* April 20, 1997.

New York Daily News, "Fran Farmer Gets 6 Mos. in Jail, Hits Matron, Fells a Cop," Jan. 14, 1943.

Oliver, Myrna. "Doug Weston, Troubadour Founder, Dies," *Los Angeles Times,* Feb. 15, 1999.

Pace, Eric. "Claudette Colbert, Unflappable Heroine of Screwball Comedies, Is Dead," *New York Times,* July 31, 1996.

Rasmussen, Cecilia. "DUI flashback: Bing Crosby in '29," *Chicago Tribune,* June 24, 2007.

———. "L.A. Brewery Was the Toast of Its Time," *Los Angeles Times,* Sept. 7, 1997.

Rennell, Tony. "The Maddest Movie Ever: Why 'Apocalypse Now' Is the Finest Movie of Modern Times," *Daily Mail,* Dec. 5, 2009.

Rushfield, Richard. "Before the Rat Pack, Another Wild Bunch, *Los Angeles Times,* July 30, 2005.

Sellers, Robert. "The Strained Making of 'Apocalypse Now,'" *Independent,* July 24. 2009.

Soble, Ronald L. "Financial Troubles Serve 'Last Supper' at Perino's," *Los Angeles Times,* May 24, 1985.

Timberg, Scott, "Tiki Tacky? Not to Fans of Trader Vic's," *Los Angeles Times,* April 7, 2006.

Vallance, Tom. "Lawrence Tierney: Obituary," *Independent,* March 1, 2002.

FILM

Hearts of Darkness: A Filmmaker's Apocalypse. Fax Bahr, George Hickenlooper, and Eleanor Coppola, directors. Lionsgate, 2010. DVD.

TELEVISION

Late Show with David Letterman, Jan. 17, 1994. Season 1, episode 95.

Late Show with David Letterman, March 16, 1994. Season 1, episode 127.

Late Night with Conan O'Brien, Feb. 14, 1997. Season 4, episode 73.

WEBSITES

BoozeMovies.com. "Cinematic Cocktails: The Buttermaker Boilermaker," http://www.boozemovies.com/2009/05/cinematic-cocktails-buttermaker.html.

Garver, William. "The Nutty Professor," Soused Cinema, ModernDrunkard.com, http://www.moderndrunkardmagazine.com/issues/53/53_soused_cinema.html.

Hall, Phil. "The Bootleg Files: Beat the Devil," filmthreat.com, http://www.filmthreat.com/features/2108/.

Kaufman, Jeffrey. "Frances Farmer: Shedding Light On Shadowland," JeffreyKaufmen.net, http://jeffreykauffman.net/francesfarmer/sheddinglight.html.

Muller, Eddie. "The Big Leak: An Uneasy Evening with the Noir Legend," Eddiemuller.com, http://www.eddiemuller.com/tierney.html.

Peary, Gerald. "Talking with Sterling Hayden." Gerald Peary.com, http://geraldpeary.com/interviews/ghi/hayden.html.

Rich, Frank Kelly. "The Great Drunk: Lushing Large with Jackie Gleason, Part Two," ModernDrunkard.com, http://www.drunkard.com/issues/03-05/03_05_great_drunk.htm.

———. "Three Drinks Ahead with Humphrey Bogart," ModernDrunkard.com, http://www.moderndrunkardmagazine.com/issues/05_03/05-03-bogart.html.

Robinson, Chris J. "Don't Be Bonin' Me: The Life of Sterling Hayden," 12gauge.com, http://www.12gauge.com/people-2003_hayden.html.

Van Doren, Mamie. "Bedtime Stories: Sex, Drugs, and Steve McQueen," MamieVanDoren.com, http://www.mamievandoren.com/bedtime archive.html.

Wondrich, David. "The Wondrich Take: Aristocrat Sparkling Punch," Esquire.com, http://www.esquire.com/drinks/aristocrat-sparkling-punch-drink-recipe#wondrich.

INDEX